GUSTAVO CISNEROS
Pioneer

 Planeta

Pablo Bachelet

GUSTAVO CISNEROS
Pioneer

Foreword by Carlos Fuentes

Translated by Edith Grossman

 Planeta

© Hispanic Publishing LLC, 2004
© Editorial Planeta, S.A., 2004
   Diagonal 662-664, 08034 Barcelona, Spain
   Translation © Edith Grossman, 2004

Original title: *Gustavo Cisneros, un empresario global*

First edition in Spanish: February 2004
First edition in Portuguese: June 2004
First edition in English: October 2004

ISBN: 0-974872-48-2
Planeta Publishing Corp.
2057 NW 87 av.
Miami, FL 33172 (U.S.A.)

ISBN (Colombia): 958-42-1060-2

COLOMBIA: www.editorialplaneta.com.co
VENEZUELA: www.editorialplaneta.com.ve
ECUADOR: www.editorialplaneta.com.ec
ESPAÑA: www.planeta.es

Printing and binding: Printer Colombiana S.A.
Printed in Colombia

Table of Contents

Foreword   9

Author's Note   15

1. Head, Heart, and Courage   17

2. The Apprentice   26

3. The Boys   37

4. A Quarry of Talents   53

5. Efficiency and Effectiveness   63

6. Multiplying Businesses   75

7. Devaluation   86

8. A Diamond on the Floor   92

9. The Storm   110

10. That Marvelous Hispanic Spirit   125

11. With Our Heads Held High   140

12. Globalized Television   151

13. The Swan's Triumph   170

14. The Internet   189

15. King of Content   207

16. An Obstacle Course   224

17. Transparency   239

18. The Vision   257

19. The Balance   270

Afterword   281

Bibliography and Sources   287

List of Individuals Interviewed   303

Index   305

To my wife, Consuelo,
for all her support, understanding, and affection

Foreword

The dictionary defines the verb "to undertake" as "to attempt and begin a work...," and it adds this caveat: "...especially if it encompasses difficulty or danger."

One could say that the dictionary had Gustavo Cisneros in mind when it added that phrase, which *Larousse* confirms in French. To undertake is "to make the decision to do and initiate." The biography of Gustavo Cisneros now being published is, first of all, a dynastic history that begins with his father, is complemented by his siblings, and is extended by his children. It is the history of an energetic youth who knew how to take advantage of the privileges granted by his inheritance and continue to grow more agile and skillful, never resting on the laurels of what has been achieved.

It is a history of risks that are rewarded, and of errors that are admitted. It is a history of opportune changes of velocity. Cisneros moves from the business of mass consumption to the business of communications, from the generation of cash flow to the generation of value. And always, before the next step, there is internal consolidation. Cisneros' entrepreneurial saga—worthy of being described by a Balzac or a Dreiser, if not by the Renaissance Fuggars—has, like every life, and above all every life of action, its lights and shadows, its defeats and victories, which are described in detail in this book.

But beneath—or above—the Cisneros saga, there are certain constants that explain better than any anecdote the personal, entrepreneurial, and collective values in the life of Gustavo Cisneros. A vertical strategy: each company should empower the other, and distribution should integrate vertically with content. Early identification of opportunities. Timely correction of mistakes. Tolerating errors made in good faith. Remaining open to dissident opinions within the company. Rewarding personal initiative. Insisting on teamwork.

These are the ethical and operational bases that explain the success of Gustavo Cisneros. He takes risks, but first he consolidates achievements. At times he dives into the pool at night without knowing if there is any water in it. He searches unceasingly for financial and operational equilibrium. That is: he proposes a model of democratic entrepreneurial organization that extends from the center to the periphery, thereby allowing the periphery an extremely high degree of autonomy.

One could claim that everything I have said simply goes without saying in a modern enterprise. If today it is taken for granted, if it is the norm, let us think for a moment about the negative Latin American tradition of the absentee landowner, the *latifundista* and the system of mortmain, the Ibero-America of stagnating riches, passive renters, dozing, if not venal, bureaucrats. And tyrants and petty despots, "masters of lives and property."

It is true. We in Latin America have not overcome all our evils. One might say that some are inherent, our curse, but the biography of Cisneros categorically negates this kind of fatalism. It demonstrates the organizational capacity of Latin Americans, the determination not to accept any problem without immediately offering a possible solution. It creates a corporate culture that allows Latin Americans to realize that on the other side of the artistic and literary culture that is our most profound and longest-lived tradition, there is now a comparably deep and enduring entrepreneurial culture. The burning question continues to be why we do not know how to transfer to politics the virtues of our aesthetic and entrepreneurial cultures.

There is a dramatic recurrence of our political vices. When we believe we have consolidated imperfect but healthy democratic systems, the microbe of authoritarianism reappears with a melodramatic gesture, an operetta balcony, a condottiere's costume, and demagogic speechifying. How can we fortify democracy against the authoritarian virus?

I believe that the life and work of Gustavo Cisneros, in a variety of ways, can offer us some answers. The first is to see to it that our societies have a powerful educational base. We must penetrate the forest and the "sacred mountains" to which Guillermo de la Dehesa refers. Poverty does not create markets, Carlos Slim never tires of telling us, and Gustavo Cisneros concurs: there is a deadly relationship between low levels of education and poverty. We Latin Americans must wield our pencils as if they were daggers. Education assures that the creative energies of our compatriots can be released. Education liberates the personal talents and abilities of citizens who in no way are condemned to ignorance and destitution.

In his cultural work, as well as in his educational initiatives, Gustavo Cisneros has found a magnificent ally in his wife, Patricia Phelps de Cisneros. The Mozarteum, which introduces and promotes musical culture among young Venezuelans. The visual arts initiatives based on the works in the Colección Cisneros. The rescue of Amazonian ethnographic objects. The collection of hundreds of thousands of photographs taken in the south of Venezuela. Patty Cisneros understands culture as an ongoing gestation, and she assumes the responsibility of bringing together the works of a culture that is popular and unique—works that, in the long run, belong to the community.

There is, then, this base for local development. Basic education. But in a world of technical and educational development as rapid and globalized as the one in which we live, the base of local education faces two challenges. First, knowing that our education is ongoing. It does not end dramatically in the sixth year of primary school, which often is the limit for millions of young Latin Americans. It does not end even upon receiving a university degree. Education ceases only when life is over.

Second is knowing that local education must modernize in order to confront the challenges of rapidly developing technologies. Bill Clinton recalled, in an address to the General Assembly of the United Nations, that when he assumed the presidency of the United States in 1992, there were only fifty sites on the World-wide Web. When he left the White House eight years later, there were 350 million. Let us calculate the leap we can expect in the next ten or twenty years.

The technological revolution embraces both the local village and the global village. In nations with an extensive agrarian population, for instance in Latin America, the techno-informational revolution can radically alter living conditions. Access to the Internet transforms the relationship between agricultural supply and demand. It brings up-to-date information to rural workers. By means of a connection to the sources of information, the *campesino* can receive news in schools, community centers, and health centers. The pocket Simputer even overcomes the barrier of illiteracy by converting text into words.

On an international level, it is a question of acceding to a globalization that is not imposed but generated from within. Gustavo Cisneros has globalized his companies in two ways: from the periphery to the center, and from the center to the periphery. He has insisted on the qualitative evolution of his companies, providing them with increasingly advanced technologies. The new digital-information society has been used by Cisneros to multiply services through a unique technological platform. Barriers of and to information fall away. Latin America cannot, yet again, "come late to the banquet of civilization," as Alfonso Reyes once said.

Democracy is consubstantial with modern civilization. Gustavo Cisneros, *nolens volens*, represents a value and a political role in his native Venezuela. The cycle of boom and bust, the mirages of petrolification ("the devil's deposits"), the decadence and frivolity of political parties and personalities created a suitable vacuum for the customary return of the eternal Latin American temptation to authoritarianism in the figure of Hugo Chávez. Elected like Hitler, histrionic like Mussolini, a populist like Perón, Chávez has unleashed (because he has not controlled it) a tide of divisions, economic regressions, and social illusions that could be contagious in an Ibero-America that congratulates itself on being democratic but also asks itself when it will have bread, a roof, a school, health care.

Winning the battle against the authoritarian temptation is a duty of democratic citizens in Latin America. Gustavo Cisneros occupies the democratic center and for this reason suffers attacks, calumnies, and other assaults from the Chavista basement. In the face of Chávez' divisive policies, Cisneros is situated in a center not of insipidities but of commitments. A dangerous center—dangerous for demagogic authoritarianism. For Cisneros represents the capacity for organization that the authoritarian government lacks. He represents social balance as opposed to divisive disequilibrium. He represents the creation of sources of work and wealth in contrast to sterile bombast and the squandering of resources.

Gustavo Cisneros is a transatlantic entrepreneur. His relationship with Spain signifies the abolition of the ocean: the caravels have round-trip tickets. He is an inter-American entrepreneur. His presence on the continents of the New World—Ibero-America and Anglo-America—turns him into a man ahead of his time in mutually beneficial relationships, as he has demonstrated in multiple negotiations with North American companies, which never assume weakness or ceding of rights on our part, but rather an equality that is rational and honorable.

The creator of a business culture, a man ahead of his time in a political culture of equilibrium, a promoter of an educational culture that leaves no one behind, a defender of the Spanish language in the heart of Anglo-America, Gustavo Cisneros descended one day to the cavern of Sarisariñama, deep in the Venuezuelan jungle. Just as a character of Sir Arthur Conan Doyle's descended to the center of the earth and, when he touched it, heard a shout of pain. In his descent to the cavern, perhaps Gustavo Cisneros heard a shout of joy: "A fierce measure of manhood," as Rómulo Gallegos exclaims in the pages of *Canaima*.

CARLOS FUENTES

Author's Note

I met Gustavo Cisneros in 1998 while on assignment for *América-Economía* magazine, reporting on the phenomenon of the day, the "convergence" of the Internet with traditional mass media. The article, "Citizen Cisneros," told the story of a man who was staking out territory in the frenetic world of media and technology, at a time when one purchase followed the other, each more spectacular than the one before.

Cisneros spoke of expanding his operations in Argentina, of his fondness for television, of a business philosophy that sought to integrate his companies vertically, to produce not just the content for TV, but also the means to distribute it. This, he told me, was what his father had done with Pepsi-Cola in Venezuela.

Trimmed to some three thousand words, the article was just a preamble. Behind it lay the powerful story of a man who wanted to stay ahead of the entrepreneurial and political currents of the day. This was comparable to a child on the beach who trips over a stone and starts digging, only to discover a rock weighing several tons.

Over the past three decades Cisneros, with his heart set in Caracas but his mind tuned to New York, worked to anticipate the great waves of globalization that swept over Latin America and the entire world. Working with his brother Ricardo, he succeeded in constructing one of the few truly multinational business empires in Latin America. This book recounts the trajectory of Gustavo Cisneros, from the early days when his father, Diego, told his son that he would teach him to be a "leader of men," to his tireless and insistent efforts to create a single modern digital platform to disseminate television programming throughout Latin America.

A family tragedy meant that Gustavo Cisneros took on the leadership of the family group when he was barely twenty-five, filled with dreams of diversifying operations into supermarkets, telecommunications, and breweries. Step by step, Cisneros would meet his own challenges, and discover how to balance these achievements with his social commitments.

His determination to stay one step ahead of the times and of trends would lead him to acquire department stores in Spain in the early 1980s—by using a financial formula virtually unknown in Europe—and to defend an entrepreneurial project before a skeptical Prince Charles of England. This book attempts to explain what lay behind Cisneros' marathon negotiations to join with the Australian media magnate Rupert Murdoch, or how the violent looting that gripped Venezuela on February 27, 1989, influenced his decisions.

Cisneros has taken part in some of the boldest, most spectacular deals in Latin America, Spain, Portugal, and the United States, always in companies that produce those things that accompany us in our daily living, such as soap operas, golf balls, the Internet, supermarkets, and soft drinks.

It is a story that helps us understand the complex variables that intervene in a globalized economy, within the unique context of Latin America. It is a story of achievements and also of difficulties, an eventful course marked, on occasion, by controversy.

The book is based on more than sixty interviews, including several with Cisneros. He was cautious. He demanded that his family's privacy be respected. And he did not want these pages to settle old scores.

The result may be useful to those trained in the ways of business. But it is also for others who wish to comprehend our world and our time through the perspective of an entrepreneur who has given shape to one of the most powerful business organizations in Latin America.

1.   Head, Heart, and Courage

"Gustavo, did you see the article in the *New York Times* on the Fogg Museum?" asked Patricia Phelps de Cisneros.

Gustavo Cisneros and his wife, Patricia (Patty), were in Casa Bonita, their vacation house in La Romana, in the Dominican Republic, which also serves as an operations center for his organization. That day they received two excellent pieces of news, and a third that worried them.

Patty Cisneros was delighted as she looked at the image sent to her by e-mail on that morning of August 17, 2001. It was a reproduction of the first page of the *New York Times* Friday "Weekend" section.

The article, entitled "A Universe of Art, Centered in Boston," featured a photograph of *Composition in Blue, White, and Red* by Alfredo Volpi. It was a typical creation by the Brazilian painter, a geometric design of subtly contrasting rectangles and colors. That painting was one of sixty works from the Colección Cisneros on exhibit at Harvard University's Fogg Art Museum.

The review in the *New York Times* touched a special chord in Patty because it recognized the quality of Latin American art, stressing the "particular nature of Latin American abstract art, its breadth and variety, and its relationship to the European avant-garde."

Patty Cisneros began collecting art in the 1970s in order to be "surrounded by beautiful things." Encouraged by her husband, whom she defines as "the visionary," while she describes herself as "focused on execution," she hired curators to supervise the care and coordination of the works.

Pieces by Joan Miró, Pablo Picasso, and Max Bill, among others, were acquired. Also acquired were works by Latin American painters that represented the style of art known as geometric abstraction; its sculptural variant, kinetic art; and other modern movements. Through the Fundación Cisneros, Patty helps to ensure that these works in the Colección Cisneros are used to help increase worldwide awareness of the achievements of such Latin American artists as Jesús Rafael Soto, Carlos Cruz Diez, Lygia Clark, and Joaquín Torres-García, among others.

The positive reception of these works at the Fogg Art Museum meant that Patty was succeeding in her commitment to the heightening appreciation of Latin American art. She had plans to open a show in São Paulo and another in Río de Janeiro in 2002. Buenos Aires and Montevideo would come in 2003, to be followed by Lima and Santiago in 2004.

The other good piece of news came from Spain. King Juan Carlos had approved a decree granting Cisneros Spanish nationality. This is an award given by the monarch to outstanding figures who have contributed to unity among Hispanic nations, to the expansion of their language and art, and to Spain's rapprochement with the rest of the world. It recognized Gustavo Cisneros for his work in extending the reach of the Spanish language by means of the telecommunications industry. That year the King also honored, among other personalities, the great Chilean painter Roberto Matta.

The third piece of news received by Cisneros was disturbing. His agreement with the magnate Rupert Murdoch to offer a single platform for digital television in Latin America was in danger. Murdoch had been patiently negotiating with General Motors to acquire control of Hughes Electronics, which in turn owned DirecTV Latin America, the satellite television company in which the Cisneros Group had invested in order to offer satellite television service in Latin America. DirecTV Latin America needed to merge with its competitor Sky, owned by Murdoch, in order to earn a profit, in this way realizing Cisneros' longstanding dream of working in partnership with Murdoch. But Charlie Ergen, an individual not well known outside the pay-television industry, had made a generous offer to Hughes Electronics to acquire DirecTV, stealing the deal out of Murdoch's hands. If General Motors accepted Ergen's offer, it would destroy Cisneros' plans to work with Murdoch in Latin America through News Corp.'s acquisition of Hughes.

Perhaps it was not the best time for great corporate alliances, Cisneros thought. The world economy had grown sluggish and market indexes were falling, wiping out part of the profits earned in the previous five years, during the height of investment in technological infrastructure.

Cisneros knew how to wait. He knew how to be prudent. It was one of the many lessons his father had taught him.

In the face of the new times he had to confront, Gustavo Cisneros remembered in particular the work of his father, Don Diego.

Gustavo Cisneros was born on June 1, 1945. He was the fourth child of Diego Cisneros and his wife, Albertina Rendiles. Diego Cisneros already headed one of the great entrepreneurial groups in Venezuela. In the same year that Gustavo Cisneros came into the world, Diego Cisneros had succeeded in displacing the powerful Coca-Cola with an unknown drink, Pepsi-Cola. Gustavo Cisneros feels that he owes his father much more than the businesses he created. As Gustavo Cisneros recalls, the broad, pluralistic thinking of Diego Cisneros was shaped by the circumstances of his life, difficult at first, but which kept him in touch with different countries and cultures. Diego Cisneros was born in Havana on September 27, 1911, the child of Diego Jiménez de Cisneros and the Venezuelan María Luisa Bermúdez Martínez. Three years later he lost his father. His mother, left with economic uncertainty, decided to move to the Caribbean island of Trinidad where some of her family lived.

Trinidad was the home of Diego and his brother Antonio for the next thirteen years; at that time, the island was like a world apart from the South American continent. As a British colony it enjoyed political stability. María Luisa enrolled her sons at St. Mary's College, run by the Irish Catholic Order of the Holy Spirit. The boys enjoyed the best of the English educational tradition abroad: discipline with tolerance, a good amount of sports, and academic rigor.

From the time he was young, Diego worked as well as studied. When he was a teenager he obtained his first job at an optician's office that needed someone bilingual in English and Spanish. He already showed a good business sense. When he was sixteen he sold homemade ice cream on the street. "It was my first experience in doing something to satisfy a public need," he would later recall.

In September 1928, when Diego was seventeen and had finished his studies, his mother decided to return to her native country. Young Diego fell in love with Venezuela, and especially with Caracas, which was then a small city of 150,000 inhabitants. Built on the slopes of the beautiful El Ávila mountain, Caracas was a peaceful place, with narrow streets and a few French-inspired public buildings that contrasted with its colonial architecture.

The Cisneros brothers rapidly obtained employment. Antonio was hired by Shell Oil Company. Diego, after a short time at the Royal Bank of Canada, began to work in a Chrysler dealership that sold International trucks. One morning a former employee came to ask for credit that he would use to convert three International trucks into buses that would cover the Plaza Bolívar-El Cementerio route. Cisneros listened to the details of the deal and sensed an opportunity in public transportation. In the months that followed he saved all he could until he had the thousand *bolívares* ($153) needed to acquire a heavy-duty truck. A contractor paid twenty *bolívares* ($3) for each trip, which was enough to cover expenses and payments on the vehicle. Antonio also joined the project, and the brothers proposed converting the truck into a bus for public transportation.

It was Diego's task to obtain the operating permit from the Justice Department of Caracas. At that time, meeting with a public official was a complicated matter. After a good deal of persistence, Diego finally got an appointment with the secretary to

Governor Rafael María Velasco. Having arrived at the agreed-upon hour, Diego was stopped by a stubborn and ill-humored police officer who would not let him pass, disregarding the verification of the appointment that Diego showed him. The angry protests of the young entrepreneur earned him five days in a cell at Caracas police headquarters, and left Diego Cisneros furious with the authoritarian and arbitrary system of law enforcement then in place in the country.

A few months later, after persistent efforts, the Cisneros brothers obtained a permit to operate a route in Catia, a marginal neighborhood the west of the city. The truck Diego had purchased was renamed "*El Expedito*," or Speedy, and overhauled as a bus.

That was the seed of the Cisneros Group of Companies. The experience in public transportation would mark the entrepreneurial future of Diego Cisneros. He learned to attract passengers by making certain that the buses were always shining and the passengers comfortable. Diego Cisneros was obsessive about the importance of meeting the needs and desires of consumers.

Among the many things that Gustavo learned from his father, he recalls: "He taught us to pay attention to details, to put all our energy and vitality into any business we undertook, no matter how small."

In 1938, Diego married Albertina Rendiles Martínez, who was his wife until his death forty-one years later. She was a practical and affectionate woman, a complement to her husband who had a dreamer's adventurous streak. They were a good team.

"Mamá was calmer, with her feet on the ground. Perhaps she knew more about many things because she saw through people more quickly. Papá took everyone at face value until they proved otherwise. He was very American, an absolute optimist. Mamá was much more reserved, often rightly so," remembers Gustavo Cisneros.

In 1935 the dictator Juan Vicente Gómez died, and Venezuela began to experience changes that ultimately led to the establishment of a democratic regime in 1958. Diego Cisneros' life also entered a new phase. Tired of struggling against the obstacles imposed by municipal governments, in 1939 he decided to withdraw from the business of transporting passengers and devote himself to the sale of replacement parts for vehicles. A short while later he founded D. Cisneros & Cía., a firm that eventually sold merchandise ranging from refrigerators to trucks. Diego Cisneros was now a well-to-do businessman, but it would be Pepsi-Cola that would launch his greatest success.

His brother Antonio had tasted his first Pepsi-Cola in 1939, during his honeymoon in New York. The World's Fair was the great attraction in the city at that time. The exhibition was filled with inventions of all kinds, like the box that received images transmitted from a distance and was called a television set. But Antonio was powerfully drawn to the sparkling flavor of Pepsi-Cola. He refused to budge from the offices of the manufacturer until he was assured of the contact that eventually would allow him, with his brother Diego, to negotiate the concession for bottling and distributing the drink in his own country. It was a great event for Pepsi-Cola. Until that time the company distributed its product only in the United States and Cuba, where operations were managed directly by the main office.

Pepsi-Cola Venezuela would acquire mythic proportions. Venezuela was one of the few countries where sales of the soft drink surpassed Coca-Cola's, and in the most overwhelming way, until it became the most profitable international concession for the American company.

Don Diego demanded the same passion he brought to his work from his employees, and especially from his managers at the bottling plant and in other businesses. He would often say: "You cannot have a successful business if you don't have all three: Head, Heart, and Courage."

Aware that the key to the soft-drink business is distribution, he designed a marketing strategy that guaranteed that his products were always available and, above all, ready to be purchased: "The message has to be constantly before the consumer," and "A cold drink is a sold drink," were two of his maxims. Moreover, he instructed his salespeople to memorize the five fundamental principles of William Forsythe, a well-known master of marketing technique at the time, which he adapted to his own company. Perhaps the most important of these was the third: "In every retail outlet where Pepsi-Cola is sold," it said, "there should be a sign outside, another inside, and a cooler to keep the bottles cold."

In this way Pepsi-Cola began to generate resources that permitted Cisneros to diversify his businesses and holdings. This was how several plants of Liquid Carbonic were born, as well as distributorships for Studebaker cars and Tío Rico Ice Cream. In fact, the 1959 edition of *Economic Geography of Venezuela* listed his companies as one of the principal economic groups in the country.

Then, in 1960, the Cisneros Group acquired the concession for Venevisión, its first television station and network. This enterprise, in fact, profoundly influenced Gustavo Cisneros, and provided the impetus for the changes that would determine the new direction for the Cisneros Group during the 1990s.

The purchase of Venevisión was a result of the political turbulence of those years, and of the perseverance of Albertina Cisneros. She watched more television than her husband and did not like what was broadcast on Channel 4. The television station, then called Televisa of Venezuela, had declared bankruptcy and, as a result of a court ruling, the unions had taken control of operations.

The president at the time, Rómulo Betancourt, had his hands tied because no entrepreneur was willing to assume the risk of buying the station and network. Don Diego, however, was listening to his wife and began to watch more television. He liked the dynamic nature of the medium, but it was clear to him that the managerial structure he had at Pepsi-Cola could not be used to run something like this. He needed a partner.

Diego was a friend of Goar Mestre, one of the first moguls of Latin American television, who had the stature of the Brazilian Roberto Marinho, Sr., founder of the Globo Network, and of the Mexican Emilio Azcárraga Vidaurreta, creator of Televisa. In 1943, Mestre paid $50,000 to acquire CMQ, a television station in Havana. From there he acquired almost all the radio and television stations in Cuba, earning the nickname "the Czar." He lost his position with the arrival of Fidel Castro, and moved to Argentina, his wife's native country. There, in partnership with CBS, he created Channel 13, which would stay at the top of the ratings for eleven consecutive seasons.

Diego and Goar could not reach an agreement for managing Venevisión together, because the latter wanted to control the business, and his corporate partner, CBS, was already negotiating a joint venture with the well-known and locally important Vollmer family for the acquisition of another Venezuelan channel.

Diego Cisneros would finally find the ally who would help in the Televisa of Venezuela deal: the American Broadcasting Company, ABC, which was then trailing its competitors NBC and CBS. Its president, Leonard Goldenson, had a good relationship with Diego Cisneros. Like him, the American was a businessman who had made his first inroads into television when he acquired ABC for $24 million in 1953.

Goldenson advised Don Diego regarding the purchase of rights to syndicated programs and Hollywood movies. As a consequence, the entrepreneur felt he had backing and decided he was ready to take part in the bidding for the purchase of Televisa of Venezuela.

That decision was a relief to President Betancourt, whose response was: "The state would look favorably on you and other private business people investing in the television sector."

The bidding took place on June 7, 1959. The Cisneros-ABC partnership won by paying a little more than 3.8 million *bolívares* ($1.1 million). Most of the shares were in the hands of Diego Cisneros and the same group of shareholders who had been with him at Pepsi-Cola. The new channel, Venevisión, Channel 4 in Caracas, began broadcasting with a capital of 4.5 million *bolívares* ($1.3 million) and 800,000 *bolívares* ($239,000) in paid advertising each month, an unheard-of sum in those days. Venevisión's inauguration was celebrated on February 27, 1961, with great fanfare that captured the attention of the country. The actress Joan Crawford, a member of the board of directors of Pepsi-Cola International, and the winner of an Oscar in 1945 for the film *Mildred Pierce*, was one of the celebrity guests. A veritable who's who of Venezuelan society attended the event that day in

Colinas de Los Caobos, and among other attractions they enjoyed the voices of Lucho Gatica and Olga Guillot.

The first logo for the channel was a playful tiger. It soon would be an icon known to millions of Venezuelans. The vision and boldness of Diego Cisneros, united with the knowledge, experience, and determination of his managers, soon made a huge success of Venevisión. The station diversified its programming schedules to meet consumers' preferences, showing family series like *My Friend Flicka*, the soap opera *La Cruz del Diablo*, and local shows such as *Casos y Cosas de Casa*. A new way of producing television was born in Venezuela.

As the popularity of the new channel was growing, Goar Mestre finally arrived in Venezuela to manage its competitor, Venezolana de Televisión, Channel 8. Allied with the Vollmers, and with Time-Life and CBS, Mestre attempted to out-perform Venevisión. But the programming team at Venevisión had a better grasp of the preferences of the Venezuelan viewer. Despite all his efforts, Mestre could not surpass the popularity of Venevisión programs like *Venemaratón* and *Festival Criollo*, two that were most emblematic of the Venezuela of that time, and when the Vollmer family stopped supplying capital, Mestre withdrew from the Venezuelan venture.

As some of Diego's collaborators confirm, he had always seen qualities in his son Gustavo that he knew would help him run the television enterprise one day. Gustavo was sharp, he possessed the same curiosity that characterized Diego, and from an early age he had shown a special interest in the small screen. Diego Cisneros saw that Venevisión would do well in the hands of his fourth child.

The truth is that Gustavo Cisneros could not imagine doing anything else; from the time he was a boy he was trained by his father in the corridors of Venevisión. "I grew up in the media. It is an industry I know and understand...I'm in love with television."

2. The Apprentice

Gustavo Cisneros smiles as he remembers that it was rarely necessary to remind the eight Cisneros children to do their schoolwork. They took it for granted that they had to do it, and they did. Diego Cisneros and Albertina Rendiles imposed that duty with their presence. Cisneros studied at San Ignacio, a traditional and demanding Jesuit school in Caracas. From the beginning of his schooling, he was on the honor roll and did outstanding work in history and mathematics, a curious combination "typical of a Gemini," he says. Along with his academic obligations he had a love for sports.

Cisneros liked school. The director, Brother Bonnet, was a charismatic teacher who used to say that he "would never allow the school to crush individuality."

His classmates remember Cisneros as a good student and a good friend, though somewhat "pugnacious." The Cisneros house in Los Palos Grandes was open to friends, a place where there was always Tío Rico ice cream—manufactured by one of Don Diego's enterprises—and ice-cold Pepsi-Cola.

Gustavo Cisneros' childhood home was filled with the comings and goings of relatives and friends. "The doors were always open. You could bring friends, and the friends of friends," remembers Cisneros.

He also recalls his father's important guests. "Any interesting foreigner coming to Caracas would come to the house." The young Cisneros liked to listen to them. He was struck by the enigmatic

Commander Edward Whitehead, president of Schweppes, with his impeccable clothes and characteristic beard, and Pepín Bosch, head of Bacardi, the leading producer of rum.

Another frequent guest was Rómulo Betancourt, one of the founders of Latin American social-democratic thought. Betancourt and Diego Cisneros had met in the 1930s, when Betancourt's office was in the same building where Cisneros had a car dealership. This was many years before Betancourt became president (1959–64) and put an end to the dictatorship of Pérez Jiménez.

"There were breakfasts, or lunches, there were social gatherings," Gustavo Cisneros remembers about these guests, and the children had an open door to come in, sit down, and listen. Politics was a recurring subject, since Venezuela was experiencing difficult but dynamic times. Between 1936 and 1952, there were two coups, and 159 political parties, electoral groups, and pressure groups were formed. Gustavo Cisneros remembers his home as nonpartisan. Diego Cisneros tried to listen to everyone, a trait that his son would inherit. "It was a very independent family, taking something from here and something from there and not prejudging."

Diego Cisneros, of course, had his own political ideas. He had joined the Mont Pelerin Society, an organization founded by the liberal economist Friedrich Hayek to promote economic freedom. The Society would embrace eight winners of the Nobel Prize in Economics, including outstanding thinkers like Milton Friedman. Cisneros, as a forthright defender of democracy and freedom, was opposed to revolutionary ideas.

Still, "all the political colors of those days, within the democratic sphere," came to the house, states Gustavo Cisneros. "And Papá always had something good to say about them. I learned that everyone has something to contribute. There wasn't the political division that became so strong later in Venezuela. Because they were open-minded, we didn't hear Papá or Mamá express prejudices because people had a different color, religion, or ideas."

Cisneros' qualities, his devotion to the Catholic faith, and his outstanding academic record, attracted the attention of the school's administration. When he finished the sixth grade, Father Fernando María Moreta, S.J., his spiritual adviser, sent for him.

"Gustavo, you're doing well at school," he said, "and I want to congratulate you."

"Thank you, Father," the boy responded.

"You have special qualities, my son," the priest continued, "and the house of God could derive much benefit from them. Would you consider studying at a seminary?"

Cisneros felt flattered.

"Maybe...I'll think about it."

That same night he talked it over with his parents. A week later, he found himself on a plane heading for the United States. Although Don Diego Cisneros never interfered with the professional choices of his children, it was clear to him that a boy of twelve was not prepared to make so important a decision. He preferred him to make a mature judgment after weighing the options.

Don Diego wanted his children to have the same kind of multicultural education that he himself had enjoyed, which had been an enormous advantage in life. It had allowed him to feel English in Trinidad, Cuban in Havana, American in New York, and Venezuelan in Caracas.

After an intensive program in English, Gustavo finished a junior-high program at Nyack Boarding School, in New York, and preparatory school at Suffield Academy, in Connecticut. The change in language did not affect Cisneros' grades, which continued to be good, and he even won the prize as best in his class in history.

He stayed in touch with his father through letters, telephone calls, and trips to Caracas during school vacations. Diego Cisneros also traveled to New York frequently and would often spend the weekends with his son. During vacations, instead of engaging in the pastimes appropriate to his age, Gustavo preferred to accompany his father to inspect one of the Pepsi-Cola plants or to work at Venevisión. "It amused people that I was there, and I wasn't a bother." He paid careful attention in order to absorb all he could from his father and the environment. At times, when they were alone, he would offer suggestions or criticisms.

"Don't criticize, give solutions," his father would respond with firmness. Gustavo Cisneros remembered this "as good advice for any boy."

When he had completed secondary school Gustavo returned to Venezuela intending to begin the study of law at the Universidad Católica Andrés Bello. In eighteen months he obtained a Venezuelan baccalaureate diploma and completed the first year of law school, but the field bored him. Although he was doing well, he could not see himself practicing law and did not see it as his vocation.

His return to Venezuela allowed him to reaffirm contact with his country and become more involved in his father's business. Gustavo Cisneros points out that "contrary to what one might think," following in his father's footsteps was his own decision; it was not imposed on him.

"My father would have gladly accepted his children studying medicine, like our grandfather, or even becoming priests," he says.

A photograph of Gustavo Cisneros in 1963, taken during a celebration at D. Cisneros & Co., shows him at eighteen: confident, with his father's warm smile, attractive, and impeccably dressed. He would not leave his father's side. Diego, impressed by the boy's curiosity and his passion for business, kept him close in order to train him.

"When I was fourteen," Gustavo Cisneros would recall several years later, "I accompanied my father to a dinner at the Hotel Delmonico in New York, where he said to me: 'Gustavo, I'm going to teach you to be a business leader.'"

Upon completing his first year of law school at the Universidad Católica, Cisneros chose to return to the United States, and in June 1965 he enrolled at Babson College, in Wellesley, Massachusetts, a college town located approximately fourteen miles from Boston. The school was founded in 1919 by Roger Babson, a financier and conservative presidential candidate, who imparted to the college a serious character focused on the challenges of business.

Babson, which was rooted in the best New England tradition, was a pleasant place. Harvard University and Wellesley College, both of which were nearby, had large, vibrant, and diverse student bodies.

When his brother Ricardo joined him at Babson in 1966, and they rented a house in the neighboring town of Framingham, Gustavo stood out as a good host at the parties they gave.

He seemed to have time for everything, from going to a party on Friday to meeting his father at the Hotel Delmonico when Diego was traveling on business or for pleasure. He was a well-organized student who did not have to stay up all night to cram for exams. He would even remind his friends when they seemed to be avoiding their responsibilities: "Let's go, guys, it's time to study," he would tell them. He continued to receive good grades.

In their free time, the Cisneros brothers organized teams to play dominoes. "Gustavo and Ricardo were an impossible combination to beat," says Johnny Fanjul, Cisneros' friend at college and a member of a Cuban family that had owned large sugar plantations on the island. "When it's time to play, he plays hard, and when it's time to work, he works hard," the Cuban recalls.

Babson continued to mold the intellectual personality of Gustavo Cisneros. He particularly remembers Professor Robert Wertheimer, a German Jew who had fled the Nazis. He had an elegant and special way of convincing his students that "individuals and states should not respond to planning but to incentives." Today this may seem an obvious piece of advice, but not at a time when Ché Guevara was considered a hero, the Soviet Union was in fierce competition with the United States in the race to conquer space, and powerful bureaucrats in Moscow, Beijing, and New Delhi were establishing economic five-year plans.

Diego did not spoil his children with great luxuries; this was evident even in their allowances, which, without being frugal, did not reflect the family fortune: each brother received $15 a week, as Ricardo Valladares, an old colleague, recalls. This led the brothers at an early age to develop small businesses, for example, a snow-removal service during the harsh Massachusetts winters.

Cisneros was fiercely loyal to his friends. In February 1968—when there were only three months to graduation—Johnny Fanjul had a traffic accident after a party and was taken to the hospital with two broken legs. In an act that would reinforce their mutual affection, Cisneros was the first to go to the hospital to donate blood. Then he tended to his friend's anguished parents when they arrived from Miami.

"He was a natural leader," says Fanjul. "He was aware that he had a mission."

When he was in Caracas during the summer the young Gustavo Cisneros plunged into his father's exhausting work schedule. Diego's workday began before sunrise. After reviewing his schedule at home, Diego would go to his center of operations, the Central Office for Technical Advice and Assistance, known by its Spanish acronym, OCAAT.

The creation of OCAAT was one of Diego's managerial accomplishments. As his business organization grew, it became increasingly challenging for Diego to manage its divisions. The organization was integrated vertically through satellite businesses that revolved around and supported Pepsi-Cola: there was no key supply needed by the bottling plants that was not in his hands. The bottles were produced by Produvisa, the caps by Tapas Corona, the sugar by Central Azucarero Portuguesa, and the carbonic gas by Liquid Carbonic: all companies affiliated with the Cisneros Group. In order to grow in the market, Don Diego created Concentrados Nacionales to develop the Hit line of soft drinks that included pineapple, lemon, orange, and *frescolita* (red cola) flavors; by 1970 these companies would be joined by Gaveplast, which supplied plastic cartons for transporting the bottles. Through this vertical integration, Pepsi-Cola was assured a constant supply of raw materials in a country where shortages could suddenly occur when least expected.

OCAAT oversaw the common functions of the different divisions, such as auditing, human resources, and legal services. In that period of his apprenticeship, OCAAT was, for Cisneros, a window onto his father's dynamic world of business.

While he liked Pepsi-Cola, the young Gustavo Cisneros felt a special affinity for Venevisión. Diego would go to the station in the mid-afternoon, and his son would get there early to have Diego's work schedule ready for him. Gustavo did not become bored: "I was an ongoing student of how to get things done," he recalls.

It was during his summer work that Gustavo detected the storm clouds beginning to threaten the Group's business. The shareholding structure of the Pepsi-Cola empire had become complicated. Cisneros family members—that is, Diego and the heirs of his late brother Antonio—shared control of Pepsi-Cola in Venezuela with other families who had been with them from the beginning, including the Pérez Benítezes, the Paríses, the Monsantos, and the Brillembourgs. The Monsanto family had significant influence on the Caracas concession, one of the four "mother" regions depended upon by smaller operations that were added as production and distribution increased. The Monsantos also controlled Valencia, while the Cisneros family presided over the eastern operation based in Barcelona and the western operation in Maracaibo.

The difficulty lay in the fact that Caracas, unlike the other regions, was not managed directly by the Cisneros family, and it was having problems; this is why Diego convinced his partner, Roberto Monsanto, to let him intervene at the plant. Diego appointed men he trusted and improved distribution and marketing, bringing the output of the Caracas bottling plant up to the level of the rest of the country.

Roberto Monsanto, perhaps uncomfortable at what had happened, asked Diego to give his managers an opportunity to run the operation again. Diego agreed, but on the condition that Estanislao Pérez, a young executive who had earned Diego's respect because of his managerial talents, would keep his position.

The problems in Caracas were not the only source of differences between the two families. Supported by other shareholders, the Monsantos disagreed with the strict policy of capital reinvestment implemented by Diego. At the time, costly technological changes were being effected at the plants, and operations in Colombia and Brazil had to be financed. In what would be the Cisneros Group's first steps outside Venezuela, Diego wanted to expand Pepsi-Cola throughout Latin America.

"Papá was an international entrepreneur," says Gustavo Cisneros, "a Venezuelan ahead of his time. He began investing in Venezuela, and by 1947 he was already bottling in Colombia. He had firmly established himself in Brazil, and he wanted to establish businesses in the United States. We [his children] had very solid conversations about planning, about what to do in the future. I was already talking about the need to move into supermarkets and breweries."

In view of such ambitious projects, there was no room for dissension in the ranks of the shareholders, and Gustavo Cisneros was concerned about how these differences of opinion drained his father.

"Papá," he said to him one day, "these discussions with the other shareholders can't go on. Why don't we buy the Monsanto share?"

"Perhaps you're right, Gustavo, but I ask you to be patient," his father responded affectionately. "I can handle these things."

The truth was that as long as Diego was at the head, the Monsantos would not be prepared to go beyond verbal criticisms. No one doubted the charisma, capacity for work, and drive of Diego Cisneros. What he could not imagine was that because of personal circumstances, his son would be responsible for doing battle in the conflict that threatened to divide Pepsi-Cola Venezuela, undoing years of work by the brothers Diego and Antonio. This situation would become one of the first trials by fire of the younger Cisneros generation.

In 1968, Gustavo Cisneros graduated *cum laude* from Babson College. The school yearbook says simply that he received his degree in "Economics." His expression in the yearbook photograph is serene and intense. Immediately afterward Gustavo headed for the offices of ABC to serve an internship. He wanted to prepare himself for taking control of Venevisión, since that was where he felt he could make the greatest contribution. The commercial strength of the medium and its potential for internationalization was already becoming apparent.

Cisneros' arrival at ABC could not have happened at a more opportune time. In the late 1960s there was a good deal of adrenaline in the veins of television channels in the United States. No longer a cottage industry, television had become a huge business generating revenues of more than $1 billion a year. Some five hundred channels distributed the programming offered by ABC, NBC, and CBS, the three major networks. At that time ABC was the smallest of the three, but its president, Leonard Goldenson, the same man who had advised Diego at Venevisión, had the vision and forcefulness that would move the network into first place, and he was a tireless innovator. Goldenson had already acquired the rights to broadcast Monday-night football games, a custom that has been maintained over time. He foresaw the value of sports on the small screen, and years later he founded the sports channel ESPN for cable television.

Goldenson was Gustavo Cisneros' mentor, and when he was not available his assistant took on the role. Since the operation was small, there were no layers of bureaucracy to restrict Cisneros' initiative.

"They let me do whatever I wanted, from operating the camera to editing and handling the cables. It was all very fast," he says.

In the meantime, Gustavo was in constant communication with his father. In June 1969 they met in Wellesley to attend Ricardo's graduation from Babson College. Diego was content, because here were the successors to whom he would entrust the future of the Group. He had once told Estanislao Pérez, one of his closest collaborators at Pepsi-Cola, "Gustavo will open new paths for the group, and Ricardo will take care of consolidating them." Ricardo, who is more reserved than his older brother, feels more comfortable in the world of numbers.

At ABC, Cisneros worked in the network offices in Detroit, Chicago, New York, and Los Angeles, and he still remembers how much he enjoyed his internship. The Venezuelan had first-rate colleagues at work, some of television's true champions. Outstanding among them were Michael Eisner, who would later head the Walt Disney Company, and Barry Diller, who would build the Fox and USA networks. At that time these innovators were also beginning their careers, and for the past forty years they have maintained their friendship.

Shortly before Christmas 1969, Cisneros received a call from his father asking him to return to Caracas. Diego was concerned that his son was being seduced by American television. When he expected him to be in Los Angeles, he would turn up in New York. Now he needed him at his side.

Gustavo Cisneros' plans took an unhappy turn at the end of February 1970. He was working at Venevisión when he received a call from the regional vice president of Pepsi-Cola in Maracaibo.

"Gustavo, I'm calling because of your father," he said in a worried voice.

"What's happened?" Gustavo asked.

"Diego isn't feeling well, but we're certain he'll be better soon."

That did not happen. Diego Cisneros suffered a heart attack. He was fifty-eight years old.

He was unconscious when he was brought to the San Román Clinic in Caracas. In addition to the heart attack, he also had had a stroke. The doctors presented a discouraging picture to Doña Albertina and the eight children who had gathered there. There was nothing else the the physicians could do. The treatment Diego required was highly specialized; he would have to be moved to the United States, but there was a chance the trip would only complicate his precarious situation. The specialists recommended that he remain hospitalized in Caracas.

However, the entire family agreed that it was worth it to attempt the trip. They knew the entrepreneur would prefer to die fighting.

Outwardly, Gustavo Cisneros appeared calm and practical, but on the inside he was devastated. Even today it is difficult for him to reconstruct the sequence of events during those months in 1970.

At the end of March the family took Don Diego to New York's Rusk Institute. He not only survived the move, but his prognosis was fairly positive, though his rehabilitation would take at least a year, perhaps two. In May, Gustavo Cisneros rented a small apartment in New York to be near his father.

Gustavo Cisneros Rendiles and Paticia Phelps Parker were married on June 10, 1970, at Saint Patrick's Cathedral in the heart of New York City, the place where they had met coming out of Mass nine years earlier. It was the same church where, in 2003, Guillermo Cisneros—the son of Gustavo and Patty—married Adriana Catalina de Santiago Atencio, a Venezuelan. Patty was the daughter of William Phelps, a member of the Phelps family, the founding owners of Radio Caracas Television. Her family settled in Venezuela in 1896, when her great-grandfather, the eminent ornithologist William H. Phelps, came to the country and conducted groundbreaking work.

Gustavo and Patty had a simple ceremony. Their wedding trip was interrupted by news of the failing health of Patty's father and they returned immediately to Venezuela. William Phelps died a few days later.

Gustavo was just twenty-five years old. Sorrow would bring the young couple even closer together, and oblige Cisneros to take the entrepreneurial reins of the group earlier than anticipated.

3. The Boys

In mid-1970, Diego, who was recovering from his stroke, decided to send a recorded greeting to his managers, who were meeting at the Macuto Sheraton Hotel on the coast of La Guaira, near Caracas. The message was brief and his voice somewhat tremulous:

"I have never felt closer to all of you than during these two weeks when you have been together at this convention," he said. The most emotional moment came at the end: "I wish that all of you had a single heart, a single body, so that I could give all of you a single embrace." People rose to their feet. Tears fell from some eyes.

His father's illness meant that Gustavo had to assume—and quickly—the presidency of Venevisión, but Pepsi-Cola Venezuela was a source of concern.

By this time Roberto Monsanto, the transportation entrepreneur who had been partners with Diego Cisneros for three decades, had died. Naturally, one would expect that over the course of so many years the two men had experienced occasional differences, but these had always been resolved in order to find a solution. Now, Julieta Monsanto, Don Roberto's oldest daughter, had decisive influence in the Monsanto group, but his various heirs held differing opinions regarding the path they should follow. The intricate shareholding structure of Pepsi-Cola Venezuela, in which some families controlled one region but not others, made innovations difficult, especially if these involved new investments.

The various groups fought to take control of a new plant, and the directors' meetings were "pitched battles," as Gustavo recalls.

Some of the families began to insinuate that Diego should resign the presidency of the company due to his illness. Gustavo and Ricardo could not allow this to happen because, to a large extent, the company had reached its powerful position as a result of their father's sustained efforts.

Toward the end of 1970, Diego returned to the office part-time. But beneath a cloak of normalcy, upper management was weakened by internal differences. The company was divided according to the number of shares held by each family. The Cisneros family was in charge of operations in the west and east of the country, while the other shareholders controlled the central region, which included Caracas and Valencia. For a business whose success depended essentially on distribution, it was a hopeless arrangement: a truck with a salesman on board could not leave its own territory, even when there was a need to do so. In reality, Pepsi-Cola Venezuela had disintegrated into several companies.

Gustavo decided that he had to buy the Monsanto shares. The problem was the price being asked. Even so, he was prepared to pay it. Fortunately, Coca-Cola had wonderful relations with Gustavo and had begun talks aimed at having the Cisneros family assume the franchise in Venezuela. This possibility played a part in persuading the Monsantos to sell their shares in Pepsi-Cola. In fact, Coca-Cola had already ceded the Venezuelan territory to Cisneros, and with that front covered, Gustavo was able to commit the resources to buy back the shares.

Gustavo persuaded his first cousin, Oswaldo—a son and heir of Antonio Cisneros—to join him in the operation. Oswaldo was cautious and hesitated at first, but eventually he agreed. This was the moment when the team of Gustavo, Ricardo, and Oswaldo Cisneros, which would go on to achieve significant successes, began to take definitive shape. It was also at this time that Gustavo sought the advice of Pedro Tinoco, a banker and corporate lawyer who had worked with large corporations in the United States during the 1950s. An old collaborator in the Group describes him as "Gustavo's great colleague and counselor, his business adviser." Over the years, Tinoco would become a mentor to the younger generation. Within the Cisneros Group he would be known by the nickname "Buddha," because of his temperament, entrepreneurial astuteness, and ability to decode human beings and the nature of power. He was both a financial adviser and legal counselor. Gustavo Cisneros remembers him as a completely loyal and devoted person with a great ability to provide guidance on how to accomplish goals while minimizing risks and costs.

Cisneros' next step was to talk with Luis Antonio Pellicer, the vice president of Pepsi-Cola. As Roberto's nephew, Pellicer enjoyed the confidence of the Monsantos.

"He was a key man for me," says Cisneros. "Pellicer convinced the Monsantos to sell, persuading them that with the money from the sale they could do much more in the United States than in Venezuela."

Following the separation from the Monsantos, Oswaldo became head of a unified Pepsi-Cola. Trained from the ground up by various Pepsi managers, he was considered one of the group and therefore the ideal person to run operations from then on.

Diego Cisneros created an atmosphere in which his two sons could channel their entrepreneurial restlessness. Gustavo was working at Venevisión, and Ricardo was training at an automobile dealership.

In August 1972, in a simple office in the Fertec building on Avenida Libertador in Caracas, the corporate entity GURI, for "Gustavo and Ricardo," was born. They were joined by Estanislao Pérez and Oswaldo Cisneros.

"Even then we were thinking about department stores, supermarkets, radio, the computer revolution," recalls Gustavo Cisneros.

The new division, which became the legal and financial department of the Cisneros Group, was a miniature reflection of OCAAT, the office that coordinated the various activities of Pepsi-Cola in Venezuela. At GURI, strategic plans and budgets were developed for the companies, with periodic reviews.

Gustavo Cisneros, as the president of the leading television channel in the country, had a great advantage: access to bank financing for the purchase of companies. One of the first enterprises acquired was Gaveplast, which manufactured plastic cartons for transporting bottles of Pepsi and other products. The business was part of Diego Cisneros' plan to vertically integrate all the companies surrounding the world of Pepsi-Cola, from the manufacturer of caps to the sugar supplier. The next to be added was Pharsana de Venezuela S.A. (1973), which sold Chicco baby products, an Italian brand. Another business brought in by the younger Cisneros generation was O'Caña, a liquor distributor founded in 1973. The petroleum boom had increased the demand for all consumer goods.

Gustavo Cisneros did not want to undertake the O'Caña business by himself. He chose to organize a group of partners, each of whom would contribute his specialty. Gustavo was, in the words of one collaborator, "the orchestra conductor," the strategist.

Gustavo and Ricardo Cisneros, and Estanislao Pérez, traveled to Europe to obtain distribution rights for various wines and liquors. Although the brothers were not yet thirty (the "old man" of the group was Estanislao, who was thirty-seven), they were preceded by an impressive record that included the presidency of Venevisión and the fact that they were the principal shareholders in the only Pepsi-Cola bottler in the world that could surpass Coca-Cola. They would soon acquire the rights to brands like Dimple whiskey, Mumm champagne, and Paternina and Sansón wines, with financing provided by the suppliers themselves, who were impressed by the backgrounds of these young men. They began operations in 1974—José Irimia was the first general manager of the new firm—with a purchase of 3,000 cases. Then, an advertising campaign on radio and television helped O'Caña to increase sales sharply, and by the early 1980s they were selling as many as 120,000 cases of Scotch a year.

There were also missteps. Gustavo Cisneros decided to manufacture a white rum, but Venezuelan consumers, accustomed to the dark variety, did not accept the new product. The Bacardis, commented Cisneros in a recent interview, "are the people who know the most about rum in the world; we had the best distribution channels and were successful in marketing and advertising. But being the best rum-maker in the world was not the same as being the best rum-maker in Venezuela. For Venezuelans, the taste of the Bacardi white rum was not as desirable as that of Venezuelan dark rum, and we failed miserably. I sold my shares, and with that money I bought a significant interest in Cacique, which at that time was the best rum in the country and the one that was exported the most. Eventually we sold it to Seagrams with a very good return."

As their businesses grew, Gustavo and Ricardo expanded the personnel at the Cisneros Group and had to move to larger offices on the Paseo Las Mercedes, in Caracas. These new offices would become the headquarters for the Cisneros Group in Venezuela for the next thirty years. As for their brothers, Diego Alberto was working at Pepsi-Cola in Valera, a small town in western Venezuela, Carlos Enrique was at Pepsi-Cola Brazil, and Antonio José and Gerardo were studying in the United States.

The offices on Paseo Las Mercedes consolidated resources to provide the necessary financial support to the entire Cisneros Group. At its height, at the beginning of the 1990s, the organization had 150 employees, including auditors, analysts, and attorneys. One of the defining characteristics of the Cisneros Group was, and continues to be, the separation between its financial and operational arms. In general, those responsible for supervising the accounts of the various enterprises were called "financial managers," in contrast to those in charge of management, who were called "operational managers." This separation between the financial and operational functions was not new. It was, for example, a characteristic of the American company General Electric. There, a general manager could dispense with any employee in the company except his vice president for finance, a prudent means of control.

Generally, no operational manager likes to have a financial manager looking over his shoulder, checking his figures, and reporting to a superior somewhere else, and for this reason the two groups frequently clashed over the next two decades. But in retrospect, the mechanism imposed discipline and accountability on an organization headed by a man like Gustavo Cisneros, whose mind bubbled over with creative energy.

"I've watched this competition from the beginning, and it's healthy," says an executive who has been with the group since 1978. "There is self-auditing, requiring the companies to exercise control over themselves."

Gustavo himself referred to Ricardo and his people as his "filter." In fact, the operational-financial duality reflected the division of roles between the two brothers, though it would not be correct to define Ricardo exclusively as a financier since he also had operational roles. According to an executive close to the group, Gustavo is more interested in strategy, while Ricardo favors tactics.

In this way, each brother complemented the other's abilities. Gustavo was the architect who designed the property, organized its spaces, and designated the builders, while Ricardo made certain that the edifice had no structural faults and kept within budgets and established timetables. When he perceived an error, he had the right to veto Gustavo's design. Without actually planning it, as the years passed the older brother would be the public face of the Group, the one with the title of CEO. Ricardo, given his reserved nature, preferred to tend to the finances. It was a family alliance based on mutual respect, just as Don Diego had visualized it.

In the mid-1970s, when he was barely thirty years old, Gustavo undertook the new challenge of entrepreneurial growth and diversification. He had great confidence in the potential of his partnership with Ricardo, and that was the message he wanted to transmit to the new executives in the Cisneros Group. Alejandro Rivera, a current adviser to the office of the president at the Group, recalls his first interview with Gustavo Cisneros: "He told me that he did not want all his eggs in one basket, that he wanted to expand the group into new areas."

The challenge stimulated him, coming from a businessman who was already diversified, with a television channel, soft drinks, liquors, radio stations—the Radiovisión network—and, as will be seen, a chain of supermarkets. Then Gustavo Cisneros added:

"I promise you a great deal of work, but we're trying to organize things so that we can go home at five o'clock."

From then on the norm would be twelve-to-fourteen-hour work days, because just as the staff was about to go home Gustavo would pull some project out of his sleeve, and they would have to work like madmen all over again. But during those years, what did it matter! They were young and ready to conquer the world. "All the important American bankers who visited us in Caracas were expecting to see older people, and what they found were youngsters," says Cisneros.

Strategically, Gustavo Cisneros was using the youth of the leadership team as an asset in his public relations, something he had managed with natural talent from the beginning. He would tell his guests and possible partners: "As you can see, we're all very young here, and if we're successful now, that's the best guarantee that we can go on being successful for a long time to come."

While the Cisneros Group began to put down roots in a variety of businesses, Gustavo continued to head Venevisión, the enterprise that occupies a special place in his heart.

During those years the channel experienced a stellar run. Programming, directed by Enrique Cuzcó, was first-rate. "What I know about programming, I fundamentally learned from Cuzcó," says Cisneros.

Cuzcó and his predecessor, Héctor Beltrán, had competed with two formidable rivals: the Phelps family in Radio Caracas Televisión, and the "Holy Alliance" of Vollmer-Mestre-CBS-Time Life. Of the twenty most-watched programs in 1965, eighteen were transmitted by Venevisión.

"Television requires a balance between iron administrative discipline and a high degree of creativity," says Cisneros. In an environment where "everyone feels like an artist," it is important not to lose sight of creative people and to always give them the support they need to do their work. If a channel loses favor with its public and its advertisers, repositioning it is an arduous task.

These difficulties, inherent in the business, favored the consolidation of private television in Latin America at that time. In Mexico, Emilio Azcárraga Milmo, known as "the Tiger," was the absolute master of the dial with Televisa. The Marinho family, with Globo, similarly dominated in Brazil. The same kind of consolidation had occurred in Venezuela as well. But advertisers took advantage of the stiff competition to negotiate discounts, and discounts on top of discounts. The cost of advertising in Venezuela, measured by audience share, was one of the lowest in the world.

With Mestre out of the picture in Venezuela, Gustavo Cisneros put an end to discounts. In his position as president-owner, he sat the various executives of the channel around a table so that they could resolve their differences. He encouraged more harmony between the sales teams and the programming people, who had separated into their respective domains. Economic losses began to reverse. It was a good managerial school for Cisneros. "TV is such a dynamic activity that it prepares you for any other business," he states.

Paradoxically, a new problem appeared: how to capitalize on success. According to statistics at the time, Venevisión had cornered 80 percent of the viewership. Gustavo Cisneros, never complacent in the face of success, knew that Venevisión could not grow any more in Venezuela. If he wanted it to grow, he had to conquer new territories outside Venezuela.

"From the first day I walked into Venevisión, I wanted to transform the channel into something different, something international," he says. "We always thought about expanding internationally, growing in production, in sales, and when we were allowed to, investing in communications media in other countries." From that time on Cisneros would confront a new challenge that he had to decipher, define, and realize: a channel in the United States and a television enterprise for the entire continent. In the meantime, he could export programs.

During those years it was uncommon in Latin America for a channel to program content from other channels. Rather, artists were traded. In 1970 this situation changed, and Gustavo Cisneros lost no time in calling an old friend in Costa Rica.

"Mr. Fanjul? One moment, Mr. Gustavo Cisneros is on the line."

"Juanito! Do you have a television nearby?" Cisneros asked in great excitement.

"Of course I do. What happened?"

"Turn it on...I just sold my first soap opera!"

His business success made Cisneros happy, and with reason: Venevisión International had sold the soap opera *Esmeralda* to a channel in Costa Rica. Written by Delia Fiallo, this was the starting point that would bring Venevisión into the international circuit of Latino soap operas, or *telenovelas*.

Soap operas, a cornerstone of television in Latin America, already occupied a place of honor in regional programming when Gustavo Cisneros became president of Venevisión. The pan-regional soap opera, however, had not yet been born. But that would change during the 1970s. Since then, for better or worse, the soap opera has been consecrated as the great contribution of Latino television to mass entertainment on an international scale, and Cisneros knew how to capitalize on the phenomenon.

By the mid-1970s, in fact, the Group was making strong progress. Five years after his return from the United States, Gustavo Cisneros had placed Venezuela, by means of Venevisión, on the international circuit, which had been his idea from the beginning, and the Cisneros Group was in the process of full diversification. This was the context that led to his interest in the petrochemical business.

Petroleum began to be important in Venezuela in the 1930s, when it definitively displaced traditional products like coffee and cocoa. In 1934, petroleum generated the equivalent of $42 of fiscal income for each Venezuelan. In 1973 that income had reached $583. A year later, thanks to the oil boom of the previous year, it had climbed to $1,540.

The president who inherited this bonanza was Carlos Andrés Pérez, of the Democratic Action Party. His election, in December 1973, initiated the era of bipartisanship in Venezuela when he received 49 percent of the votes while Lorenzo Fernández, of the COPEI party, received 37 percent.

Gustavo Cisneros had an idea that could generate an attractive business and would also allow him to participate in the country's development during this nationalist fervor. Pérez may have understood Latin American politics, but he was not very familiar with the nuances in the functioning of the modern developed societies to the north.

The president received Cisneros in his office in Miraflores, the Venezuelan presidential palace. Gustavo wanted to invite the government to participate in a project that involved the Cisneros Group and some foreign partners in operating three new petrochemical plants that would produce thirty-six chemicals, from caustic soda to benzene. The investment, he said, exceeded $500 million, and the figures in the preliminary studies carried out by Purvin & Lee, the advisers he had hired, were promising. If everything went according to plan, they could begin production in 1978.

"The only way this will be politically viable is if we can count on the support of the government," Cisneros told the president.

"At what percentage?"

"50-50."

The president seemed to like the idea, and Gustavo explained the details. In July 1975 the initial technical studies were supposed to be completed, at a cost of six million *bolívares* ($1.4 million). He planned to recruit the largest chemical and petroleum companies and have them participate in the project, called Pentacomplejo Petroquímicos, or Pentacom.

Until then the state-run petrochemical industry, managed by the Venezuelan Petrochemical Institute (IVP), had been inefficient. Bureaucracy, poor management, and even pressures to sell some of its products at less than the market price had weakened it. Once, after a visit to one of its plants, Carlos Andrés Pérez criticized the performance of the IVP, which some interpreted as an invitation to the private sector to intervene.

Cisneros had taken up the challenge. In his plan, the government would contribute financing and raw materials for the plants, while the international petrochemical firms would operate them and sell the products abroad. And Gustavo Cisneros would be the orchestra conductor who would coordinate everything. With the president's endorsement, he held in his hands a business that could surpass Pepsi-Cola. In February 1975, Pentacom made its public debut. The magazine *Bohemia* referred to the project as "the most powerful entrepreneurial association ever achieved in Venezuela." Cisneros had convinced eighteen colleagues, including his attorney-mentor, Pedro Tinoco, to participate by contributing ten million *bolívares* ($3 million) to cover the costs of the technical studies for the project.

Gustavo Cisneros admits that he never imagined the political storm the Pentacom project would create. It was not enough to have convinced the Venezuelan president. Pentacom, according to one deputy, was a maneuver intended to "filter the interests of transnational companies into an industry that is vital to the development of our country." Another accused Pentacom of being "a vulgar maneuver by the bourgeoisie." As a consequence, a great debate began as to whether the petrochemical industry, classified as a "basic industry," ought to remain in the hands of the government. Some saw Pentacom as a facade for a secret pact between the entrepreneurs and President Pérez.

Cisneros vehemently defended his project. There was absolutely no pact, he insisted. On April 16, 1975, he revealed to a congressional subcommittee the conditions for the project, specifying that ownership of each of the plants would be determined by the government, which also had the authority to select the foreign firms that would contribute their technical and marketing skills.

"Pentacom is not imposing decisions on the government," he said. "Just the opposite: it is designed to operate under the premise that it is the government that decides. I would go so far as to state that the failure of the petrochemical industry in Venezuela is not so much the consequence of the government's inefficiency, but of the lack of support it has received from the private sector."

Until the moment Cisneros attempted to drive the project forward, the Venezuelan petrochemical industry had achieved only symbolic production of very few products, and had accumulated losses of some $200 million since its founding in 1953. In March 1975, in statements to the newspaper *La Verdad* in Caracas, Cisneros argued that his project was "a viable solution that could be implemented without disrespect to any previous effort." He said that Venezuela had the potential to develop a large-scale petrochemical industry, "without this jeopardizing her well-known conservationist course with regard to our nonrenewable natural resources."

Cisneros saw the need for integrating the private sector into the petroleum industry, an idea fully accepted today but resisted then.

The political storm frightened potential partners. Of the thirty-three companies contacted, only four were openly enthusiastic (W.R. Grace and ARCO Chemical among them). According to Purvin & Lee, responsible for first contacts abroad, five acknowledged having interest "but with reservations" (Shell was in this group); another five did not wish to express a definite opinion, but showed "some interest" (DuPont, BASF, Hoechst, among others); seven rejected the idea outright.

Cisneros understood that politics was sinking his project. His father had warned him not to become involved in doing business with politicians. The son had pushed the project forward because technically Pentacom was not part of the governmental sphere, though he realized later it was a minefield of political interests.

"An important sector of the country wanted us to triumph and gave us a good deal of encouragement," Cisneros recalls, but he was not prepared to waste more energy on a discussion that would drain time and resources.

On May 2, 1975, Cisneros sent a letter to the newspaper *El Nacional* to make public his withdrawal from the Pentacom project. He regretted that Pentacom "had become the motive for sterile controversy and political complications resulting from distorted interpretations." He also indicated that "the decision to withdraw was due to the fact that circumstantial political passions and causes prevented a calm and rational analysis of the project."

Pentacom was a serious disappointment for Cisneros. The bitter taste of this failure sharpened his desire to internationalize and taught him to separate good relationships with governments from business. He was ahead of his time with his vision of the petroleum business. However, the polemic engendered by the project made it clear that conditions were not yet ripe to undertake it successfully.

Cisneros had put the Pentacom episode behind him when he received a call from Pedro Tinoco, who offered him a deal that would significantly empower the Group in Venezuela:

"I'm speaking to you as a representative of the Rockefeller family," he said.

In the mid-1970s, Rodman Rockefeller, a member of the renowned American political and industrial dynasty, was having difficulties with the International Basic Economy Corporation (IBEC). IBEC originated in Nelson Rockefeller's affinity for Latin America. Nelson had been coordinator of inter-American affairs for President Roosevelt during the Second World War. When the conflict ended, Nelson was concerned that the United States might lose interest in the region, and he founded IBEC as a vehicle for promoting commercial relations between North and South America. Over the years it formed 133 enterprises in thirty-three countries, in areas ranging from the sale of food products to financial services. Despite being so diverse a group, with some ups and downs, IBEC was reporting profits.

The Rockefellers had always had a special affinity for Venezuela, where they had established such enterprises as Leche Carabobo, the Avila Hotel, and the CADA supermarket chain.

IBEC operated without problems between the 1950s and the 1970s. But after that time, the region no longer needed active promotion, and the Rockefellers decided to sell their companies. Furthermore, Venezuela had joined the Andean Pact, a treaty that promoted nationalization of foreign investments. "The writing was on the wall, and it said: Leave!" Rodman Rockefeller, Nelson's son, would later say.

CADA was the Rockefellers' jewel in Venezuela. Shopping in CADA was like shopping in a supermarket in Chicago or Los Angeles. It represented what was most modern in the field at the time. Rodman and Harvey Schwartz, his assistant in charge of negotiations, spoke with their minority partners to offer them shares in IBEC, but these partners prolonged the negotiations, knowing that time was in their favor. Eventually, they speculated, the Rockefellers would find themselves obliged to sell at bargain-basement prices.

On the advice of Tinoco, whom Rodman considered "a valuable friend and one of the most brilliant people in Venezuela," the Rockefellers extended the offer to other Venezuelan groups, but "no one in the country was thinking about a modern transaction," says Schwartz. "They all spoke in terms of book value, which made no sense because the shares were worth much more."

Negotiations between the Rockefellers and the Cisneros Group were not smooth, although the Americans were pleased to deal with counterparts who employed modern concepts when it was time to calculate the value of companies. In the final moments of their conversations, the two groups went into different rooms in Tinoco's offices, while the lawyer diligently went back and forth between them. Gustavo Cisneros, taken with the elephant-patterned tie that Schwartz was wearing, sent his tie to Schwartz as a signal that he was ready to sign an agreement, and so that Schwartz , in turn, could send back his tie. The American executive gave Tinoco the elephant tie that Cisneros wanted, and the agreement was concluded.

Days later, one of Cisneros' assistants was sent to London to resolve the final transactional details. In addition to the various assets held by IBEC in Venezuela, the Cisneros Group bought 20 percent of IBEC's parent company. This became the largest commercial transaction in the history of Venezuela.

Cisneros had fulfilled one of his great desires: to acquire a chain of supermarkets and thereby deepen the Group's diversification in mass consumption. This acquisition transformed him into the largest private employer in Venezuela, and in 1976 *BusinessWeek* included him in its list of the eight most influential Latin Americans in the world.

CADA's crown jewel was its forty-eight supermarkets, which employed 2,300 people and generated sales of 300 million dollars a year. But the acquisition was in reality a package that included fifteen soda fountains, a coffee-processing plant, a bread factory—the first of its kind in Latin America—and a chain of supermarkets in El Salvador.

Subsequently the deal would expand with the acquisition of a cattle ranch, Mata de Bárbara, in the state of Barinas, Venezuela. Cisneros decided to attempt an experiment there that had nothing to do with agriculture.

The young entrepreneur and his wife were convinced that education could help overcome the problems of underdevelopment in Venezuela. "Levels of education and poverty are closely related, and the development of our region depends, in large measure, on the instruction we give to our citizens," he says, regarding the reasons that led him to initiate a literacy program among the *campesinos* of Mata de Bárbara.

Cisneros knew the work of a priest, Monsignor José Joaquín Salcedo, who directed an innovative program of long-distance education that had been producing good results in Colombia since 1947. Gustavo Cisneros suggested to Patty, who was interested in education and literacy programs, that she redesign the program for Venezuela. She had dedicated the early years of her marriage to caring for her three children—Guillermo, Carolina, and Adriana—and she wanted to take on a challenge that would help to improve the quality of life in her country.

Patty considers Monsignor Salcedo as one of the people, after her father and Gustavo, who has had the greatest influence on her life.

The Venezuelan version of the program, called ACUDE, an acronym equivalent in English to "be productive," or "respond," consisted of a kit of phonograph records and printed material, which cost very little, thanks to subsidies. Patty wondered if the workers on Mata de Bárbara would participate in the program. When she arrived to teach the first lessons, she was impressed by the reception. Some forty *campesinos* between the ages of eighteen and twenty-six, looking weather-beaten but strong, showed up. Some, as if they could not contain their desire to learn, held pencils in their fists as if they were daggers.

In addition to teaching the mechanics of reading, ACUDE attempts to improve the quality of life and the self-esteem of the *campesinos*, linking reading with content that deals with hygiene and health. In parallel classes, women were taught to cook vegetables and other nutritious foods of the region. There were also classes in chess, and a soccer field was built, all within a framework aimed at fighting poverty by attacking the obstacles that stand in the way of individual self-improvement.

"The struggle against poverty demands, first of all, respect for individuals, for their dignity and their potential," says Patty Cisneros. "Rescuing self-esteem is a first step; developing aptitudes and creating the conditions for material prosperity are also essential. The process should move forward on all fronts simultaneously."

The Mata de Bárbara experiment achieved its objective of teaching literacy to the inhabitants of that rural area. In the years that followed, from the offices of the Cisneros Group on Paseo Las Mercedes, Patty and Gustavo Cisneros worked to expand ACUDE throughout the country, under the direction of Mario Martínez, who had been a priest. So that it would not be perceived as a public relations instrument, Gustavo Cisneros rarely appeared to promote the program, and he always insisted that someone else serve as its president. From 1991 to 1994, the kit was revised and the improved version distributed to more than 800,000 people, until technology, as well as changes and circumstances in Venezuela—as will be seen—dictated its retirement.

"How can we combat poverty and provide a large number of people with access to a better standard of living? In my opinion, the answer lies in education," says Patty Cisneros.

4. A Quarry of Talents

> You always have to arrive before the competition... either you arrive first or your problems multiply.
>
> GUSTAVO CISNEROS

Gustavo Cisneros decided to present the executives at CADA with a challenge. He told them that he wanted to expand the operation from forty-eight to one hundred branches. It was not a whimsical idea but the product of careful planning.

It was a good moment to be in a business oriented toward consumption. Driven by petrodollars, the *bolívar* became a currency as hard as iron, keeping the same currency value exchange of 4.3 *bolívares* to the dollar that it had had since 1964. With salaries adjusting to inflation, by 1975 the purchasing power of each Venezuelan was equal to that of a Japanese. At the end of the decade, each Venezuelan enjoyed a per capita income higher than that of its Latin American counterparts, and on a par with that of the Spaniards, according to the World Bank. It was the period of shopping trips to Miami, in a fever of consumerism known as "*Dame Dos*"—"It's cheap, I'll take two!"

Imports doubled between 1973 and 1975, reaching $5.4 billion. Two years later they would double again.

The supermarket business is sustained by the volume of sales, and in the Venezuela of that period there still existed a good number of towns that were inadequately served. Wherever CADA went, the people's quality of life improved.

"In how long a time?" asked the manager of the chain.

"Five years."

"A hundred supermarkets?"

It was an enormous challenge, considering that it had taken CADA twenty years to open forty-eight branches.

Cisneros contacted key people in the United States to help in the work he had assigned his executives. He turned to the Food Market Institute, an industry association whose directors recommended the implementation of certain basic concepts in the supermarket business. It was better to have a single center for buying, warehousing, and distribution than dozens of supermarkets making requests on their own. A greater volume of purchases meant more discounts from suppliers. And so, in 1981, Cisneros opened a new distribution center in Cagua—in the state of Aragua in north-central Venezuela—which was unusually large for the industry at the time.

As a way to encourage his employees, Cisneros spared no expense in training his personnel. In 1976 he sent twenty-five executives to the annual Food Market Institute trade show in Dallas so that they could become familiar with the latest trends in the industry. The executives found in Publix supermarkets an ally that helped them in their apprenticeship. The Florida-based enterprise knew how to remodel an establishment without interfering with the customers. In Venezuela, these renovations took months. Renovations at Publix, on the other hand, took weeks, and were carried out without having to close the store.

The advantages of CADA included its debt-free balance sheet and its potential for generating positive cash flow. A supermarket is essentially a volume business. It receives payment in cash at the registers and pays its obligations to suppliers in installments in order to maintain inventory. This method of operation, accompanied by a constant increase in sales, generated the financial resources that were used to expand the supermarket chain.

On October 2, 1978, Gustavo Cisneros and his team celebrated the thirtieth anniversary of the chain. In his speech, he said, "We are proud to inform you that, according to the figures indicated on our computers, CADA serves a million consumers a month." He also emphasized that from the time the Group had taken over the business, sales had doubled. The entrepreneur went on to announce that 97 percent of the goods bought by CADA carried the stamp "Made in Venezuela." This was lauded by the government, which at the time was implementing a program to reduce imports.

Gustavo Cisneros, convinced that entrepreneurial freedom and political freedom ought to travel hand in hand, took advantage of the celebration of the thirtieth anniversary of CADA to organize a Colloquium on Autocracy, Democracy, and Totalitarianism in order to discuss these subjects. Prominent among those attending were the economist John Kenneth Galbraith, Arthur Schlesinger, the Harvard University historian, and Felipe González, the young president of the Spanish Socialist Workers Party.

This was an opportunity to broaden Venezuela's perspectives on the world. Moreover, Cisneros, an unconditional defender of political and economic freedoms, felt great pride when he saw that his country was enjoying democratic stability in a region afflicted by authoritarian regimes.

CADA was the key to opening new doors. Cisneros began to apply the formula his father used to make Pepsi-Cola a success, that is, he looked for a way to integrate his enterprises vertically. He owned the largest supermarket chain and the principal television channel in the country. Now he could focus on acquiring suppliers, because the CADA-Venevisión combination provided the platform for the mass-marketing of brands that no competitor could match.

For example, the factory that produced Fisa Kapina beauty products, which represented the Helene Curtis International line in Venezuela, was experiencing financial difficulties when Gustavo Cisneros bought it in 1975. From then on, and under the operational leadership of Gustavo's brother Carlos Cisneros, Fisa Kapina reversed its fortunes and began to turn a profit. Housewives who watched soap operas on Venevisión could learn the virtues of Heno de Pravia, a bath gel, and Finesse shampoo. Moreover, the popular beauty contest Miss Venezuela, broadcast by Venevisión, also promoted the brand's products. Helene Curtis sales in Venezuela skyrocketed. During that period of expansion, another of the Cisneros brothers, Antonio José, who was a vice president of operations, assumed control of the division that covered the entire eastern part of the country.

"They are unique," a manager at the headquarters of Helene Curtis in the United States told the *Wall Street Journal*. "They have the Miss Venezuela pageants and use the winners to publicize our products. They own the media and a large part of the distribution. How can you lose in that position?"

Gustavo Cisneros kept the original managers, who were now supported by CADA and Venevisión and supervised from the central offices of the Group on Paseo Las Mercedes. With the increase in sales and cash flow, the businesses themselves eventually covered the payments for the initial acquisition. The system was simple but efficient, and he would repeat it in his international ventures a few years later. Gustavo and Ricardo and their team elaborated a simple five-point guide to help determine whether an operation was of interest. To be considered for purchase, the company had to:

1. Be oriented toward mass consumption
2. Be a leader in its market
3. Produce products simple to manufacture
4. Maintain a positive cash flow
5. Bring in its own management

The acquisitions made between 1975 and 1988 added a large shopping basket of products to the Cisneros Group, ranging from Cherry Blossom creams for polishing shoes to Apple computers. Totally new brands were also launched, which rapidly became leaders, thanks to the Venevisión-CADA combination, later joined by Maxy's Department Store. This is what happened with the Cotton Candy line of children's clothing in the mid-1980s; the brand, unknown until created by Cisneros, moved to the front ranks in its market. Another important innovation involved the Burger King franchise. When the Cisneros Group acquired the CADA chain in 1976, there were initially fifteen "soda fountains" attached to the supermarkets, conceived and designed according to the most modern standards of the time. These installations subsequently multiplied until there were thirty-two units throughout the country. Gradually, over time, the original concept went out of fashion as habits of consumption and life-styles changed, and the demand for "fast food" increased. This required, among other things, faster service and lower costs, with a reduced menu, less—or no—need for table service, and the elimination of traditional tips. Gustavo Cisneros decided to make the move from soda fountains to fast-food franchises, and Burger King, Pizza Hut, and Taco Bell were selected as the options offering the greatest possibilities to the customer. These were the first three fast-food franchises in Venezuela, with the first Burger King site operating in the CADA branch located in the district of Las Mercedes in Caracas, the first Pizza Hut opening simultaneously in Caracas and Maracaibo, and the first Taco Bell appearing in Caracas. Today, the Pizza Hut franchise in Venezuela is still managed by the Cisneros Group.

Within the Group the feeling prevailed that nothing was impossible. It even organized a small operation to bring miniature Canadian pines for Christmas to the tropical climate of Venezuela. Many trees died on the way when they were transported by ship, but a manager discovered that the trains that ran from Florida to Canada with refrigerated cars full of oranges and grapefruit returned empty. They took advantage of this unused capacity to fill the trains with pines, which were loaded onto planes in Miami, with Caracas as their final destination. In the CADA stores, each pine was sold for from $5 to $20. "The size of the CADA stores made it worthwhile," says an executive.

As time passed, the men and women of the Cisneros Group became so skilled in business planning that if an enterprise met its goals in the first quarter, it almost always did so for the next three quarters as well.

With the exception of CADA, of which it controlled 70 percent of the shares, the family owned 100 percent of the shares in the Group's other enterprises. To compensate for the lack of financial controls imposed by stock-market investors, the Cisneros Group worked with banks, which functioned as external guardians. Pedro Tinoco always advised the Cisneros brothers to pay the banks promptly and to inform them well in advance of any problem. "We have always maintained good relations with the banks, and we allow ourselves time to explain our transactions to them," says Cisneros.

This relationship would be fundamental for the Group years later, when it began to invest in international markets.

As the Cisneros Group expanded its operations in the field of mass consumption, Gustavo Cisneros did not lose sight of Venevisión. He wanted to acquire assets that could be effectively marketed through the strength of the channel. At the beginning of the 1980s, he found two such assets: Rodven and the Organización Miss Venezuela.

At the end of 1978 he met with Rodolfo Rodríguez Miranda, the son of Rodolfo Rodríguez García, the executive vice president of Venevisión at the time. The younger Rodríguez presented his idea: a factory that would produce vinyl records. After presenting the project and agreeing to bring in half the capital, he asked Gustavo Cisneros: "Would the Cisneros Group be prepared to bring in the other half?"

"You know, Rodolfo," said Gustavo, "the opportunities in this business are not in the manufacture of the records but in the rights. Let's work together, but to build an integrated record company." That is how Rodven was born.

The first vinyl records came off the press in July 1981. The factory was profitable, but Cisneros had been right: in reality, the money was in producing the music, not the plastic that recorded it. At that time an album sold for four dollars, of which one dollar was paid in rights to the owner of the license and a sizable portion of the remaining three dollars was invested in sales and distribution. What was left for the manufacturer of the records was a small fraction of the profits. Rodríguez decided to buy the rights to some popular music classics, which he compiled together into one album. Called *Momentos*, it is still the top-selling album in the history of Venezuela.

The next step was to obtain licenses from the large record companies in the United States to distribute the productions of international stars in Venezuela. The music market was different at that time. Large American labels like EMI and CBS lacked local representation and operated through licenses. Rodríguez learned that practically all the licenses were in the hands of three local labels. The young man found no way to enter the market.

"Let me see what I can do," Cisneros told him.

Cisneros called his friend Nesuhi Ertegun, president of the board of directors of Warner Elektra Atlantic (WEA) to negotiate a contract, which they signed a month before the opening of the disc factory. With support from the Group's stations and some advertising space on Venevisión, Rodven soon became the leading company in the market, a position that it maintained for the next twenty-five years. Following the contract with WEA came those with Ariola, EMI, and the Spanish Hispavox, owner of the rights to artists such as Rafael and José Luis Perales.

The next phase consisted of producing home-grown artists and selling their licenses outside the country. With the exception of José Luis Rodríguez, known as "El Puma," there were no world-famous singers in Venezuela, a fact that increased the market's potential.

The first talent that Venevisión brought to Rodven was Guillermo Dávila, who, until his appearance on the soap opera *Ligia Elena*, had been a stage actor of limited prominence. The soap opera's theme, "*Sólo pienso en ti*" (I Think Only of You), was a smash hit; the singer's melancholy eyes drove the girls wild. The soap-opera album sold 300,000 copies in Venezuela, and would be popular as well in Puerto Rico and Central America. Applying the same plan used with Dávila, the Rodven-Venevisión partnership would achieve several number-one rankings on the best-selling album charts.

As the years passed, Rodven would eventually close the circle, acquiring a chain of record stores and the production company Big Show Productions.

Just as *Esmeralda* marked Venevisión's entrance onto the stage of international soap operas, the Miss Venezuela pageant, acquired by Gustavo Cisneros in 1980, signified another rung in the internationalization of the Group, which, incidentally, helped to popularize the belief that Venezuela, in addition to oil, has the most beautiful women on the planet.

Cisneros decided early on how to direct the management of this new enterprise. First, he made sure to free the event from the intervention of corporate bureaucracies; then, he used it as a tool to enhance the potential of local talent, inside and outside the country; finally, he gave creative freedom to Osmel Sousa, director of the Organización Miss Venezuela.

Gustavo and Patty Cisneros, who knew Osmel through his work as a society reporter for a local newspaper, knew that Sousa's real passion was the feminine aesthetic. When Cisneros acquired Miss Venezuela, he named Osmel director.

"You have carte blanche to do whatever you like," he told him.

Employing a format similar to that of a major-league baseball team fed by the minor leagues, Osmel organized castings in the largest cities in the country. Since then, more than five thousand girls every year have registered for the competition in the hope of becoming the next Miss Venezuela. However, after an arduous selection process, only twenty-eight young women are accepted, and for almost a year they are trained at contest headquarters in Caracas by a team of stylists, designers, instructors in public speaking, modeling, general culture, and languages, sports trainers, and a qualified medical group. Osmel Sousa invests more than $60,000 in the formation of each participant.

Seventy beauty titles, outstanding among them four Miss Universes, five Miss Worlds, and three Miss Internationals, make Sousa the most successful director of beauty pageants in the world. This recognition, as Osmel himself emphasizes, has been possible thanks to the support offered by the Cisneros Group, especially Gustavo Cisneros.

"They have always allowed me immense artistic and operational freedom," says Sousa. "They have always liked what I've done, and that is wonderful for any person working with the company," Sousa declares.

For Cisneros, the Miss Venezuela pageant is "one of the businesses that best promotes the country's image in the world." The four-hour event, which is rebroadcast in one hundred countries, takes in an amount, in the form of advertising revenues, that easily covers a budget of some $4 million. Furthermore, the competition is a quarry of talents. Countless producers come to Sousa's rigorous training sessions to identify promising young women to join the ranks of show business. Thanks to the Miss Venezuela pageant, Venevisión is showcase for pretty faces with talent. Contestants have gone on to careers in diverse fields. Maite Delgado, for example, is a successful television announcer, Bárbara Palacios has been an outstanding businesswoman, and Irene Sáez, who has held the positions of mayor and governor, was a candidate for the presidency of the country in the 1998 elections. The Miss Venezuela pageant and everything that surrounds it constitute an example of synergy within the Cisneros Group, combining the talent of a producer like Joaquín Rivera—who brings magic to the show—with the sagacity and good judgment of Osmel Sousa, and adding to that, Venevisión's professional management.

In view of the successes they had achieved, the Organización Miss Venezuela decided to introduce a male version of the pageant: Mr. Venezuela. With a kind of glamour different from that of its feminine counterpart, the event, to which more than four hundred men have applied, is a platform for promoting careers in modeling or acting.

More than beauty contests, the Organización Miss Venezuela has erected a structure that benefits not only the Cisneros Group but the careers of the contestants, and of a group of experienced professionals ranging from producers and masters of ceremonies to fashion designers. In fact, the great names in Venezuelan couture owe a good deal of their international prestige and prominence to the Miss Venezuela pageant. Outstanding among them are Margarita Zingg, Angel Sánchez, Mayela Camacho, and the late Guy Melliet.

By the 1980s, Gustavo and Ricardo Cisneros had generated a synergistic entrepreneurial network that fed and nourished the growth of the Group. Venevisión provided a showcase for talents from Rodven and the Miss Venezuela pageant, and for the rest of the products manufactured by the Cisneros Group, while CADA operated a vast distribution network. All the parts benefited all the other parts, and together they generated more income than they did as individual entities.

In 1985, the *Wall Street Journal* reported that the Cisneros Group had generated revenues of $4 billion. Gustavo Cisneros, in addition to putting into practice what he had learned from his father about OCAAT and the vertical integration of the enterprises surrounding Pepsi-Cola, had successfully diversified even further the Group's operations, which now included everything from the manufacture of beauty products to the sale of champagne. For their part, his brother Ricardo and his financial executives, together with the bankers, kept the companies under control with updated financials. The Group was in a state of equilibrium.

5. Efficiency and Effectiveness

In July 1980, Diego Cisneros died in Caracas. His illness had taken away his mobility but had not dulled his intelligence. Gustavo Cisneros kept him up-to-date on the business and asked his advice, but never burdened him with problems. "He gave great importance to a positive attitude toward life," says Cisneros. "He emphasized that it was good to be a critic but better to be a builder."

Gustavo Cisneros never misses an opportunity to pay tribute to Don Diego as the inspiring figure in his entrepreneurial development. From his father he inherited his "curiosity about how the world works and to what end, and a desire to do something of value beyond the purely material."

He attributes to Diego's teaching his determination to turn the Cisneros Group into a group of companies of international scope, transforming its Venezuelan management into a globalized and multicultural one. Diego Cisneros insisted that his children have loyalty and vision.

One of Don Diego's most relevant characteristics was his obsession with detail, to the point where he personally supervised plants, the administration of offices, and the work of the managers in each area. The real reason for the zeal with which he looked after his businesses was in order to optimally satisfy the needs of his customers, whether it was for a soap opera or a bottle of Pepsi-Cola. Diego Cisneros knew that if he failed in some detail, the error could be magnified by the time the product reached the consumer.

His inspections of bottling plants—without prior notification—were like those of a sergeant inspecting the barracks in the morning. "The plant had to be immaculate," recalls a manager from that time. "We respected and feared Don Diego because he was very demanding."

During his visit, Don Diego would fire questions at the manager. What was the degree of carbonation? And the result of the Brix test for density? Questions about the results of quality control tests were so detailed that the managers had to carry them out themselves in order to feel secure in their responses. Like his father, Gustavo Cisneros would conduct unannounced inspections, from supermarkets to the kitchens of the Burger Kings. If he found anything wrong he made his observation directly to the person responsible, and, like his father, after listening and issuing instructions, he would encourage the manager to improve his work.

Another characteristic shared by father and son is the consumption of information. Gustavo Cisneros does it voraciously. He is interested not only in the general aspects of a topic but in the details, which might appear less significant. This passion to be informed means that even today a select team of managers is required to report their itineraries a week in advance to guarantee that they can be reached if needed. A phenomenal memory, which his subordinates have learned not to underestimate, helps Cisneros to remember facts and dates that are key to the Group.

"Gustavo Cisneros has an impressive capacity to learn," says Cristina Pieretti, executive vice president of operations in Venezuela. "This translates into an organization where if the chief has the capacity to learn, the employee also has the capacity to learn."

Cisneros' personal characteristics also contribute to the ability to supervise the Group. Gustavo does not sleep much—those close to him say between five and six hours a night though it seems like less—and he is a man overflowing with energy. According to Sandra Zanoletti, his personal assistant for almost two decades, if he stands up twice during a working meeting, it is a clear sign that he is bored. He has no patience with airlines, and since the 1970s planes, and later helicopters, have been a part of the Group's work arsenal.

Headquarters of D. Cisneros & Cía., distributor of Studebaker cars and other U.S. products for which the company had guaranteed exclusivity throughout Venezuela (mid-1940s). The seed of what would become the Cisneros Group was planted here, in the Quinta Crespo area of Caracas.

Gustavo Cisneros, the fourth of eight children, at age five (May 1950).

Diego Cisneros, father of Gustavo and founder of the Cisneros Group of Companies, with Carlos, Gustavo at age seven, and Marion, their sister, at D. Cisneros & Cía.'s headquarters, launching a new Studebaker model (1952). From an early age, Cisneros began to show interest in his father's business.

Gustavo Cisneros, who played right forward position, with the soccer team of the St. Ignatius of Loyola school, Caracas (March 1953). Cisneros constantly emphasizes teamwork.

Close friends exchange greetings: President Rómulo Betancourt, a champion of democracy in the Americas, and Diego Cisneros, on the occasion of the wedding of his daughter, Marion Cisneros, Caracas (February 5, 1960).

Gustavo Cisneros (second row, fifth from the left) with the soccer team of Suffield Academy, where he completed preparatory school (April 1964). Sports have been a constant in Gustavo Cisneros' life.

On the day of his graduation *cum laude* from Babson College, Wellesley, Massachusetts, Gustavo Cisnero with his brother Ricardo (June 1968). The brothers' college years provided them with a strong academi foundation as well as opportunities to experiment with business initiatives.

On the day of his graduation from Babson College, Ricardo Cisneros with his brother Gustavo (June 1969). The two would form a solid managerial team.

Ricardo Cisneros (second from left) on the day of his graduation from Babson College, with Antonio José, Gerardo, Diego, and Gustavo (June 1969).

Patricia Phelps de Cisneros and Gustavo Cisneros, lifelong companions, on their wedding day, in St. Patrick's Cathedral, New York (June 10, 1970).

Diego and Gustavo Cisneros at home in Caracas (September 1970). For Gustavo, his father was a guide, an example, an indispensable adviser, the person who bequeathed him an entrepreneurial vision.

Cisneros and Fidel Castro, in Varadero, Cuba (February 1973). At the request of the Venezuelan government, Gustavo Cisneros participated in the process of reestablishing diplomatic relations between Venezuela and Cuba. Cisneros' views as a supporter of democracy and freedom of speech have always been on the other end of the political spectrum from those of Castro.

Three generations: Diego, Gustavo, and Guillermo Cisneros, in Los Roques, Venezuela (April 1974).

Diego Cisneros and his sons, Antonio José, Ricardo, Diego Alberto, Carlos Enrique, Gustavo, and Gerardo, at the family residence in Caracas (September 1974).

Cisneros visits Rómulo Betancourt, founder of democracy in Venezuela, at "Pacairigua," the residence of the Venezuelan president in Caracas (November 1977). On that occasion, Cisneros invited the renowned statesman to participate in a colloquium on democracy.

Gustavo and Ricardo Cisneros at a meeting of the board of directors of Venevisión (October 1979). The younger Cisneros generation was taking control, and Gustavo used the youth of the directors of the organization as a public relations asset, promising his associates that many years of success lay ahead of them.

Gustavo Cisneros in the Cabinet Room at the White House, with President Ronald Reagan, Secretary of State Alexander Haig, Jr., other high-ranking North American dignitaries, and business representatives from Latin America, in a conversation on free trade in Latin America (1981). The meeting resulted in greater understanding on the part of the United States leadership of the challenges and opportunities in Latin America and contributed to the start of the Caribbean basin initiative.

Cisneros returns to his alma mater to deliver a speech as a founding member of the International Academy of Distinguished Entrepreneurs of Babson College, Wellesley (April 15, 1981). At the time, Cisneros was the youngest entrepreneur to be inducted into the Academy. Marcus Wallenberg, Swedish entrepeneur and honorary inductee, is seated at left.

Albertina Rendiles with her son, Gustavo, at the Cisneros Group's Christmas celebration in Caracas (December 1982).

Gustavo and Patty Cisneros with His Majesty Juan Carlos and Her Majesty Sofía, King and Queen of Spain, at "La Viñeta" in Caracas, the residence for heads of state invited to Venezuela (July 1983).

Cisneros, after receiving the Order of Isabel la Católica from His Majesty the King of Spain, delivers his acceptance speech in Caracas (May 16, 1984).

Patty and Gustavo Cisneros with the Spanish ambassador, Amaro González de Mesa, on the night Cisneros was honored with the Order of Isabel la Católica. For his entire career, Cisneros has been dedicated to unity among Hispanic nations, the expansion of their language and culture, and building bridges between Spain and the nations of Latin America.

Cisneros, as owner of the chain of Galerías Preciados stores, projects the new image of the company at one of its stores in Madrid (September 1984).

Patty and Gustavo Cisneros in Parima, Venezuelan Guayana, visiting an indigenous Yanomami community (February 1985). For decades the Cisneros couple has contributed to the preservation of the cultures of Venezuelan ethnic groups.

Cisneros and Arthur Ochs Sulzberger, owner of the *New York Times*, salmon-fishing in Alaska (August 17–24, 1985). Fishing is one of Cisneros' and Sulzberger's lifelong passions.

His Holiness Pope John Paul II holds a private audience for Patty, Carolina, Gustavo, and Guillermo Cisneros at Castelgandolfo, Italy (September 17, 1985).

Ricardo, Marion, and Gustavo Cisneros, photographed on Calle Serrano, in Madrid, on the day of the relaunching of the Galerías Preciados department stores (April 1986).

Gustavo Cisneros addresses the plenary assembly of the Pontifical Commission on Social Communications in Vatican City (March 18, 1987). Cisneros has insisted on the relevance of communications media as channels for the transmission of a humanistic message of peace and harmony among nations.

Gustavo, Patty, and Adriana Cisneros, with Zubin and Nancy Mehta, at "El Cedrito," Galipan, in the mountains north of Caracas. The distinguished conductor, invited by the Centro Mozarteum, led the New York Philharmonic in Caracas and offered a master class to the Youth Orchestra of Venezuela (July 1987). Mehta has become a tireless fighter for peace in the Middle East.

At the exact point where the borders of Venezuela, Brazil, and Guyana meet: Peggy and David Rockefeller, Elaine Wolfensohn, Max Ravard, Courtney Neeb, Patty, Carolina, and Gustavo Cisneros (March 1988). The rapprochement between Venezuela and Brazil, and the harmonious development of their border areas, is a matter of keen interest to Cisneros.

In Beijing, in the Great Hall of the People, Patty and Gustavo Cisneros with the man who transformed the People's Republic of China and began its opening to the free market: the great reformer Deng Xiaoping (May 24, 1988).

Patty and Gustavo Cisneros host a luncheon at "La Ribereña," their residence in Caracas, for Colombian President Belisario Betancur and former President Alfonso López Michelsen, joined by Venezuelan Cardinal José Ali Lebrún, Venezuelan President Jaime Lusinchi, and former Presidents Rafael Caldera and Luis Herrera Campins (July 21, 1988).

But in 1980, with fifty enterprises under his control, and with hundreds of managers and thousands of employees, the operation had become too large and diversified to watch over with the personal meticulousness that was his father's managerial style. Gustavo Cisneros was aware that he needed to design another form of organization.

Cisneros knew that the future of his companies rested, in the final analysis, in the hands of his employees. "The fundamental difference between one organization and another lies not in financial or fixed assets but in the talents of its personnel," he said in a speech delivered in 1981 at Babson College on the occasion of his designation as a member of that institution's Academy of Distinguished Entrepreneurs.

He wanted the support of a first-rate consultant to find a new form of organization, and to do that he contacted Dr. Yehezkel Dror, an internationally renowned social scientist at Hebrew University, in Jerusalem. In the book he published in 1970, *Mad States,* Dror predicted a challenging future for humanity in which a few fanatics would have the ability to destabilize the world order. He called them "true terrorists," as opposed to those whose actions were motivated by money.

Dror was more than an expert in international relations. He also studied the methods by which governments are able to organize and act effectively. Throughout his career he advised more than thirty governments and international organizations, among them the office of the English prime minister, the European Union, and several Israeli governments. Cisneros was interested in meeting him. He was struck by the efficiency of the Israeli government. Cabinets and prime ministers came and went in the midst of wars and other upheavals, but the government continued to operate.

"Something like that isn't an accident," said Gustavo Cisneros. "Ben Gurion might have been a great general, but he wasn't really a manager...Golda Meir perhaps even less so."

In November 1974, Dror came to Caracas. The businessman was charmed by the academic, who gave him an in-depth analysis of the explosive situation in the Middle East, the Jewish-

Palestinian question, and terrorism. When he had satisfied Cisneros' concerns, they proceeded to analyze the best way to organize a complex entrepreneurial structure. The academic explained how the office of a prime minister ought to function.

"Ideally," he said, "it should have some twenty or twenty-five well-qualified people from varied backgrounds who bring a diversity of opinions."

To coordinate the personnel, a special assistant is needed, a chief of staff.

Some years later, Cisneros hired another consultant who essentially made the same recommendation. A native of Germany residing in the United States, Peter Gabriel had the advantage of knowing Venezuelan idiosyncrasies. He had worked as a consultant to McKinsey & Company in Caracas during the 1950s, when American companies were investing in the oil industry. He later moved to the United States to advise corporate figures of the stature of Tom Watson of IBM and David Rockefeller of Chase Manhattan Bank. Like Dror, he held a doctorate from Harvard and he was dean of the business school at Boston University, where Antonio Cisneros, Gustavo's younger brother, had earned his degree.

Gabriel advised him to increase the capacity of Castor Trading—a company created to centralize the purchase, storage, and exportation of merchandise from the United States for CADA and other companies, and directed for some time by Johnny Fanjul—and assign it more managerial functions.

On the other hand, Gabriel agreed with the idea of a chief of staff who would channel all of Cisneros' creative energy and focus it throughout the Group. In his opinion, Cisneros ought to separate personnel and entrepreneurial matters.

Dror and Gabriel provided Cisneros with a sketch of the ideal structure, although putting that idea into practice was another task altogether. The great obstacle lay in finding a suitable candidate to fill the position of chief of staff.

"Given the complexity of managing my schedule and my time, we needed a person with judgment who was both efficient and effective. It was very difficult to find all that in a single individual," says Cisneros.

Furthermore, that person was not going to be a mere figure-head. Gustavo Cisneros delegates responsibilities, something he does almost intuitively. "He knows to whom to delegate, depending on the responsibility. He differentiates between those who are good at execution and advisers; the former excel at making things happen, the latter warn of risks along the road and minimize them as much as possible," says Carlos Bardasano, an executive in the Group.

The person had to possess a great capacity for work in order to keep up with Gustavo Cisneros' pace, in addition to having good business training. In actuality, many people possessed those two attributes, but not many could also manage people effectively.

After some experiments that did not work out, it was not until 1982—eight years after Cisneros' first conversations with Dror—that a young Venezuelan named José Antonio Ríos filled the position. Gustavo Cisneros had heard about Ríos, the world-wide manager for Viva la Gente, a nonprofit organization that put on concerts for young people that carried a message of peace and good will. Struck by the fact that it was a Venezuelan who ran the organization, Cisneros located him and offered him a job with the Group.

"I'm happy at Viva la Gente and I don't want to leave," Ríos told him.

"Some day you'll get tired of your work, and when that happens, call me," was Cisneros' reply.

Two years later, when his third child was born, Ríos was ready to move on to a higher-paying corporate career. Cisneros asked him to have an interview with Gabriel. The consultant was favorably impressed by Ríos' intelligence, education, and articulate manner.

Cisneros finally had his chief of staff.

"We can both succeed," he told Ríos, "but obviously we don't know each other yet. I'm going to give you a title that can mean everything or nothing: you're going to be director of the office of the president. What you do with the title depends on you."

"Become involved in the office, in the projects we have. Some need the international experience of people like you. In three months we'll see if you're interested."

Ríos spent three years working shoulder to shoulder with Cisneros in his first position with the company. Together they transformed the family style of the Group into something that was closer to the idea of an American corporation.

Gustavo and Ricardo Cisneros put into effect a managerial and corporate concept that they called "decentralized centralization," defined in their own words—in a 1990 interview—in this way: "Each company in the Group operates autonomously, but finances and planning for all the companies are unified in the executive center of the Group. A planning team elaborates short- and long-term plans for each company, plans that are compared to results every six months to make certain that objectives are achieved. To this is added our long-term plan, which sets forth the global strategy that our group of companies should follow."

Cisneros had never been very attached to corporate titles and formalities, but the implementation of this nomenclature would help him regulate his growing operation.

He would be the president, Ricardo the executive vice president. Under them there would be a vice president of operations and a vice president of finances for Venezuela. The United States businesses operated under a similar structure.

That was the upper echelon of the Cisneros Group. "There were always four people who were informed about the key action items, the four principals, who could vary, although Ricardo and Gustavo were always there," says one manager.

Under these vice presidencies there would be six divisions in Venezuela: food products/mass consumption; commerce; information/telecommunications; communications; aluminum; and mineral development. The general managers of all the companies reported to the vice president of operations, and the financial managers reported to the vice president of finance. This was the corporate structure in effect, with modifications, until 1993.

With his office of the presidency firmly established, Cisneros could demand the seal of perfection from his Group. He is a man who works hard, unwilling to leave things to chance or improvisation. He never attends a meeting without prior preparation, which he requests from his chief of staff or whomever he thinks is expert on the agenda item. If he is meeting with a guest, he asks in advance for a resume and any other key details. Cisneros prefers to listen. His interventions tend to be brief and his questions precise. If someone has an idea he likes, he shares it enthusiastically, just as his father did. At the end of a meeting, he always asks the opinion of each person present, including the secretary taking notes. And it is the chief of staff who is responsible for the follow-up.

More than anything else, Cisneros demanded that his chief of staff keep him informed. Peter Tinoco, who once held the post, recalls how demanding his boss could be. Every three months the companies in the group submitted their financial reports, following the guidelines of the Cisneros Group. Peter evaluated them and sent them on to his superior. One day Gustavo Cisneros called him on the phone:

"Peter, I'm looking at the report from CADA...Why did their tomato inventory go up?"

Tinoco did not have the slightest idea why CADA was accumulating more tomatoes than usual. He had to be honest because his boss had a special nose for detecting when someone was trying to deceive him. Everyone knew that Cisneros could ask a question whose answer he already knew just to find out if his people had done their jobs. Cisneros despises dishonesty.

"I won't lie to you, Don Gustavo. I don't have the slightest idea."

There was a silence on the line that seemed very long to Peter. Then Cisneros spoke in a tone of voice that made it clear that what he was going to say was important.

"But Peter, you're here because you're my eyes. You have to be informed."

From that time on Tinoco asked about everything, no matter how insignificant a detail might seem.

"You always have to be informed," says Tinoco. "His communication style is direct." Reports had to be written on one page, two pages maximum. "Don't explain the situation. Be direct."

Cisneros also used the position of director of the office of the president to test talent. The office has been occupied by people who today are trusted executives, like Steven Bandel (president and chief operating officer of the Cisneros Group), Carlos Bardasano (vice president of the Cisneros Group), Luis Emilio Gómez (vice president of legal affairs), Peter Tinoco (executive chairman of the Fundación Cisneros and president of Venevision Productions), and Eduardo Hauser (vice president of AOL Latin America).

"My office is a useful place for measuring aptitudes and developing skills," says Gustavo Cisneros. "Whoever is successful there can qualify for a position with greater responsibility. It's a problem for me, because when one leaves I have to begin all over again."

In addition to its informational and operational tasks, the office carries another responsibility that is key for Cisneros: managing his growing network of contacts throughout the world. Like his father, Gustavo Cisneros is convinced of the need to talk to people, face-to-face.

To that end, he set up a complex team of fifty people in the New York and Madrid offices, with results that astounded people who met with Cisneros. "He is very organized, and there are a good number of people working behind the scenes to make certain that things go smoothly," said Tom Hicks, a Texas banker who would become Cisneros' partner at the end of the 1990s.

Cisneros seems to know everybody. One executive recalls the time she located Shoul Eisenberg, to request help for the Cisneros Group in a project that Gustavo Cisneros wanted to undertake in China. Eisenberg was an Israeli multi-millionaire who made his fortune in commercial exchange. His contacts in Asia allowed him to act as an intermediary for potential investors on that continent. He was involved in a number of projects, including an electricity-generating plant in the province of Shandong. No one knew more about the devices of power in Beijing than this aged survivor of the Holocaust. When the executive introduced herself, Eisenberg's response surprised her.

"Ah! You're from the Cisneros Group? And how is Gustavo Cisneros?"

The executive never imagined that Eisenberg knew him.

Cisneros is disciplined in the art of cultivating relationships. Don Diego possessed an overwhelming charisma that allowed him to lead great groups of workers, talking to them man-to-man. Gustavo Cisneros, on the other hand, prefers small meetings where he can demonstrate his innate charm; he is not likely to become involved in polemics, not even with his closest friends. One of them describes him as a "diehard busybody." He inquires, he engages, and he listens. It is an uncommon characteristic in a businessman. "I've met at least two-thirds of the powerful men in Latin America," says Violy McCausland, a Colombian investment banker who would participate in various large transactions with Cisneros in the 1990s. "Most of them are intensely concerned with themselves. Cisneros is just the opposite. He is intensely focused on you, your opinions, what you think."

This broad network of contacts and friends—ranging from journalists like Barbara Walters to musicians like Julio Iglesias—helps Cisneros to form an analytical mental picture of the world. It is as if he were attending an ongoing tutorial. He, in turn, rewards his interlocutors, sharing his considerable experience and knowledge of business and politics in Latin America. Moreover, Cisneros is loyal to his friends. For example, he never failed to stay in touch with J. Richardson Dilworth, the right-hand man to the Rockefeller family, who helped orient him in New York at the end of the 1970s, even though Dilworth was suffering from a disease that kept him away from public activities for more than a decade. When Dilworth died, Cisneros was an usher at his funeral.

To understand the world of business, Cisneros cultivates relationships with the most outstanding people in the entrepreneurial world, such as Roberto Goizueta, the late chairman of Coca-Cola. He learns from world figures like Michael Armstrong, the former head of AT&T, and Michael Jordan, the former head of CBS Westinghouse. All of them have played fundamental roles in the development of his organization because, like him, they are individuals who think about the future and a great market without frontiers.

Cisneros broadens his knowledge of international politics by participating in the Council on Foreign Relations, a U.S.-based organization that seeks to improve understanding of the world and to contribute new ideas to Washington's foreign policy. He is a member of the Committee of International Advisers at the Council, whose members—all foreigners with outstanding political or entrepreneurial careers—are called on to enrich the institution's international perspective. Gustavo Cisneros "likes the storm of varied substantive ideas to understand new aspects of economic and social development," says Beatrice Rangel, an adviser to Cisneros.

Another feature that the Cisneros brothers would implement in the Group is what the managers term "rotation." Upper management is divided into two kinds of executives: specialists and generalists. The first group can spend years leading a company, as is the case of Guido Tonitto, the head of NCR Venezuela, or his partner Rodolfo Rodríguez at Rodven. Generalists are trained to be more versatile in the functions they fulfill. An executive can experience abrupt changes in direction or area, in different businesses within the Group. For example, Victor Ferreres began his career at NCR—a computer company—then moved to a coffee factory, a television channel, a satellite television operation, and today he heads Venevisión. Carlos Bardasano began at Pepsi-Cola, was executive vice president and general manager of CADA, and from there he moved to the presidency of Venevisión before occupying his present position as vice president of the Cisneros Group and head of international television operations. With rotation Cisneros makes certain that his employees stay motivated, while at the same time maximizing the strengths and minimizing the limitations of each of them.

Along with rotations and ad hoc teams, Cisneros uses another strategy to keep his executives sharp. He sets goals for them that are almost impossible to reach.

"He tests you at different moments to see how you're doing, making you work like a madman," says one former executive. "You're involved in everything from the sublime to the ridiculous," he adds, recalling that in a single day he might spend time with the president of Venezuelan in the morning and help to clean a studio at Venevisión in the afternoon. A manager with a "stratified vision" of "a hierarchical order" would refuse to do that.

"Gustavo is looking for people who will get into a cab to take a document to a notary if that's what's needed."

Another of Cisneros' favorite tools is the creation of ad hoc teams for specific projects. In order to evaluate an acquisition, he can bring together a person from Miami, another from New York, and a third from Caracas. When the work is completed, the team is disbanded.

"Having a static team doesn't work," says Cisneros. "We want to be very enterprising. The way to do that is to put the best people together on a team even if it subsequently disbands. It's part of our managerial success."

Another of the characteristics of the Group, says Steven Bandel, is the autonomy with which executives operate: "They can take risks; furthermore, we count on that, a balance between prudence and daring."

Cisneros is demanding, but he is also generous, and not only in financial terms. "There are a series of unwritten guarantees in the Cisneros Group, and one of them is stability," says José Antonio Ríos, who would leave the organization amicably after fourteen years for a position in the Spanish company Telefónica. "At the top executive levels, people leave because they want to. You have to struggle to leave the Group. It's part of the family atmosphere. Gustavo Cisneros knows the spouses, families, and children of each one of his executives very well, and this gives top staff a good deal of confidence."

At times Cisneros can criticize a subordinate harshly, but he is careful to balance this with kind words for each of his collaborators, from his chauffeur to his highest executive. He is generous with his employees, especially when they experience a family or medical emergency. In 1983, Estanislao Pérez went sailing around Puerto La Cruz. He was suddenly taken ill, and was in very poor condition when he reached the clinic. Cisneros immediately sent his plane to move him to a hospital. For months he followed his recuperation very closely, until Pérez was completely cured.

Cisneros leaves his personal mark on the Group by recruiting managers who are versatile and adaptable to the dynamics of the market. By demanding hard work combined with rotating positions and mental flexibility, he felt that he had created a team ready to take on the Group's next challenge: to transform a Venezuelan organization into an international one. This would not have been achieved with management that was traditional, hierarchical, and accustomed to preestablished procedures. By the early 1980s, Cisneros was very close to realizing his dream of making a vigorous entry into the United States.

6. Multiplying Businesses

The entrance of Gustavo Cisneros into the American market was not the result of luck or chance. Before making his first investments in the United States, the entrepreneur had cultivated close relationships in that country for many years. Cisneros wanted to grow in the north, and from there move into other areas. He understood the importance of the U.S. market and its influence on the rest of the world.

New York, a city where the dynamics of daily life speeds up time, suited Cisneros' energetic personality perfectly. "It was a city that used to change every five years and now it's every two. If you leave for a time, when you return the players have changed. It's the most dynamic capitalist society in the world."

Manhattan is a place for connecting with people who, like Gustavo Cisneros, have their eyes fixed on the world and the future. The contacts he would establish there would set him apart from the typical South American businessman who has made his fortune by limiting himself to an exclusively national sphere.

New York is a city densely populated with bankers, and there Cisneros strengthened his friendship with two men who would help him in his entrepreneurial ambitions: George Moore and David Rockefeller.

Moore and Diego Cisneros belonged to what Gustavo Cisneros calls a "mutual admiration society." When Cisneros moved to New York in 1970 to be with his ailing father, George Moore was about to retire as president of the First National City Bank of

New York. The banker knew everyone on Wall Street, but above all he knew about banks. His career began, when he was twenty-four, at the City Bank Farmers Trust Company, which after several mergers became Citibank in 1968. He considered sleeping more than five hours a day a "waste of time." Cisneros describes him as "a dynamo." Moore moved up at a time when banking was in the hands of only a few families. When he took over a division, he would clear away the bureaucrats and replace them with young people fresh out of business school who were as ambitious as he was. In the late 1950s, when he was managing the institution's domestic operations, he introduced First National City Bank of New York into the arena of mortgage financing and consumer loans. In 1959, when he was fifty-four years old, he became president of the bank. Moore opened branches in Europe and Latin America as if they were fast-food restaurants. Married to a Mexican woman, he played a key role in making Citibank a global enterprise, which attracted Cisneros. In 1967, Moore was named chairman of First National City Corporation.

When Moore retired from the bank at the age of sixty-five, Cisneros convinced him to take advantage of the international contacts he had made in his fruitful business career and begin a second career as a consultant. Gustavo Cisneros was one of his first clients.

In 1977 the banker called Cisneros to talk to him about a small bank in Nashville, Tennessee. For a person accustomed to New York, like Gustavo Cisneros, Nashville—more famous for its country music than its financial or banking potential—sounded somewhat alien. But Moore explained his idea. He was president of the board of directors of the Tennessee Valley Bankcorp, a trifle compared to Citibank (though it had more assets than all the banks in some Latin American countries), but with a privileged position in the heart of the United States. At that time banks could not have branches outside their home state, but Moore was betting that the government would eventually lift that restriction, "and the value of Tennessee Valley Bankcorp shares will skyrocket," he told the Venezuelan entrepreneur.

The Cisneros Group, together with an important group of Venezuelan financiers, made a significant investment in the Tennessee Valley Bankcorp and became the principal stockholders, with 25 percent of the shares. Moore's experienced eye had not been wrong. Six years later the great banking consolidation in the United States began, and the investors sold their shares, at a good price, to Nations Bank. At this stage, Ricardo Cisneros represented the interests of the group of investors and established a network of alliances and relationships in the southern United States.

By 1979, Moore had moved to Sotogrande, in southern Spain, but would continue to counsel Gustavo Cisneros. He would be a valuable adviser when the moment came for Cisneros to move into that country in 1984 with the purchase of Galerías Preciados—one of the most controversial and daring investments of his career.

Moore had retired but continued working. In 1987, at the age of eighty-two, he founded the Gibraltar Trust Bank, Ltd., an offshore bank created in conjunction with Credit Suisse (today CS First Boston) in the British colony, causing some friction with the Spanish government, which at the time was very sensitive regarding the sovereignty of that small enclave. "This will be my last bank, unless they ask me to create one in heaven or in hell," he told the *New York Times*. There was still time before that happened. He died in April 2000, at the age of ninety-five.

The Cisneros brothers considered Moore a mentor and guide.

"We loved him dearly, and he had a great influence on me. He knew all the important families in the world and always told them to expand outside their own countries so as not to fail if there were a depression or a dictator came to power. He was very insistent about that," Gustavo recalled.

The friendship Cisneros cultivated with David Rockefeller, the other banker of his father's generation, would develop on another plane. What Moore had done with Citibank, Rockefeller did with Chase Manhattan Bank, an institution from which he would retire definitively in 1981. But in reality Rockefeller was a more than a banker; he was a philanthropist and a born "people person."

David Rockefeller, a man so modest he always wore the same style of suit and shoes, wanted to transmit his philanthropic values to his Latin American friends. John D. Rockefeller, David's grandfather and founder of the group in the late nineteenth century, proclaimed that with wealth came a responsibility for doing good. He had donated half his fortune—close to 540 million dollars, a colossal sum of money at that time—to a variety of charities. For his part, his grandson David was a founder of the Council of the Americas and the Trilateral Commission, chairman of Chase Manhattan Bank and The Museum of Modern Art in New York, a skilled amateur sailor in his free time, and a pillar in the worlds of finance and philanthropy.

The Rockefellers became intimately identified with Wall Street, and were always open to philanthropic works, and in the case of Nelson Rockefeller, David's brother, to politics. Even their investments in Latin America were vehicles designed to increase cooperation between North and South America more than initiatives for making money.

David in particular acted as a Renaissance Maecenas. Under his leadership, Chase Manhattan Bank would accumulate an impressive collection of 17,000 works of art. The banker had inherited a love of modern art from his mother, Abby Aldrich Rockefeller, who was one of the founders of The Museum of Modern Art (MoMA) in New York.

Rockefeller reserved a special place in his life for Gustavo and Patty Cisneros. When Cisneros was still very young, Rockefeller invited him to join the council of international advisers of Chase Manhattan Bank. The banker had created this group as a small forum where his important clients could gather to meet one another, discuss business, and advise the bank on international matters. Rockefeller would take his guests to exotic places for their exchange of ideas. For Cisneros, the council at Chase was a place to meet distinguished entrepreneurs, like J.R.D. Tata, the head of one of the large entrepreneurial groups in India, and W. K. Pao, the Hong Kong shipping magnate. Cisneros shared with them his knowledge of Latin America, a region that was a great mystery to many of them.

Moore and Rockefeller were not one-dimensional stereotypes obsessed only with fattening their end-of-the-year statements. They enjoyed the success of their businesses and at the same time relished mingling with people who had novel ideas and original points of view. They had a global vision of the world and promoted philanthropic causes. These individuals, along with the international opening initiated by Diego, made Cisneros into a different kind of entrepreneur.

The presence of Gustavo Cisneros in New York would allow him to relate to the world's financial elite, keeping him abreast of the trends that determine business throughout the world.

"Every Latin American entrepreneur ought to have a liaison office in New York," David Rockefeller would say.

In time, Rockefeller would convince Wall Street that Cisneros headed a group that was international and not exclusively Venezuelan. "The problem is that even if your assets are outside Venezuela, the bankers take into account the risks in your country of origin to determine the cost of capital. The struggle was to have them see us as an international corporation and not a purely local one," says Cisneros. In brief, this would mean access to cheaper and more abundant capital.

In New York, Cisneros would develop the mentality of an investment banker. The investment banker differs from his counterpart, the commercial banker. The former earns his profit through the fees he receives for putting together transactions (such as the acquisition of stocks) and the capital gains he can generate by purchasing a company, restructuring it, and then selling it for more than the purchase price. In the late 1970s, few Latin American entrepreneurs thought about creating businesses with the idea of selling them later.

"We learned that if we wanted to do it well, we had to develop our own intellectual capacity for knowing how to buy and sell, for creating the analytical design of a firm," says Gustavo Cisneros. In fact, Cisneros' greatest success in business would come not only from the profitability of his companies but fundamentally from his ability to sense the right moment to sell them.

Gustavo Cisneros considered the idea of founding a large investment bank for Latin America. He abandoned it only when his friends on Wall Street warned him that it was a cyclical business, and he would have to dismiss a good number of people during the lean years. "That didn't sit well with me," he says.

Cisneros' dream of expanding his organization internationally experienced a crucial moment at 1:35 in the afternoon of February 3, 1981, when the *Dow Jones News Service* published a simple, four-paragraph article entitled "Beatrice Foods Completes Sale of Soft Drink Division." All-American Bottling Corporation, the article said, would pay $105 million to keep a handful of plants that bottled soft drinks and mineral water.

Beatrice Foods was a large food-products company in the United States, the owner of brands such as Louis Sherry ice creams and Erckrich meats. But who was behind All-American Bottling Corporation? Proprietorship of the corporation, as far as the public was concerned, belonged to Forstmann Little & Co. and to unidentified "private investors."

Although Forstmann Little was a small, unknown investment bank, it would become a major beneficiary of the acquisitions and mergers about to occur on Wall Street. The "private investors" were, in reality, the Cisneros family, with the name All-American Bottling (AAB) being Ricardo Cisneros' inspiration.

Until the acquisition of AAB, whose revenues were approximately $200 million a year, the Cisneros presence in the United States had been discreet. Gustavo Cisneros and a group of associates, Pedro Tinoco among them, traveled frequently to the United States, looking for businesses. At first it was difficult, as a participant in these excursions recalls. Having money was not enough to penetrate the business circles that formed on Wall Street. The bankers had to be convinced of the group's seriousness and solidity. For a few years, Gustavo "devoted himself to studying the business environment," one executive recalls.

Fortunately for Cisneros, the frenzied period of leveraged buyouts (LBO), a phenomenon that would change the face of

Wall Street forever, was about to begin, and the purchase of AAB reflected that change. His friends and advisers George Moore and David Rockefeller had been bankers during Don Diego's time, and like him they insisted on the need to broaden the horizons of business and convert the entrepreneur's social commitment into action. They helped to open doors for Gustavo Cisneros and provided contacts all over the world. But Moore and Rockefeller had headed institutions that made money in the same way that Mayer Amschel Rothschild had done three centuries before: by making explicit the difference between what they paid for their deposits and what they charged for their loans.

Now a new way of financing business acquisitions, and a new kind of banker to go along with it, were about to burst onto the scene.

An LBO is nothing more than buying a company with loans supported by a pledge of the company's own assets, which means that the contribution of the purchaser's capital is minimal. When carried to the extreme, the debt financing for an LBO transaction is equal to the value of the company's assets, so that nothing is paid for with equity. Investors, of course, lend their money based on the reputation and expertise of the management and the company's potential for improvement and growth. At that time, the diversified conglomerates that had emerged in the United States during the 1960s had fallen into disrepute and were divesting themselves of assets in order to focus on their core business. Management of the assets that were being sold could be acquired by means of an LBO. Financial firms like Forstmann Little, and its great rival Kohlberg, Kravis, Roberts & Co. (KKR), organized the financing, and often participated as direct investors.

Derald Ruttenberg, an outstanding businessman and Cisneros' friend and fishing and hunting companion, had supported and encouraged the Forstmann Little initiative in late 1978. The financial firm was headed by the brothers Teddy and Nicholas Forstmann, and William Brian Little, a partner from Merrill Lynch. Teddy was the visionary of the group; he was also a good communicator and a man journalists liked to interview. It was at Ruttenberg's request that Gustavo Cisneros met with Teddy Forstmann in mid-November 1980. Teddy was not yet a star banker. He had recently acquired Kincaid Furniture Co., a small firm that designed and manufactured furniture, and that would rocket him to fame: for each dollar he and his partners invested in it, they eventually earned eleven.

"Gustavo, I have a great deal with a bottling company, but I don't know anything about the business. I need a partner and a manager," Teddy told the Venezuelan entrepreneur.

Beatrice Foods wanted to sell eleven plants that bottled brands such as Royal Crown Cola and Seven-Up, and employed two thousand people.

The Venezuelan's face lit up. He had been trying to convince Oswaldo to sell Pepsi-Cola operations in Colombia and Brazil and refocus on the United States. He could even persuade Pepsi-Co to let him bottle the cola in the United States, a market where, unlike Latin America, Pepsi-Cola was a consolidated brand.

Gustavo Cisneros said goodbye to Teddy and called Ricardo.

"We need to raise $100 million," he said.

Cisneros would make his first large purchase in the United States with the support of a French bank. The Banque Worms had followed the business path of the Venezuelan group and was prepared to approve a line of credit for the Group. Alejandro Rivera, the head of finances, had at his disposal $15 million as a cushion to fall back on.

Five days after the deal with Worms was closed, Ricardo came into Rivera's office.

"Alex, we have the possibility of buying some bottling plants in the United States, and we need you to raise $10 million: it's urgent."

"Where do you want me to deposit the money?" was Rivera's reply to a surprised Ricardo.

With the $10 million lent by the French bank, which had no idea its funds would provide the seed for a great international move, the Cisneros brothers had the money to begin negotiations for acquiring the Beatrice bottling companies. They still needed $90 million. They went to Manufacturers Hanover Trust, which had financed part of the construction of the CADA distribution center in Cagua, and the parties enjoyed mutual respect. The bank told them yes but asked the Cisneros brothers to contribute $25 million.

Gustavo Cisneros turned to his network on Wall Street. He spoke to the people at Chase Manhattan Bank, who agreed to lend the Group $25 million, with the shares of CADA owned by the Cisneros brothers as security. In this way they succeeded in obtaining the capital, which in reality was all debt.

The total cost was $125 million.

PepsiCo never granted the Group the franchise for bottling its own cola. Without a strong brand, Gustavo Cisneros felt that the chances for growth were limited, and he sold the company in 1987, as discreetly as it had been bought, to a bottler in Oklahoma who paid the same $115 million that the investing group had paid. But in their almost seven years as owners of the company, the Cisneros brothers managed to have the All-American Bottling cash flow pay the debts to Manufacturers Hanovers, Chase, and Banque Worms. The money obtained from the sale was debt-free, an excellent deal. In his speeches to the community of investors and bankers, Cisneros would recognize that he had taken out eight times the money that had been invested.

In the years that followed, Cisneros would close deals that were more spectacular than All-American Bottling. But in a sense, AAB is one of the most significant transactions of his business career. First, AAB confirmed that Cisneros could participate without major difficulties in the United States market. And second, it served to convince the community of bankers and investors in New York that he was one of them. Until the acquisition of AAB, in the eyes of important Wall Street investors, Cisneros was one among several Latin American business groups with capital whose owners were developing their operations in New York, London, or Madrid. Although more cosmopolitan than most, and more successful than many, Cisneros was, when all was said and done, part of a Venezuelan group preeminent in Latin America. The overwhelming success of AAB—which was also a pure LBO play—would place Gustavo Cisneros in the entrepreneurial major leagues, on a world scale. From that moment on, Cisneros

would occupy a prominent place in the address books of investment bankers looking for a buyer or investor for their businesses.
AAB was the key that opened the doors to multiple deals waiting
to be undertaken.

A retrospective analysis of the acquisition and sale of AAB
makes it seem like an easy transaction; it was, however, a very
daring move, since the brothers put up their shares in CADA as
security for obtaining credit. If things had gone badly with AAB,
they could have lost a part of their supermarket chain in Venezuela, and the Cisneros story would have taken another direction.
Gustavo Cisneros wagered on a well-planned risk and succeeded
in acquiring another valuable asset for the Group.

On December 2, 1982, Cisneros invited his closest associates and their spouses to the Valle Arriba Golf Club in Caracas to
celebrate "the most successful year in the entire history" of the
Cisneros Group. He was extremely happy.

"Tonight I feel exceptionally pleased and proud," he said in
his welcoming speech. "I am pleased to be able to share this with
so valuable a group of executives whose great professionalism and
dedication have made them a team for success."

They were words spoken with sincerity. Despite the fact that
1982 was an "extremely difficult year for economies throughout
the world," given the Mexican debt crisis and the recession in
which all of Latin America found itself, the Cisneros Group had
invested approximately $100 million.

In the next two months, he told them, the Group would
open two new supermarkets; Pizza Hut and Taco Bell would make
their first appearance in Venezuela; and the ribbon would be cut
for a new bread factory (the largest in Latin America) and for the
Pharsana factory, which manufactured baby products. In addition, O'Caña would have new offices in February.

Cisneros mentioned the executives of All-American Bottling,
who had been brought in especially for the occasion. In the United States, the Group had just acquired Micro Online, a chain of
retail stores that sold computers and component parts.

"The organization," he emphasized, "is an authentic *multinational* Venezuelan enterprise." He stressed the world "multinational," and those present—among them his mother, Doña Albertina—applauded.

"My friends," he concluded, "with the example of Don Diego Cisneros, our founder, and with the goodwill and enthusiasm of all of you, we will continue to triumph."

In 1980, Cisneros had told the *Miami Herald* that he was in the midst of a ten-year plan to raise the Group's international revenues to $1 billion, the equivalent of half of all revenues calculated for that year. The focus of the plan was on the United States, the Dominican Republic, El Salvador, Panama, Brazil, and possibly Jamaica.

"We are not in a hurry, and we understand that we must be patient," he told the newspaper. "If we are cautious and establish a solid base, then a couple of mistakes will not do us much harm."

In much less time than that, the Group would achieve a much more formidable profile than even Cisneros himself had imagined.

7. Devaluation

At the beginning of 1983, Gustavo Cisneros, along with his brother Ricardo, met with President Luis Herrera Campins in La Casona, the official residence of Venezuelan heads of state. The economic situation in Venezuela was critical, and they wanted to know what the government planned to do, and if there was a risk of devaluation. After nineteen years of monetary stability, it was difficult to imagine that kind of scenario.

While they were waiting, they saw Arturo Sosa, the minister of finance, leaving the president's office. Sosa was close to the Vollmer Group and a friend of Goar Mestre, the former owners of Channel 8. Cisneros valued him as a friend.

"Hello, Gustavo; what brings you here?" Sosa asked.

"We came to see the president to discuss the economy."

"Good," said the minister of finance, "let me know what you find out because I have no idea what's going to happen."

Cisneros could not believe what he was hearing. Sosa, a trusted colleague of the president, had always been known for his clear, common-sense ideas about the economy. The entrepreneur was concerned about the influence that the president of Banco Central of Venezuela, Leopoldo Díaz Bruzual, might have on Luis Herrera. Unlike Sosa, Díaz Bruzual, nicknamed "the Buffalo," was known to be confrontational and not inclined to cooperative action. The meeting with President Herrera did not reveal many clues about the future. Cisneros was worried when he left: "This is going to blow up," he said to himself.

The explosion, in fact, took place on Friday, February 17, 1983, a date that Venezuelans would remember as "Black Friday." Banco Central adopted a measure that turned out to be worse than the devaluation that everyone had feared. In an effort to contain inflation and not jeopardize the campaign of the government candidate in the elections that would soon be held, the financial institution issued two-track exchange rates of 4.3 and 6 *bolívares* to the dollar, respectively, to pay for essential imports. Nonessential imports would be subject to free exchange, which immediately reached 10 *bolívares* to the dollar. Banco Central also created the office of Regulation of Differential Exchanges (Recadi) and imposed price controls for six months, which then were adjusted according to the value of the dollar. That marked the beginning of a spiral of inflation and devaluation that would adversely affect the lives of Venezuelans for the next twenty years. The excessive dependence on the petroleum industry and the enormous economic power of the state had created the conditions for a persistent overvaluation of the national currency as well as a severe lack of competitiveness, in general, in the Venezuelan industrial sector.

Despite the government's efforts, Jaime Lusinchi, the opposition candidate from the Democratic Action Party, was elected president. Lusinchi maintained the system of multiple exchange rates, with devastating results. Between 1981 and 1985 the economy shrank almost 15 percent. This was followed by a period of recovery. However, the annual inflation rate skyrocketed until it reached 40 percent by the end of the 1980s.

All of this signified a hard blow to the nation's businesses, including those belonging to the Cisneros Group, which had to import many items, from programming for Venevisión to heavy machinery for its factories. As a result, the Group's access to dollars was limited to an amount calculated on the basis of the previous year's purchases of imported goods. This meant that every additional dollar had to be negotiated with Banco Central, which had lost its independence from the executive branch. With the recession eroding gross margins, the Group initiated a plan to reduce expenditures. It halted the expansion of CADA, and devaluation decreed the end of Castor Trading. To put it simply, it made no sense to have a purchasing office in the United States if Venezuela was restricting imports. In its place, Finser (an acronym for Financial Services) Corporation was created to serve as an operations center for the increasing number of executives who traveled to Miami to supervise international businesses.

Companies had to use their ingenuity to survive, emphasizing factors such as marketing, advertising, and efficient distribution of products. An example was O'Caña.

Devaluation was an almost mortal blow for O'Caña which, because it was the first company created by the Cisneros brothers, occupied a special place in their hearts. The price of imported liquors, which did not qualify as essential products but were the company's mainstay, increased exorbitantly. Concerned by the growing difficulties in accessing foreign currency in Venezuela, European suppliers denied the company credit. Since it was a business with low turnover—a $50 bottle of whiskey is not sold every day—cash flow dried up.

The solution was to manufacture more liquors locally in order to broaden the range of O'Caña's own products, led by Cacique rum and Sagrada Familia table wine. Now Gustavo Cisneros wanted O'Caña to develop a deluxe Venezuelan whiskey. The company, which had warehoused large quantities of alcohol fermented from rice in oak barrels, proceeded to mix one-third rice alcohol with two-thirds alcohol derived from imported malt. Bottled and labeled locally, Cisneros obtained his made-in-Venezuela whiskey. Unforeseen circumstances had demanded innovation.

The new liquor was given the name Black Horse, a brand name that Cisneros had registered some years earlier. Black Horse was not their only creation. Korzakoff Vodka, Britannia Gin, and Leclerc Liqueurs also appeared, all manufactured with the same aged rice alcohol. In view of continuing credit limitations and their negative impact on expansion, Cisneros chose to sell the company at a profit.

The obstacles during this time accentuated Gustavo Cisneros' search for new challenges. His motto was—and continues to be—"From crises bigger and better opportunities emerge." A determined optimist, Cisneros refused to be discouraged despite the difficulties, and he searched for opportunities. In 1983, a few months after the devaluation, he acquired the Sears Roebuck of Venezuela chain of multipurpose stores. The transaction, which seemed promising from every point of view, presented only one problem: the Sears trademark could be used for two more years, but at the end of that time a fortune in royalties would have to be paid to continue using the name. This obstacle did not stop Cisneros, who resolved to create his own brand name in spite of the voices saying that such a change was extremely risky.

"We are sufficiently creative to overcome challenges," he told the group of executives in charge of the operation.

After an exhaustive market study, the name Maxy's was chosen to replace that of Sears. Most of the consumers consulted had associated the name with the concept of a multipurpose store.

Once again the publicity mechanisms of the Cisneros Group were put in motion. Participants in the Miss Venezuela pageant visited Maxy's to promote the Group's products and the new name. Maxy's resounded in all the media—press, radio, and, of course, TV through Venevisión. Only eight months after the change, a survey revealed that the positioning of the Maxy's brand name clearly eclipsed that of Sears, which had passed into oblivion.

Early in 1984, despite the crisis in Venezuela, Cisneros called four hundred of his executives to a convention at the Macuto Sheraton, in Caraballeda, on the Venezuelan coast. In the midst of a festive atmosphere that Venevisión's production team created with musicians and dancers, a spontaneous and informally dressed Gustavo Cisneros spoke to his people:

"The Cisneros Group is the largest group of privately held companies in Latin America. With its fifty-three companies, and you, its 35,000 employees, this year we expect to generate 11,500 million *bolívares* ($927 million)."

The basic purpose of the convention was to infuse the new managers with the spirit of the Group. Ricardo Cisneros spoke about its entrepreneurial philosophy, sketched the portrait of an executive in the Cisneros Group, and explained the Group's diverse operations. Once again Gustavo Cisneros felt that the occasion was perfect for offering a tribute to his father. Images of Diego Cisneros were projected, and Gustavo recalled for those present his father's philosophy, his devotion to work and to democratic principles:

"My father, Diego Cisneros, left a permanent mark on the world in which he lived, on the Venezuela where he struggled so hard, and on us, his children and associates, who today, with dedication and pride, are developing and expanding the fertile creation that he left us."

In the mid-1980s, the Cisneros Group was at the pinnacle of business activity in Venezuela, famed for its capacity to revive the most moribund companies. In 1986, Banco Provincial was attempting to resolve the difficult situation of Yukery, a consumer-products company that controlled well-known brands such as Gerber's baby food. Devaluation had affected its operations, and the government feared the imminent firing of its three thousand workers. The Cisneros brothers, who saw a good business opportunity in the company, decided to acquire Yukery, and the banks agreed to refinance the debt. In the hands of the Cisneros Group, with its robust CADA-Venevisión combination and close supervision by Ricardo Cisneros, the enterprise turned around.

All of these accomplishments created a solid reputation for Gustavo Cisneros as an executive linked to business success, and the entrepreneur suddenly found a line of multinationals knocking at his door. Al Feria, the manager in Latin America of the fast-food chain Burger King, was delighted with the performance of the Venezuelan franchise in the hands of Gustavo Cisneros, because he supplied everything that was needed. "Take bread: they own the bakery," he admiringly told the *Wall Street Journal*. Cisneros also supplied mustard, ketchup, mayonnaise, meat for the hamburgers, soft drinks, cash registers, coffee, and even the machines for making milkshakes. Moreover, thanks to the soda fountains acquired from the Rockefellers as part of the CADA package, he already had locations. Radiovisión and Venevisión completed the business by broadcasting Burger King commercials.

Many foreign firms, regardless of how large and prestigious they were, wanted to work with the Cisneros Group, even if not solely. Digital Equipment, looking for an exclusive representative for its products, made an exception for Gustavo Cisneros, who already handled Apple and NCR.

Devaluation was a challenge that put the tenacity of the Cisneros brothers to the test. By the mid-1980s, even though the Venezuelan economy was still reeling, the Group was growing by leaps and bounds. Venezuela was becoming too small for the brothers. "There were sixty companies, and fifty affiliates," recalls José Antonio Ríos, the head of operations for the Group. "There were 35,000 employees in a country as small as Venezuela, in a group led by a young, dynamic person like Gustavo, with the capacity for investment and the capacity to attract investments."

"Every day it became more necessary to expand business abroad," Ríos reflects. The call to internationalization became more urgent. In 1984, Cisneros would embark on one of his greatest entrepreneurial challenges, something that would demand the maximum managerial skills of the Group.

8.   A Diamond on the Floor

The economic turbulence plaguing Venezuela did not block Gustavo Cisneros' plans for international expansion. In the mid-1980s he felt prepared to repeat the LBO formula he had employed successfully with All-American Bottling. Using some of his own capital, combined with a significant percentage of debt, he could acquire companies that promised excellent results.

In the last four months of 1984, Cisneros completed transactions that defined more forcefully the Group's international profile and would transform it into one of the largest manufacturers of sporting goods in the world. It would end with a real estate deal in Europe that would bring him, by the most intricate routes, to a crucial meeting with Prince Charles of the United Kingdom.

Dan Lufkin, co-founder of the investment bank Donaldson, Lufkin & Jenrette, approached Gustavo Cisneros to offer him a deal that fit very well with the strengths of the Group: it was oriented toward mass consumption and would have a significant cash flow.

Lufkin had a company called Q Holdings, which he had acquired in 1982. It had previously been called Questor; it was listed on the stock exchange and was fairly well known, even outside its home city of Tampa, Florida. Lufkin did something else besides change its name. He and his fellow investors delisted the company (taking it private) in order to break it up and sell its divisions at a profit.

The most attractive piece of Q Holdings was Spalding. The company was the equivalent of McDonald's in the sporting world, as American as apple pie. It was founded in 1876 by A.G. Spalding, a pitcher for the Boston Red Sox. For years the firm was the only manufacturer of the balls used in major league-baseball. As time passed, Spalding diversified its products.

There were more than enough buyers for Spalding, but Lufkin wanted the sporting goods company to be sold in a single package with Evenflo, a manufacturer of baby products.

To Lufkin's joy, Cisneros agreed to buy the package: Spalding and Evenflo. The baby products business was not a problem since the Cisneros Group already had experience with Chicco in Venezuela, which facilitated Evenflo's assimilation into the Group.

When it was time to set the price, Lufkin and Cisneros agreed on $350 million.

Initially they tried to finance the purchase entirely with debt, but the financing bank, Citibank, wanted to see capital on the table. The Group offered $30 million, which did not satisfy the bank either. In the end, the operation required the Cisneros Group to contribute $65 million of its own funds.

The purchase of Spalding and Evenflo was financed as follows: $250 million lent by Citibank, $35 million in financing by the sellers, and $65 million in capital from Cisneros. On September 12, 1984, the agreements were signed, barely nine months after the acquisition of Sears in Venezuela. These were two large businesses that had to be digested.

"We're not going to look for more companies or make further acquisitions until we have assimilated Sears and Spalding," Cisneros announced to a group of executives shortly after signing the acquisition of Spalding.

There was a feeling of relief. At last, they thought, a little calm.

"Unless," the entrepreneur added, "I see a diamond on the floor. In that case, I'm going to pick it up."

Cisneros' statement was prescient. In October, when the Spalding and Evenflo transaction had been completed, Gustavo Cisneros went to Aspen, Colorado, where he received a call from a representative of First Boston Corp. "Gustavo, the department store chain Galerías Preciados is for sale in Spain. That's why I'm calling you."

The Venezuelan entrepreneur respected the bank's judgment. Two days later he had the prospectus for Galerías Preciados in his hands. The project attracted him immediately.

The case of the Galerías Preciados chain had become a drama in Spain. Founded in the 1930s, it was adversely affected by the Spanish recession of the 1970s and was taken over by a bank, which in turn sold it to José María Ruiz-Mateos in 1981. Ruiz-Mateos was an aggressive and controversial entrepreneur from Jerez who headed an enormous group of 730 corporations and 18 banks. Rumasa (for Ruiz-Mateos SA) accounted for 1.8 percent of the Spanish gross domestic product.

At that time Ruiz-Mateos was immersed in complex controversies with the Spanish government, in particular with the new administration headed by Felipe González, who had assumed the office of head of state in December 1982. Banco de España had ordered an audit that eventually revealed an operation on the edge of a financial abyss. If the group collapsed, it would drag down with it several banks as well as its 60,000 employees. The audit, conducted by Arthur Andersen, verified that only 165 operations in the group were genuine. Rumasa was expropriated in February 1983. Ruiz-Mateos alleged political persecution and fled Spain (a year later he would be captured and extradited).

Pedro Pablo Kuczynski, of First Boston, had the job of selling everything that could be sold, and Galerías Preciados was one of the money-losing assets in the lot. The *Wall Street Journal*, quoting one of the people in charge of the sale for the Spanish government, called the chain of department stores a "lost cause." It would not be possible to get rid of it "even if we wanted to give it away." With 15,000 employees in twenty-nine stores, the operation showed losses of $50 million a year and it had to compete with Corte Inglés, a solid rival that reported substantial profits. To top it all off, there were doubts regarding the stability of democracy in Spain and the economic agenda of the socialist president Felipe González.

Even so, Galerías Preciados, with sales amounting to more than $700 million a year, was still the fifth-largest operation of its kind in Europe. The challenge of trying to restore its splendid past was too attractive for Gustavo Cisneros. He knew President González, whom he considered a sensible politician. He recalled his participation in the colloquium on democracy held in Caracas six years earlier. He was convinced the Spanish president had ideas favorable to a free-market economy.

Cisneros met with his business associates to inform them about the matter.

"We have a challenge, it's a company that has been offered to all the businesspeople in Spain, and nobody wants it. They've offered it to the principal department stores in Europe, and they've turned it down. They've offered it to Corte Inglés, and they didn't want it. They've offered it to people who have very important department stores in the United States, and they're not interested. And now they're offering it to department stores in Latin America," said Cisneros.

The list of disadvantages relating to the business was overwhelming, added to which was the political uncertainty hovering over the country. The company was strangled by debt and the rigid labor laws in Spain prevented a reduction in the payroll.

"But," Cisneros told them, "I've thought of a strategy to deal with the situation."

He sent two of his executives to verify the condition of the Galerías Preciados stores. Two weeks later they returned with their report: the stores were somewhat deteriorated but were situated in strategic locations. A few were even national monuments.

The second part of the operation, and the most critical, was to evaluate the situation with Galerías Preciados' creditor banks. If the financial institutions had no faith in Cisneros' plan and in the entrepreneur, then there was no chance at all. He also needed to determine if Spain was a reliable place for investing. For both things he turned to an old friend, the former Citibank executive George Moore, who knew more about Spain than many Spanish investors.

"George, what's going on in Spain?" he asked after explaining that he wanted to buy Galerías Preciados.

They spoke about the success of the Spanish political transition. The backbone of stability in the country was its vigorous middle class, the product of the economic boom of the 1960s and early 1970s. These people had a good deal to lose with a populist government or a return to dictatorship. A success for the Spanish economy in the post-Franco era was the Pacts of la Moncloa, signed in October 1977 by politicians, businesspeople, and workers' organizations. The unions agreed to lower their salary demands in exchange for certain additional social benefits and the passage of a Workers' Statute. The government implemented a fiscal reform, and inflation, which had been rising for a few months that year, began to come down. The Pacts of la Moncloa generated a positive economic climate that cleared the way for the building of Spanish democracy in the years that followed.

Cisneros closely followed events in Spain, where he always felt at home. The new constitution, approved in 1978, withstood the attempted coup on February 23, 1981, an occurrence that served to strengthen public approval of King Juan Carlos, the key figure in the success of the transition. Spain joined NATO that same year (with final approval in 1986) and passed the Basque and Catalan statutes. In political terms, Moore and Cisneros agreed, the country was very solid. But after Felipe González's impressive victory in the October 1982 elections, the focus of the debate moved from the political to the economic sphere. González's acceptance had been preceded by an ideological, even radical, commitment. He had promised, for example, to create 800,000 jobs in state administration through direct public investment.

Moore's opinion was reassuring. He had a good deal of confidence in Felipe González, who was only forty-two years old in 1984.

"Look," Moore told Cisneros, "nothing's going on here, Spain is a great opportunity. I have friends here who are frightened by the socialist government, but in fact his government plan is market friendly."

Cisneros told him that he was interested in approaching the Spanish banking community because Galerías Preciados owed more than $600 million. Moore put him in touch with the most important bankers in the country. Gustavo and Ricardo Cisneros first visited Alfonso Escámez, the president of Banco Central, in this case a private institution. Cisneros explained that he wanted to bring modern marketing techniques to the operation, as he had done in the United States and Venezuela; he would launch an intense television campaign, which was unusual in Spain, and he would improve the variety of products. The labor question was the most complex to resolve, since the principal union had communist leanings and was combative; but faced with imminent liquidation, Cisneros was confident it would be inclined to negotiate a cutback.

Escamez promised his support and opened other doors in Spanish banking. They spoke with Claudio Boada, president of Banco Hispano, which a few years later merged with Central, giving rise to Banco Central Hispano. Boada transmitted encouragement to Cisneros regarding Spain's economic future. He said he knew Felipe González's economic team. "They believe in capitalism," Boada told Cisneros.

They spoke to the brothers Jaime and Emilio Botín, of Bankinter and Banco Santander respectively, who also agreed to participate in the rescue of Galerías Preciados. Gustavo and Ricardo Cisneros returned from Spain with lines of credit totaling more than $400 million. Gustavo Cisneros, who also met with Miguel Boyer, President González's economic head, was certain that democratic institutions were going to consolidate.

Only the question of the unions remained. Cisneros sent another delegation to Spain, headed this time by his chief of operations, Jorge Massa, who was married to Gustavo's sister Anita Cisneros, and by Estanislao Pérez. They came back with an agreement: the unions agreed to reduce the company's payroll. They asked only to participate in the decisions about who would stay and who would go.

Gustavo Cisneros felt ready for the operation. He was conscious of the risk the transaction entailed, perhaps the greatest one of his life. A friend, Plácido Arango, an outstanding Spanish-Mexican businessman, had warned him that the only natural buyer for Galerías Preciados was Corte Inglés. Calculating the ratio of the number of consumers to the available square feet in department stores, Madrid had an excessive number of such stores in comparison to Manhattan, for example. Cisneros decided to move ahead; he was betting on the idea that he could bring the operation back to health and transform it into a successful project. He trusted his instincts.

At the bidding he offered a little more than $4 million. With the debts he was assuming, the offer rose to $147 million. The Roca Group in Colombia, owners of Sears in that country, was the other bidder. The government weighed what it meant to turn Galerías Preciados over to a group that generated $75 million a year, as opposed to the $4 billion of the Cisneros Group. Gustavo Cisneros won the bidding on December 6, 1984. There were no objections. On the contrary, many people saw a happy ending for the failed operation.

The Galerías Preciados financial package was structured almost entirely on the basis of monetary commitments, following the model of a leveraged buyout. The next step was to gather a team of executives who would move to Spain. Jorge Massa finally agreed and moved to Madrid with his wife. Prior to marrying Anita Cisneros, Massa had been Gustavo's classmate at Babson and had a long relationship with the Cisneros family. After six months in Spain, however, Massa returned to Venezuela and left the Group. In the months that followed, lawyers worked on a restructuring of the Cisneros Group's ownership to reflect the exit of the Massa-Cisneros branch as shareholders of the Group. This restructuring left Gustavo and Ricardo Cisneros as the principal shareholders of the Group and their sister Marion with a minority interest.

"Once the transaction is structured and completed, all that's left is to roll up your sleeves and go to work," Gustavo Cisneros told the team assigned to Madrid. Ricardo Cisneros was at its head, seconded by Humberto González in operations, and by Estanislao Pérez, who was happy to return to his native country, in the political-institutional sphere.

The Madrid team members negotiated with the unions regarding the layoff of 4,000 of the 15,000 employees, thereby easing the costs of Galerías Preciados. They brought in Spalding and Evenflo products, broadened the offering of merchandise, and improved their presentation by increasing the segmentation of their distribution in the store. Galerías Preciados launched an aggressive television campaign and upgraded the product displays. The stores appeared rejuvenated and more modern, thanks to renovations carried out by the architect Marion Cisneros, Gustavo's sister.

Reality revealed both pros and cons. On the one hand, Cisneros felt the company was where it needed to be. After three years of effort, the negative cash flow of 20 billion *pesetas* ($114 million) a year had been reduced to 3 billion ($23 million). The projections for 1988 estimated the elimination of numbers in the red. But the operational success—which began to weaken as the months passed—did not necessarily translate into a financial turnaround. The plan that Gustavo and Ricardo Cisneros had designed allowed a four-year grace period to pay off the debt. At the end of that time, the bankers were prepared to reschedule the liability, but they demanded that at least 40 percent of the debt be cancelled. In addition, they had to further broaden the range of products and consider the possibility of selling to their customers on credit, something that Corte Inglés was already doing. All of this meant a new infusion of capital. Gustavo Cisneros was reviewing the alternatives when he received an opportune call from London. "It seems that a magic wand follows along after Gustavo," says one executive, remembering the call.

Anthony Clegg, the partner-founder of Mountleigh Group, had become a minor legend in the United Kingdom. He began with an old textile factory, and from there went on to establish a dynamic real estate empire of offices and commercial centers. Mountleigh stock was, for a time, one of the ten most profitable on the London market. Clegg was fifty years old but looked younger. He loved Spain and the opportunity it represented, and he was amazed at the potential of Galerías Preciados. Of course, things had changed since the Venezuelans' arrival in the country. Spain had joined the European Union in 1986 and, led by the charismatic and eloquent Felipe González, was burying the last vestiges of Francoism. Cisneros compares the situation to what the California phenomenon represented in the United States during the 1950s. As a consequence, real estate values skyrocketed in Spain.

"All right," Cisneros told Clegg, "I'll see you in Spain."

After looking at Galerías Preciados, Clegg made his offer.

"I'll buy the whole thing from you," the Englishman told Cisneros.

"What do you mean the whole thing?"

The Venezuelan did not understand. Cisneros wanted a partner and had not thought about selling everything.

"What's your price?" the Englishman insisted.

Finally they reached an agreement. Mountleigh would pay the Cisneros Group a significant multiple of the initial investment, in recognition of the four years of work in expanding and redesigning the store, and introducing new marketing concepts.

"But there's one condition," the real estate magnate pointed out. "I want your managers to stay on at Galerías Preciados."

Cisneros had six of his principal managers living in Madrid, and running the operation: Marion Cisneros, Estanislao Pérez, Humberto González, Luis Regalado, Héctor Beltrán, and Paco Ramírez.

"I can't promise that," said Cisneros.

Clegg's answer was categorical.

"Then there's no deal. They set up the plan, and they should be the ones to carry it out."

It was a sensible proposition, and Cisneros said he would talk with his executives before giving his final answer. He did not like placing his executives in that kind of situation; he had taken great pains to have them feel comfortable in Madrid. He visited them in their homes and talked with their families to find out their concerns.

Gustavo Cisneros explained that the Mountleigh offer, though very good for the Group, depended on what they decided.

"If all of you don't want to stay, there's no deal with Clegg," he told them.

They all chose to continue at Galerías Preciados, and on September 29, 1987, the transfer was complete. Almost immediately the operation became complicated.

Cisneros' banker friends in New York celebrated the sale on account of the entrepreneur's daring and vision; in Spain, on the other hand, unforeseen tensions arose. In reality, Cisneros was caught in the middle of a political struggle between the opposition Popular Party (PP) and the governing Socialist Worker's Party (PSOE). The PP viewed the profits Cisneros would earn from the sale of Galerías Preciados as a way to cause difficulties for Felipe González, and it was suggested that the PSOE had benefited from the transaction. The matter was to the advantage of the PP because resentment already existed in Spain at the successes achieved by certain foreign investors.

The fact that a foreigner had acquired a historically important Spanish company and, in a very short time, successfully changed and improved the image of the stores—accomplished thanks to the Cisneros Group's experience in the Maxy's and CADA stores in Venezuela—generated uneasiness in Spain.

Few people pointed out that it had been necessary for Cisneros to convince a group of banks to join him in a business that no one had wanted to buy for three years. If Clegg or someone like him had not come forward, the situation could have become very difficult, especially if Cisneros failed to restructure debts. His opportunities to undertake more LBOs would have been compromised.

Because Cisneros disliked public controversy, he opted for silence. Many of his executives and friends urged him to grant an interview to the local press in order to defend his name. But he saw that he was in the middle of a dispute between the PP and the PSOE. There was no graceful exit from that quarrel. Furthermore, he believed that some people were simply reacting with a touch of envy at the excellent deal he had made.

"In Spain there is a good deal of commentary," he added, "but people with a thorough knowledge of the problem know what the real situation is."

In time, the PP found other subjects it could use to weaken the image of González, whose presidency, nonetheless, would last another nine years. Today, few remember the specific incidents of the much discussed case of Galerías Preciados. However, as a business, the sale of Galerías Preciados was a success for the Cisneros Group. Once again Gustavo and Ricardo Cisneros, and the Group as a whole, demonstrated their keen operational skills.

The second complication relating to the Galerías Preciados deal was less public but more challenging from the entrepreneurial point of view. On October 19, 1987, three weeks after the closing the agreement with Tony Clegg, the Dow Jones Index lost 23 percent of its value. It was the "Black Monday" that pounded Wall Street, and Clegg was also affected. The price of Mountleigh stock dropped by half, from 3 to 1.5 pounds a share.

"Gustavo," Clegg said to Cisneros, "I'll be honest with you, I'm in no condition to do the Galerías Preciados deal, but I love Spain. Would you be willing to take some of the stock in my company as part payment?"

The idea was interesting. It seemed that Cisneros was destined to continue his career as a entrepreneur in Europe.

"It depends," the Venezuelan answered, "but we love England."

The two businessmen returned to the negotiating table and soon reached an agreement. Instead of the 153 million pounds in cash originally agreed to, Cisneros received 30 million pounds sterling in cash, a twenty-four-month IOU of 81 million, and the equivalent of 42 million pounds in Mountleigh stock valued at their pre-Black-Monday level, which amounted to 7.2 percent of the company.

As the months passed, the Cisneros brothers began to doubt that Mountleigh could pay the IOU in the agreed-upon time of two years. The formerly glittering English real estate market was dimming and Mountleigh stock was still very depressed, especially after a stroke left Clegg incapacitated.

As a consequence, a third agreement had to be reached between the Venezuelan entrepreneur and Mountleigh. In October 1988—a year after the stock market crash—Cisneros returned the IOU to the English firm as an initial payment for 25 percent of the value of five properties it owned in London. Nominally the value of those holdings was 324 million pounds, though on occasion there is a great difference between what an accountant's books may say and the real price. The plan was that Cisneros would try to sell four of the properties. This would produce a double benefit: the Group would obtain revenues from the sales and, simultaneously, the value of Mountleigh stocks, some of them owned by Gustavo Cisneros, would rise.

Cisneros had hopes of making a good deal with the jewel in the Mountleigh crown: the famous group of buildings around Paternoster Square, which an investment bank had characterized as the "most attractive project to appear on the English real estate market in the past fifty years."

Paternoster Square, the area around St. Paul's Cathedral, is visited every year by some three million tourists who admire the Baroque church designed by the renowned English architect Sir Christopher Wren. Almost without intending to, Cisneros had become the owner of a site of great symbolic value for the British. The task of converting that into money fell to Ricardo Cisneros and William Keon, financial vice president of Finser, the Group's Miami office, who had experience in the real estate sector. Both men settled in London to supervise the small real estate empire.

Two years younger than Gustavo Cisneros, Keon managed important operations for the Cisneros Group in the United States. He supervised the finances and accounting for All-American Bottling and was in charge of tax and legal matters for the Group outside Venezuela. Keon lives in Coral Gables, Florida, but talks and behaves like the true New Yorker he is: he says things frankly, something the Cisneros brothers value. "Call me 'Bad News Bill,'" he tells them. He has no problem assuming especially complex tasks, or ones that others may find unpleasant. He has a particular way of keeping organized. His mind functions on the basis of papers, many papers. He writes down everything in his letter-size notebook. He tears out the pages and keeps them in files that are then carefully placed in one of the small towers of file folders—classified by subject—that decorate the floor of his office. Even now, in the era of e-mails and laptop computers Keon works in this manner.

For working meetings, Keon pulls out some papers and folders from his towers, places them in a small cart, and transports them along the corridors of the Finser offices as if he were a waiter bringing a meal to a hotel room. Everyone present knows that in a matter of seconds Keon can find in this apparent chaos of documents the exact paper that will clarify any doubts. He also has an extraordinary memory for figures and dates.

For fourteen months, Keon traveled every Sunday night to the Hyde Park Hotel in London and returned home late on Friday. During this period he accumulated a good part of the four million miles earned with the American Airlines frequent-flyer program. "The crews knew me," the executive says. "I spent 112 nights up in a plane."

His work consisted of contacting all the tenants, one by one, in the properties managed by the Cisneros Group, in order to renegotiate their leases so that Cisneros could decide on the properties' outcome. There were all kinds of tenants in the group, from small kiosks and boutiques to large corporations like Reuters and KPMG.

Keon sold three of the four properties that the Group wanted to sell. He also found a buyer for the Mountleigh stocks. Paternoster Square turned out to be the biggest headache.

Paternoster was bombed and completely destroyed by the Germans during the Second World War, but as if by a miracle, the cathedral remained intact. The surrounding areas, according to Keon, were redeveloped with the "kinds of buildings usually erected in the sixties"—that is, they were unsightly and boring. In the interior, their ceilings were too low, and the oppressive feeling was unbearable in the summer months because there was no air conditioning. Everyone agreed that Paternoster had to be renovated. Every English architect wanted to do it because it was a sure way of earning a knighthood.

Mountleigh had calculated that the cost of renovating the 4.3 acres of Paternoster was some 850 million pounds. The sum would be a good investment, because the potential profit—according to the value of the real estate at the time—would amount to the surprising sum of 680 million pounds, almost 1.2 billion dollars.

The first obstacle that had to be overcome was presented by Prince Charles himself. He adored the cathedral. It was where he had been married to Princess Diana and where, in time, he hoped to be crowned king. He considered the buildings around the cathedral "somewhat better than the ruins left by the Luftwaffe." Toward the end of 1987, he told a group of architects: "The buildings have ruined the outline of the capital and profaned the Cathedral of St. Paul." The problem was rooted in the fact that the prince would not accept just anything in their place; he wanted something that would meet his criteria in questions of architecture—a subject in which he has always demonstrated a special personal interest. Some editorial writers celebrated him as "the voice of the conscience of the English people."

Before Cisneros' involvement in the matter of Paternoster, Clegg had done the impossible to please the prince. He had invited seven architectural firms to a public meeting and urged them to consult with all the pertinent authorities, including the Church of England and the Royal Commission on Fine Arts. The prince rejected the seven proposals that Clegg showed him, including the entrepreneur's favorite, a project by Arup Associates. At one event he stated: "Surely this is the place and the time to sacrifice some income, if necessary, for the sake of the generosity of vision, elegance, and dignity of the buildings that will be erected. I trust they will strengthen our spirit and our faith in free enterprise, and will prove to us that capitalism can have its human side."

Clegg tried to defend himself: "Tastes change; the buildings now in Paternoster were admired in the sixties," he told the English press. In private, the prince's position was an obstacle difficult to avoid. Clegg had been ready to sell everything to a Kuwaiti investment fund, but the investors had retreated.

Cisneros tried to explain to Prince Charles the renovation project proposed by Mountleigh and the Cisneros Group. He arranged an appointment with the prince during an official visit to Venezuela in 1989, hoping that distance from his adored cathedral, and the transatlantic trip, would put him in a more open frame of mind. Cisneros, aware that he was betting one of his last chips, ordered the design of an enormous maquette in royal green, which turned out to be very beautiful, complete with cars, trees, and, of course, the cathedral, all to scale. He was certain he had a winning project.

The meeting was held at the residence of the British ambassador in El Country Club, an exclusive district in Caracas. Gustavo Cisneros made his presentation and waited for questions from the royal heir, but it did not take him long to realize that his project was in trouble. Arup had proposed 1.2 million square feet of high-quality construction for offices, a commercial center, and shops. Prince Charles found Cisneros' project too commercial. "The number of shops must be reduced," he said, and he pointed out the buildings that, in his opinion, were superfluous. The Venezuelan entrepreneur was prepared to lower density somewhat, but not to the extent of changing the project entirely.

After the meeting, Cisneros decided to change strategy and he brought John Simpson, Prince Charles' favorite architect, into the Paternoster project. Simpson proposed an alternative design of 1.1 million square feet, which was more to the prince's liking. It was at this point that Cisneros decided to call his friend John Gutfreund, the president of Salomon Brothers, and give him the task of finding a buyer for Paternoster.

At the end of 1989, Keon, assisted by Salomon Brothers, sold a majority interest in Paternoster to Greycoat Plc and Park Tower Realty, both specialists in the field. Two months later, the Japanese firm Mitsubishi Estate Co., the owner of Rockefeller Center in New York, came on board and Cisneros exited the Paternoster project completely.

Leaving Paternoster was a good decision. After ten different development projects, Mitsubishi, as the sole owner of the project, began the first demolitions in 2000. Prince Charles finally gave his blessing to the project, aware, perhaps, that if his attitude did not become more flexible—given his love of architecture and historic icons—Paternoster would never be modernized, at least not in time for his future coronation. In June 2003, Mitsubishi Estate announced that it had completed its urban development in Paternoster Square with the construction of three buildings, and was preparing to turn offices over to Goldman Sachs International and the London Stock Market, among others.

Clegg's stroke left the entrepreneur inactive for a year. When he returned he quarreled with his partners at Mountleigh, and in November 1989 he sold his 22 percent of the company just before the real estate market depreciated. Mountleigh, with net assets of 584 million pounds and debts of 590 million, declared bankruptcy in 1992.

Of the four Cisneros executives who had remained at Galerías Preciados, three returned after completing their year's stay; and the company, the source of the Paternoster transaction, after changing hands several times, was finally acquired by Corte Inglés in June 1995 for 30 billion pesetas ($247 million). The new owner reduced the workforce from 7,300 to 5,200 employees, kept the thirty stores, and did away with the name that for six decades had survived all kinds of turmoil. That same year Anthony Clegg died at the age of fifty-eight.

The experiences and vicissitudes of these years taught relevant lessons that became part of the Group's managerial code.

1. **It is common in business for opportunities to present themselves at the same time.** Gustavo Cisneros recommends prudence. Despite his image as a daring and aggressive businessman when the time comes to grasp opportunities, in reality there are many more deals rejected by the Group than are accepted. In fact, every day Gustavo and Ricardo Cisneros receive joint venture or acquisitions offers. In the mid-1980s for example, Cisneros had seriously considered the option of becoming a significant international player in the sporting-goods sector, thanks to his experience with Spalding. He evaluated with Ricardo the possibility of acquiring the Converse and Adidas brands. They were very close to buying but pulled out at the last moment.

"God took care of us!" Gustavo Cisneros recalls. "I was convinced, and Ricardo too, that the athletic-shoe business was good from the point of view of the numbers, but intuition told us that it would change, years later, into a business in which we could not distinguish ourselves." The sneaker business was turning into a volume business, where whoever manufactures for less earns money. It is a world condemned to increasingly narrow margins.

2. **Valuable contacts are a fundamental tool for identifying opportunities and bringing them to fruition.** The importance in Spain of George Moore, a family friend dating back to the time of Don Diego, demonstrates how a trusting relationship adds value to business. Gustavo Cisneros attributes so much importance to the matter that he has dozens of people, in New York and in Spain, taking care of his contacts and appointments.

3. **There should always be a clear "exit strategy" as part of a contingency plan in the face of uncertainty.** This requires creativity of the kind shown in the Galerías Preciados-Paternoster negotiation.

4. **Management is exportable.** But for this to be so, Cisneros looks for executives able to confront a variety of challenges, who feel comfortable running a company that produces bread or television programs. He challenges them continually in order to find their strong and weak points. "He likes to work in multidisciplinary groups of people of different ages," says a former collaborator. "Methodically, he asks each one of the members of a group for an opinion before reaching a conclusion, from the vice president of companies to a lawyer who hasn't even graduated yet but is there taking notes. He asks everybody for ideas because the best ideas can come from unexpected places."

A group of financial advisers reviews the numbers and maintains discipline. Even though it is a family company, Cisneros feels proud of having generated a team of professional managers who could assume more and more responsibilities as the Group added companies.

5. According to Cisneros, **"With clean hands one can endure everything, and adversities can be overcome."** Pentacom and Galerías Preciados were businesses that generated public controversy, which the Group was able to overcome because it had nothing to hide. As will be seen, Cisneros would experience other situations of public controversy, but in the long run he would emerge successful, even strengthened.

6. **A good relationship with banks is key for business.** This was what Cisneros' attorney and friend, Pedro Tinoco, insisted on. The banks were there when Cisneros began to buy companies in Venezuela, like CADA and Yukery. They were also there for All-American Bottling, Spalding, and Evenflo. Galerías Preciados would have been impossible without bankers.

Cisneros considers them, along with suppliers and unions, as essential allies.

7. **The world of business is a box filled with surprises.** "The normal thing in business is to expect the unexpected," says Cisneros. The unexpected can be a positive event, like the opportune arrival of Mountleigh, which permitted Cisneros to embark on enterprises in Spain and then England, or something less anticipated, like a devaluation followed by price controls, as was the case in Venezuela in 1983.

8. **It is advantageous to have sole control of the business' management.** From Cisneros' perspective, it gives better results than when management is shared. That lesson would be proved again in the years that followed, when the direction of his group would change in a spectacular way.

9. The Storm

Despite controls on exchange rates and prices, by 1988—an election year—Venezuela recorded an inflation rate of 35.5 percent. Lack of fiscal discipline was rampant, with expenditures that were 9.3 percent higher than income. Petroleum earnings nose-dived. Between 1986 and 1988, petroleum income averaged $8 billion a year, 43 percent less than the level reached during the previous three-year period. The flight of currency was unstoppable, and the foreign debt of $33 billion became unpayable. According to the historian Guillermo Morón, Venezuela was "immersed in a global, generalized crisis."

In the midst of this bleak panorama, optimism was reborn in the figure of Carlos Andrés Pérez, a veteran politician who was audacious and charismatic. Millions of Venezuelans remembered him as the man who had controlled the destiny of the country from 1974 to 1978, the years of its greatest petroleum boom.

There were no surprises in the December 4 elections. Pérez, the candidate of Acción Democrática, won easily with 53 percent of the votes, while Eduardo Fernández, his opponent from the Social-Christian party COPEI, had 40 percent. Counting as well on majority support in Congress, Pérez had a solid mandate for carrying out the reforms the economy needed. But the electorate had chosen Pérez on the basis of its memory of the golden years of his first government, with the expectation of experiencing a repetition of those times of expansion, which under the new Venezuelan circumstances—a country in debt, without reserves, hounded by its creditors, and with oil prices low—simply could not happen again.

Pérez understood that he could not duplicate the populist policies of increased spending of his first government, and he accepted the challenge of putting into effect a "package" of economic reforms favorable to the market, foreign investment, and fiscal discipline, all of this within the framework of one of the most subsidized economies in the world. His electoral mandate indicated that his popularity would permit him to take forward-looking economic measures, which might have severe effects in the initial stages, but would soon open the doors to a healthier and more sustained growth for an economy that urgently required profound reforms. Yet Pérez's popular support was not built on acceptance of tough measures to liberalize the economy, but on a comforting memory of his first term in the Palace of Miraflores, when an abundance of petro-dollars allowed the state to flood an economy lacking alternative support with money, to the point of asphyxiation. The fondness of the Venezuelans for Pérez would be much more ephemeral than anyone thought at the time.

The first days of the new administration gave no hint of the approaching storm. The new president's inaugural ceremony took place in the midst of scenes of reconciliation and voices of hope. Everyone congratulated the president-elect and cited the Venezuelan political regime as an exemplary democracy. It was the first official trip abroad by the recently elected vice president of the United States, Dan Quayle, who was accompanied by a large contingent of American journalists. Other figures who attended included Felipe González from Spain, and Oscar Arias, the president of Costa Rica and winner of the Nobel Peace Prize.

A few days later, Gustavo and Patty Cisneros were hosts in Caracas to the annual conference of the Americas Society, an organization founded by the Rockefellers, of which Gustavo Cisneros is a director. He gave a welcoming dinner at the Museum of Contemporary Art in Caracas, where he paid homage to his friend David Rockefeller. The most select of national businesspeople were present at the event. There, too, optimism was in the air.

With the blessing of the International Monetary Fund, on February 16, President Pérez announced a sobering package of measures aimed at eliminating subsidies for a variety of basic consumer products. He increased the cost of gasoline and transportation, and freed the price of the dollar, dissolving Recadi, to the relief of many. To stop the flight of currency, he doubled interest rates.

Pérez's announcements gave rise to perplexity and rejection among many people who felt defrauded and even deceived. Venezuela had not been prepared during the election campaign to face the truth.

In the days following these announcements, the news departments of various media outlets received troubling reports of isolated looting of warehouses and supermarkets. The directors of Venevisión thought it was the work of ordinary criminals, but in reality these were the first tremors predicting a major earthquake. "The atmosphere was saturated with gasoline," recalls one executive.

February 27, 1989, marked a crisis in the contemporary history of Venezuela. The events of that day, known popularly as "the day the hills fell down," or the "Caracazo," defined one of the saddest chapters in Venezuelan democracy. The plan for austerity measures and fiscal reform, as well as the decision to increase the cost of public transportation in the metropolitan zone of the capital, ignited a fuse of protest that turned violent. Thousands of people began looting commercial establishments, and the residents of Caracas watched in amazement as anarchy overwhelmed the city. The disturbances were eventually repressed by the military and other state security forces. Even today it is not known exactly how many lost their lives in the course of the three days of social upheaval. These events left their mark on Venezuelans, along with the fear that one day something similar could happen again.

This period and its immediate aftermath convinced Gustavo Cisneros that the time had come to put into effect one of the boldest entrepreneurial changes of direction in the history of Latin American business.

The grim days in February were a time of adjustment for the businessman and his future plans. For the first time since 1964 (the height of the struggle against Castroite guerrillas), the rights to free expression and assembly in public places were suspended in Venezuela. A curfew from 8:00 p.m. to 6:00 a.m. was imposed. Schools were closed until further notice. Some 15,000 army troops, supported by 7,000 police, guarded the city.

Numerous warehouses, stores, supermarkets, and commercial establishments of all kinds were looted, among them four branches of CADA. The store in the middle-class district of La Florida was surrounded, and the police reached an agreement with the looters, many of them women and children: they could carry out whatever they wanted, but they had to enter in small groups.

Gustavo Cisneros' ability to respond was immediate. Within two days of the disturbances, most of the CADA stores opened their doors again to the public. The gesture of the employees, who worked extra hours so that everything would be in order within so short a time, was a cause of special satisfaction for Cisneros. It showed that labor relations at the very heart of his organization were excellent: one of the few positive facts derived from the experience.

"When the problem had been solved from the managerial point of view, I began to think and meditate about what had happened, and if there was a possibility that it could happen again," he recalls.

What concerned him most was his country's future. The immigrant community was one of those most harmed by the damage, because many cafés, restaurants, and other places of business had been founded by Spaniards and Italians who came to Venezuela during the 1940s and 1950s. After February 27, many would pack their bags and return to their native countries.

In the long term, the fact that Venezuela was becoming polarized between an increasingly weak middle class and the impoverished masses had a direct impact on any investment project. Cisneros wanted a prosperous Venezuela whose citizens had significant purchasing power and therefore a high consumption rate in his supermarkets and department stores, with a positive impact on every-one's quality of life, but the signs were all pessimistic.

Even before Pérez assumed office, the Cisneros Group had begun considering the option of gradually reducing operations in Venezuela, in view of the obstacles imposed by a stagnating economy dependent on oil. The strategy developed by Cisneros twenty years earlier had come full circle. In the mid-1970s, his aim had been diversification in order to broaden the income base and give more stability to the Group. He did it first in Venezuela, adding enterprises like CADA and O'Caña to the traditional companies of Pepsi-Cola and Venevisión. Then he made inroads in the United States, acquiring All-American Bottling, Spalding, and Evenflo. The goal of deriving half of all sales from international sources had been achieved.

On a daily basis the Cisneros brothers received from three to five offers of partnership or purchase, not including projects to expand the operations they already owned. Teams of managers visited mega-market installations in Brazil and the United States to better understand the development of these stores and apply such concepts to CADA. Their experience in Europe demonstrated that the Cisneros Group had completed a successful phase, and the brothers were now concentrating on the study of new businesses. They could do this because they had the necessary cash flow, as well as experienced managerial talent that needed only to be empowered by new challenges.

The process of globalization was another reason to consider change. The world had become—according to the well-known phrase—a "global village," that is, the connections among nations, peoples, and communities had become closer, and there was a proliferation of exchanges on all levels of human life: economic, social, cultural, and political. This was an unstoppable dynamic that generated benefits and at the same time created new challenges for humanity. In this demanding and highly charged context, great multinationals increased their interest in Venezuelan companies, and the group now had to reckon with the local affiliates of Unilever and Kraft. "You can compete with Nestlé in ice cream," says one collaborator, "but you have to forget about everything else."

As a result of lessons learned from the events of February 27, Gustavo Cisneros met with some of his most trusted executives, the purpose being to refocus the direction of the Group. It would be the first of several meetings that would be held in Caracas, New York, and La Romana.

Gustavo and Ricardo were very clear about what they did not want: companies that were dependent on a single country. The only operations that should remain in the Group were those capable of expanding beyond Venezuela into the rest of Latin America, the United States, and Spain.

"A company that cannot internationalize," Cisneros told his people during a meeting in La Romana to consider long-term strategy, "will have no justification. All of you are accustomed to managing companies that generate *bolívares*; now we'll learn to generate dollars."

That determination excluded several of the flagship enterprises in the Cisneros Group. First on the list of companies to sell were the producers of foodstuffs such as Yukery, Tío Rico Ice Cream, and Atlantis, which manufactured mustard, spices, and other products for the kitchen.

It was not an easy decision.

"Let's do this without undue procrastination, because if we analyze it too much, we won't do it at all," said Cisneros.

Some assets on the sale list dated from the time of Don Diego. Rafael Odón, the vice president in charge of the entire area of retail sales, and today the president of Cervecería Regional, looked with suspicion at the sale list since it included three-quarters of the division that he headed. It was a hard blow for a manager trained in retail sales, but as a result of the twenty-one years he had worked at Nestlé before joining the Cisneros Group in 1986, he understood the need for globalization. "It's the wave of the future," he said.

Whether CADA and Maxy's could be "globalized" was a subject of debate. Giants like Carrefour and Wal-Mart were beginning to extend their tentacles into Latin America, and the destructive events of February 27 had shown the vulnerability of that sector. Still, the emotional ties to CADA were very deep, and Cisneros was prepared to explore the possibility of acquiring some operation that would expand CADA internationally.

This period would mark the boldest managerial successes of Gustavo Cisneros. His intention was to strengthen and focus the Group and lead it to new entrepreneurial accomplishments.

Cisneros' idea was to maximize the growth of the Cisneros Group in telecommunications, television, and entertainment on a pan-regional level. Gustavo Cisneros and his team worked on the concept of "entertainment." The entrepreneur did not limit this concept to programming for a television channel, the movies, or the theater; for him, soft drinks and beer, like pay television and radio, were products linked to entertainment.

The move from the manufacture of perishable goods for mass consumption to the communications media had enormous implications. In the past, a company's level of cash flow was a key indicator for the brothers when it was time to decide on a new acquisition. The financial analysis centered specifically on the amount of cash flow. Cisneros always told the bankers that he would buy a company only if its earnings were enough to finance its own growth and amortize all its loans within a period of five to ten years. It was the essence of the LBO model.

But in the communications industry, cash flow was a less important measurement tool, since Spanish-language pay television channels and regional content providers—like MTV, CNN, or ESPN—had been operating for too short a time to provide a useful cash-flow history. The question was how to evaluate their price. The answer was that it could not be done in the same way that the acquisition of a sporting-goods manufacturer was evaluated. Companies that sell pay television are not valued so much on the basis of the income they earn from their subscribers month to month as by what they are potentially capable of doing with those distribution networks, from geographical expansion to their utilization in carrying data and telephone transmissions.

In short, the Group was changing from a model based on the generation of cash flow to a model more closely tied to the creation of value. Banks would probably be less enthusiastic about making loans to fund a new documentary channel than to expand a juice-processing plant. These new businesses would demand more of the family's own resources. After the sales of All-American Bottling and Galerías Preciados, the Cisneros Group was enjoying a comfortable financial situation. The move merited the incorporation of new partners. This was not a matter of inviting in partners to participate as passive investors; it was necessary to have experienced operators as partners, including those who could bring an additional managerial platform to projects.

Since the days of Pepsi-Cola and O'Caña, the Cisneros brothers had worked very little with this kind of partner. The exceptions were limited to investments in industries that lay outside their field of direct expertise. For example, there was a plan to develop a gold mine in Guyana with Goldfields, a South African firm. They had another project for an aluminum foundry with the French firms Pechiney and Iritecna, and Techint in Argentina.

Gustavo Cisneros was aware that these changes would generate a certain uneasiness at the very heart of the Group. In December 1990, he decided to hold a conference to communicate the Group's new course in person and invite his employees and associates to embrace the new goals by working with the same dedication they had always shown. More than six hundred people met at the Hotel Macuto Sheraton, on the coast near Caracas, for what was called a "strategic encounter" of the Cisneros Group.

On the first afternoon, Gustavo shared the stage with his brother Ricardo. In his opening address, he used expressions like "a stop along the way," "renovating spirit," and "reformulating strategies."

"I want to deliver a message to you that will stimulate innovation, unorthodox thought, an anti-dogmatic attitude, the search for unconventional solutions, and options in the face of challenges."

He was planting the seeds for what was to come.

A few months later, the brothers met with a group of executives in La Romana to put into practice the new concepts that had been discussed at the convention at the Sheraton. The name of the meeting said it all: "Strategic Planning Meeting for the Cisneros Group." Ricardo Cisneros presented some recommendations that he called "strategic directions."

From this there emerged what some call "the first great restructuring of the Group." Atlantis, the company that made mustard, shoe polish, and household cleaners was transferred in its entirety to Yukery. The Atlantis distribution center was closed. "The instructions were to give maximum attention to cash flow; we had to find the greatest possible efficiency," one manager points out.

Another goal raised by the brothers was that in three years' time, the level of debt in all the companies would have to be zero. This key decision, made in 1991, avoided major problems during the collapse of the Venezuelan banking sector in 1994.

An emblematic decision during this time was the sale of the Tío Rico ice cream company to the large transnational Unilever. For years the ice cream firm had been managed locally in various countries, but the effects of globalization also transformed the competitive terrain. The transaction marked the group's first departure from the food-products segment.

In November 1991, Oswaldo, Gustavo, and Ricardo Cisneros founded Telcel, currently the leading cell phone company in the country, in partnership with the United States firm BellSouth. Cisneros was expanding his presence in technology and telecommunications, in alliance with a large multinational that would exercise operational control. It would be the recipe he would follow for more ambitious transactions over the next few years.

At the beginning of 1992, Cisneros was satisfied with the progress of the Group. The events of February 27, 1989, however, had left their mark. They had not affected his deepest beliefs concerning Venezuela's prospects, or his fundamental commitment to his country, but they had served as a lesson for reorienting the organization's future direction.

Despite the clouds that were gathering on the Venezuelan horizon during that time, Cisneros was taken totally by surprise at the news his pilot gave him on a February dawn of that year as his Gulfstream was crossing the Pyrenees en route to his house in Madrid. "Mr. Cisneros, they're asking you to communicate with Mrs. Sandra Zanoletti when you reach Madrid."

Zanoletti was his personal assistant.

"It seems there's been an attempted coup in Venezuela," the pilot added.

Cisneros felt powerless, trapped in the stratosphere while his country was in turmoil thousands of miles away. He had time to reflect on the bitter irony of what was happening. He had just come from Davos, a small town in the Swiss Alps, after attending the annual meeting of the World Economic Forum, funded by the large multinationals. Once a year this international forum gathers under one roof the most important corporate heads and political leaders to reflect on the world's future. At no other time do so many influential people from so many different backgrounds gather in so small a place.

That year, the atmosphere had been one of rejoicing and celebration. More than a thousand corporate presidents had listened to Vaclav Havel, the Czech president, speak of the "end of Communism in the history of humankind." They took note of how the South African leader Nelson Mandela acknowledged that under no circumstances would he nationalize industries, contradicting what was stated in the electoral platform of his party, the African National Congress.

Even the problem of Latin American foreign debt seemed to be nearing a solution. "The debt crisis in Latin America will end in August, when the accords are signed that will restructure debt in Argentina, Mexico, and Brazil," predicted William Rhodes, a member of Citibank's board of directors.

And now, just as freedom, democracy, and the market economy were becoming more solid than ever around the world, Venezuela had suffered an attempted coup.

Ricardo Cisneros was one of the first to recognize what was approaching. At ten o'clock on the night of February 4, a security staff member called his residence to warn him that two battalions of paratroopers—some 1,600 heavily armed men—were on their way from Valencia to Caracas, intending to take power.

Venevisión, as the leading television channel in the country, was a logical operational target in any coup attempt. The channel's security teams had contemplated that possibility and knew exactly what they had to do. One of the most incredible nights in the history of the channel and the Cisneros Group was about to unfold.

Carlos Andrés Pérez, who had also been at Davos, was lucky to be alive. The insurgents had tried to trap him at the Maiquetía International Airport, but the president always seemed to be one step ahead of them. From the airport he headed for his official residence, La Casona, but it was under attack. He fled immediately to the Palacio de Miraflores, but the rebels followed in his footsteps and he had to escape again through a tunnel, along with Vice Admiral Iván Carratú, head of the Palace Guard, and a small group of bodyguards, in two armored Ford LTDs.

The insurgents were spreading rumors that the president was dead. In a city filled with rebel tanks, the president looked for a television channel to prove that he was alive and still the head of state. In the confusion that followed, some would maintain that Cisneros put Venevisión at the president's disposal. As Pérez himself would tell the well-known Colombian journalist Gerardo Reyes, the truth was that he eventually made history on Venevisión, but his intention was to reach another station, Televen Channel 10.

"Televen is the newest station and they're probably not watching it as closely," the president told his chief bodyguard.

When they reached a highway that passes through the higher elevations of Caracas, known as La Cota Mil, an assistant passed him a telephone, saying he had a security head at Venevisión on the line.

"If you recognize my voice don't identify me," said Pérez. "Do you people know what's going on?"

"Yes, we do, the news has been reported."

"Good, I'm coming there."

Shortly before midnight the two cars reached Venevisión and President Pérez was given an office where he could make phone calls. He urgently needed to locate his minister of defense. Someone passed the news to the United States embassy, and Pérez received a call expressing solidarity from President George Bush. César Gaviria of Colombia, as well as Felipe González of Spain and other European leaders, also phoned him.

Pérez was taken to the ground floor of the station where there was a modest studio with a camera and a desk, and where an older man, the announcer on duty, was sitting. The president spoke to the Venezuelans with a face that reflected three assassination attempts and the ten-hour flight from Europe.

"He looked terrible, not very presidential. He was sweaty and disheveled," a witness recalls.

Fortunately for the channel, the engineers arranged for Pérez's image to be aired simultaneously by Venevisión and two other television channels, leaving the insurgents in doubt as to the leader's real location. This ensured that Venevisión would not be shelled immediately, and Pérez could prove that despite statements by the insurgents, he was still alive.

In the meantime, Gustavo, who was in Madrid by now, pondered what he should do. He was aware that Pérez had lost popularity in the country, but he did not consider any alternative other than supporting democracy. His father sent Venevisión cameras out to the streets during the presidential elections of 1964 to demonstrate that the country was capable of holding a peaceful election. Now, the son affirmed his adherence to his father's philosophy. Once again the Cisneros family was placing Venevisión cameras at the service of Venezuelan democracy.

Cisneros opened his address book and began to communicate. He spoke with politicians, businesspeople, and diplomats. Even at a distance he was bent upon acting as a cohesive factor for the constitutional forces, encouraging them and sending a message of confidence and loyalty to the institutions of Venezuelan democracy.

Many people came to Venevisión to express their solidarity with the president. Despite the fears of the security teams, the rebel troops never did take over the channel and the building's occupants.

Finally the president was able to locate Fernando Ochoa Antich, the defense minister, who notified him that the coup apparently was the work of a lieutenant colonel named Hugo Chávez.

Pérez was surprised.

"Who's that?"

"He came two months ago to ask for an appointment and talk about a disciplinary measure that had been imposed on him, which you lifted."

"Oh yes, yes, now I remember."

Chávez had spent almost ten years planning a coup, but the tolerance of a solid democracy missed the many signs pointing toward a conspiracy. Chávez got what he wanted. Pérez had decided that the officer could remain in the Armed Forces.

The president gave instructions for the loyal troops to deal harshly with the insurgents. "No negotiations. Give them a taste of lead."

The outcome of the coup did not reflect the amount of planning time Chávez had put into it. The paratroopers under his command became involved in street battles with the police. In addition they could not control the strategic La Carlota airport, in the heart of the capital. And although they sent a group to Channel 8, the state channel, to broadcast their proclamation, they were not able to do so because the tape had been recorded in the wrong format.

At 4:30 a.m. the president returned to the air, though this time he was in a larger studio more suited to the occasion. A flag was even found to place behind him. With no Venezuelan standard, a Colombian flag, which has similar colors, was used, folded so that no one could tell the difference. This time Pérez projected more authority. He expressed his gratitude for all the calls of support and announced: "In a few minutes I'll return to the Palacio de Miraflores, because the rebel troops have been subdued."

At 5:00 a.m. the president, accompanied by Vice Admiral Carratú, entered the Palacio de Miraflores while shots from insurgent guns could still be heard a few blocks away. At 6:40 in the morning he asked the last center of rebellion in Valencia to lay down its arms. Hugo Chávez finally surrendered at 11:30 on the morning of February 5. Loyal troops arrested 133 officers and 956 soldiers. According to the minister of defense, twenty men lost their lives and another sixty were wounded.

Gustavo Cisneros worked to defend Venezuelan democracy, but he paid a price for it.

The day after the coup, the telephone switchboards at Venevisión were filled with calls insulting the channel. The populist rejection of the image of Carlos Andrés Pérez on Venevisión was so intense that the size of the station's audience shrank.

"It was a great lesson," Gustavo Cisneros recalls. "The number of viewers went down, because people identified us with democracy. This reaffirmed our conviction that democracy has to confront social problems with urgency and efficiency."

It would take Venevisión two years to recover its traditional supremacy, which occurred in 1994, coinciding with that year's World Soccer Championship in the United States.

On November 27 of that year, a group of officers in the Air Force organized another uprising. This time the insurgents understood the need to control the mass communications media, and they took over the Mecedores transmitting station, located in the mountains that surround the city and used for transmission by television channels. They broadcast a proclamation from the studios of the state channel, urging a popular uprising. The effect on viewers was just the opposite of what the rebels were hoping for: people stayed in their houses.

A few months after these events, Pérez was accused of crimes of administrative corruption because of his handling of the government's discretionary funds, and he was forced to leave office. Venezuelan democracy, which until 1989 was characterized as one of the most solid in the region, had begun what would become a long period of instability because of an economic decline, unusual even for Latin America, which was accustomed to violent highs and lows.

In 1996 the gross domestic product per capita was 20 percent below its peak in 1978. The standard of living of each Venezuelan had returned to the level of the mid-1960s, wiping out all the gains of the petroleum boom in the 1970s.

One of the key protagonists in these events, Lieutenant Colonel Hugo Chávez Frías, would be elected to presidency of the republic in 1998. With charisma and—at the time—overwhelming popular support, the retired military man succeeded in moving forward a process that fundamentally changed all the political institutions in the country, including the constitution.

What happened in Venezuela between 1989 and 1993 reinforced Gustavo Cisneros' conviction that democracy is the only viable way to resolve the problems of his country and of all of Latin America, and that businesspeople have an unavoidable social responsibility in this regard. "Economies are improving, but people are experiencing the challenges inherent in the growth of the free market, principally instability," he said in an interview in November 1992. "The contribution that companies can make to improve the situation is to invest in educational initiatives. This will assure that today's Latin American children are prepared to be tomorrow's creative generation. When we invest in education and stay on the right path toward democracy and the free market, the development of our people will continue."

10. That Marvelous Hispanic Spirit

When Gustavo Cisneros assumed the presidency of Venevisión in 1970, he had a clear vision of his mission: "I wanted to turn the channel into something different, an enterprise of regional and even worldwide scope," he points out.

He had to wait more than two decades, until in 1992, after a long sequence of events that were resolved in his favor, Cisneros closed what would become the most successful deal of his career. This would set the stage for his meteoric rise as a media tycoon. In the early 1990s, Cisneros began to build a Hispanic communications empire.

Soap operas, or *telenovelas*, are Venevisión's great letter of introduction abroad. They are shown in the United States, Latin America, and to a lesser extent in Europe and Asia. Along with Mexico, Venezuela, led by Venevisión, was one of the first countries to distribute these programs beyond its borders. Beginning in 1970, Venevisión enjoyed great international success with *La Señorita Helena*, *La Revancha*, *Las Amazonas*, *Cara Sucia*, and *La Mujer de mi Vida*, among other productions.

The soap opera in Spanish was lagging somewhat behind its Brazilian counterpart, but the gap would close at the end of the 1980s. The period of the great global phenomenon of the Latin American soap opera was beginning, which would benefit Gustavo Cisneros. The scriptwriters—the true silent stars of the form—knew how to press people's emotional buttons. The typical script for a *telenovela* narrates a variation of *Cinderella*, in which a poor student, dressmaker, or servant manages to succeed in life and win the heart of the hero. A favorite alternative is avenging a betrayal, in the style of *The Count of Monte Cristo*.

Félix Caignet, the father of the genre, who wrote the classic *El Derecho de Nacer*, explained why his soap operas were so popular to a friend, the writer Gabriel García Márquez: "I always try to make people cry, because people love to cry."

Even the Sandinista government in Nicaragua transmitted televised Venezuelan dramas on state channels despite recognizing that they did not contribute very much to revolutionary fervor. Venezuelan *telenovelas* became strong in Spain thanks to the success of *Cristal*, by Delia Fiallo, who revolutionized the *radionovela* and in a certain sense transferred the technique to television. At the beginning of 1991 fourteen soap operas filled the screens in Spain, with productions from Venezuela, Brazil, Puerto Rico, Peru, and Mexico. Cisneros placed *Esmeralda*—another work by Delia Fiallo—*La Revancha*, *Las Amazonas*, and *Cara Sucia*.

For Cisneros this process constituted the recovery of a goal that had taken shape toward the end of the 1980s aimed at doubling the number of Venevisión production studios to ten, which would permit the addition of approximately 2,500 hours of programming a year to the library of 10,000 hours it already had by the end of that decade. This did not equal the scale of its Brazilian and Mexican counterparts, but Venevisión's works—and those of its competitor RCTV—reached some thirty countries. One out of every four soap operas transmitted in the Spanish-speaking world came from Venevisión.

"In the past twenty years we have placed more than fifty soap operas on a variety of Hispanic channels in the United States, with extraordinary success," Gustavo Cisneros declared proudly to a group of bankers in November 1992, when the sales of Venevision International, in the midst of a Hispanic boom, increased 150 percent compared to 1991.

The first president of Venevision International was Rodolfo Rodríguez, and subsequently the company has been headed by Carlos Barba, Carlos Bardasano, and, currently, Luis Villanueva.

Its soap operas were and are transmitted in markets as diverse as Turkey, Hungary, the Philippines, Greece, Lebanon, Portugal, the United States, Brazil, and Mexico. "Not even the Russians are going to save themselves from *Cara Sucia* and *La Revancha,*" Cisneros said at a meeting of executives. There will be soap operas for some time to come because the numbers are very attractive. Venevisión's strength is that it knows how to produce shows at a reasonable cost that do well beyond the local market. Manuel Fraíz-Grijalba, executive vice president of Venevisión, emphasizes: "From the point of view of the business of television, the soap opera is the best strategic product in terms of the audience, as well as finances. It requires a high initial investment, which is counterbalanced the longer the soap opera stays on the air."

In recent years, *telenovelas* have become an entertainment phenomenon that goes beyond their original audience: housewives who feel lonely at two in the afternoon. Now they are watched by people of all ages and both sexes.

Soap operas showed Cisneros that he could compete in the entertainment industry beyond the Caribbean basin. But he understood that in order to become a serious player he needed to buy a television network in the United States. That would mark the difference between being a producer of content and a true television entrepreneur.

A badly managed television network is a license for losing large quantities of money. The more distant and exotic the market, the greater the probability of acquiring something that in the end shows losses. Roberto Marinho, the baron of the Globo network, learned this lesson in 1985 when he acquired Telemontecarlo, an Italian channel that competed with the state operations of RAI, and with Silvio Berlusconi's stations. One of his sons moved to Monaco—where the channel was located even though it is Italian—to supervise the operations. The result was catastrophic for the Brazilians. In 1991, Telemontecarlo lost $55 million, and another $50 million the following year. Globo finally sold it in 1993.

The television business is a recycling of programming from one platform to another, from the first broadcast by the anchor channel—Venevisión, for example—to its retransmission in other countries or on a pay channel. In this respect television is no different from the Hollywood studios, who first send their films to movie theaters and then to other media, such as video, pay-per-view, and cable television. This is why owning more than one channel in several countries is a guarantee of distribution.

When Gustavo Cisneros gained control of the TV network Televen, Channel 10 in Caracas, at the beginning of the 1990s, he wanted to target the young adult sector, the growing middle-class technocracy emerging so powerfully in the country at that time, to complement the more popular family profile of Venevisión. Televen began to import a sizable collection of Brazilian soap operas. Their production was first-rate, filled with exterior shots that emphasized the beauty of that country. Their scripts wove together sophisticated stories through the narration of parallel plots. In fact, the audience indices for the channel increased from 2 percent to 10–12 percent, with good advances in the target audience: the professional and technical sectors of the Venezuelan population. But then, they rose no further. No one understood why. Televen organized focus groups—a tool used by marketing teams to explore the responses of clients—with a variety of viewers, and requested the opinion of experts, but a plausible explanation never emerged. With a few very notable exceptions, such as *Pantanal* or *Tieta*, the Brazilian programs had limited penetration in the Hispanic world, as if dubbing erased some decibels of emotion and took away the mystique of the show; then too, the stories were complex. "The simpler the soap opera, the better. The predictable soap opera tends to be the one most watched by the public, because people identify, participate, interact," says Manuel Fraíz-Grijalba.

At the beginning of the 1990s, Cisneros concentrated renewed energies on the task of making his way into the television market in the United States. "We always wanted to be there," says Cisneros about North America, "but we never obtained anything large enough. A small station in Florida made no sense; we wanted to encompass the entire U.S. market."

Emilio Azcárraga Milmo, the Mexican entrepreneur and principal shareholder in Televisa—and the son of the network's founder, Emilio Azcárraga Vidaurreta—thought he had a mission to take Mexican culture north, in the same way that the Americans had brought theirs south. Azcárraga Milmo shared with Gustavo Cisneros a natural gift for leadership. At that time he controlled 97 percent of the Mexican market, and in 1991 he exported 38,000 hours of programming, principally news and *telenovelas.*

Investors were delighted with Azcárraga Milmo. At the height of his power in 1991, in what would be the crowning glory of his work, they acquired 22 percent of the Televisa shares that the entrepreneur listed on the New York Stock Exchange. The proceeds from the offering were $862 million—not bad for a company that had revenues of $914 million that year.

In spite of all this, a part was still missing to complete Azcárraga Milmo's empire: the United States. He needed to increase the export of Mexican programming. To that end, in the 1970s he had launched Spanish International Network (SIN), a channel that would carry Televisa programming to the several million Hispanics who lived in the United States at that time. But there was a problem: U.S. laws required the channels (like SIN, NBC, or CBS) to be owned separately from the network of stations that distributed the signals in each city. If one did not have control of the stations, there was no guarantee that they would carry SIN's programming. Conseqently, Azcárraga Vidaurreta and Azcárraga Milmo formed a partnership with a group of American investors and René Anselmo, a broadcasting entrepreneur, to found the Spanish International Communications Corporation (SICC). SICC began to buy stations that would broadcast SIN programming, comprised primarily of Televisa productions.

Led by Anselmo, the operation began to meet the needs of the growing Hispanic market, and in 1979 Anselmo added Galavisión, the SIN cable channel.

It all collapsed in 1986. The powerful Federal Communications Commission (FCC) ruled that Anselmo was acting in the interests of the Mexican tycoon and therefore was violating regulations that prohibited a foreigner from controlling a station; he was required to sell the five stations he owned in the United States. The purchaser came as a surprise: Hallmark Cards Inc., the manufacturer of greeting cards and stationery, which at that time was embarking on an ambitious program of diversification.

Hallmark's purchase of SICC-SIN gave birth to Univision.

Hallmark had little experience in the difficult art of programming for Hispanics. The company hired Joaquín Blaya, a Chilean with a proven track record. Blaya began to implement a costly plan to produce the channel's own programming. By the early 1990s, almost 30 percent of Univision's programming was developed locally. Naturally, this did not please Azcárraga Milmo at all: not only was the channel buying fewer Televisa products, but it was also positioning itself as a possible competitor.

Blaya's aim might have been laudable, but the Chilean's plan did not work for two reasons. First, the advertising revenues in the Hispanic television market were still too small to sustain the costs of local programming. As Blaya increased sales, expenditures increased even more, and Hallmark did not have the funds needed to pay the loans it had obtained to finance the purchase of Univision. The EBITDA (earnings before interest, taxes, depreciation, and amortization), a measurement of a company's cash flow widely used by financial analysts, fell from $48 million in 1988 to $34 million in 1992. "It was a recipe for bankruptcy," recalls an executive in the Cisneros Group.

Second, to Blaya's dismay, it turned out that Hispanic viewers missed their soap operas. SIN-SICC had always satisfied their preferences, but in 1991 its audience share fell below 60 percent.

Hallmark finally understood that Hispanic television had nothing to do with the design of Christmas cards, and it put Univision up for sale. This was the great opportunity that Gustavo Cisneros had been waiting for so that he could make a solid landing in the United States.

Cisneros had observed the evolution of Telemundo, Univision's competitor in the United States. Telemundo's weakness was that it had only seven stations compared to Univision's thirteen, and a fraction of affiliated channels. This meant that no matter how popular Telemundo's programming might be, its smaller coverage relegated it to second place in terms of audience reach. For this reason it would always obtain a smaller portion of the advertising dollars allocated to the Hispanic television market, and expanding the Telemundo network was a very expensive matter.

Fortunately, Cisneros and Azcárraga Milmo knew each other and got along well. Cisneros was fifteen years younger than Azcárraga and considered him a friend. Each man respected the achievements of the other. "We understood each other, and shared many common interests. He was a very gifted man with his own way of doing things, who projected Televisa into the world, just as it had to be done," says Cisneros. They spoke frequently. Azcárraga Milmo sailed his yacht to La Romana to spend a few days with Cisneros. They both preferred New York to Miami, and the Venezuelan was a member of Televisa's board of directors. The good chemistry between them allowed Cisneros to convince the Mexican magnate that they should join forces to buy Univision.

The next step, and the more complicated one, was to find an American partner who would be acceptable to both Azcárraga Milmo and the FCC. There were not too many candidates when one eliminated those who had clashed with "the Tiger," as Azcárraga was called, or who lacked the courage to take over an operation that was practically bankrupt. Carlos Barba, recently hired by Cisneros to be president of Venevision International, had an idea. Barba knew the U.S. market because he had worked as manager of Channel 47 in New York. His boss, the owner of the station, had been Jerry Perenchio, a successful businessman with a very sharp mind for the television business. Barba and Perenchio had managed a channel that surpassed Azcárraga's SIN channel in audience ratings during prime time.

"Talk to Perenchio, let's see if he's interested," Cisneros told Barba.

The son of an Italian winemaker, Perenchio had a well-deserved reputation as an astute investor. When he ended his career as a pilot in the late 1950s, he went to work for Lew Wasserman, the legendary music tycoon and founder of the Music Corporation of America (MCA). Wasserman taught him the management principles that Perenchio would apply for the rest of his life, including his obsession with maintaining a low profile. Publicity, Wasserman would say, was for the artists, not the managers of the companies that represented them. Perenchio, convinced that individual prominence worked to the detriment of team effort, was even more implacable. His low profile generated an almost reverential mystery about him, since his career was brilliant. In the 1960s he represented actors like Elizabeth Taylor and Marlon Brando. He did not allow obstacles to deter him when it was time to innovate. During the 1970s and 1980s he formed partnerships with independent producers who had great successes on American television, with programs such as *All in the Family* and *The Jeffersons*.

Although Perenchio did not have a good command of the Spanish language, he was convinced that Hispanic television had a promising future in the United States. He invested in several Spanish-language channels, including Channel 47 in New York, and in 1986 he was close to buying SICC from the Azcárraga-Anselmo partnership, but negotiations broke down at the last moment. Energetic and dynamic, he himself takes charge of reviewing the numbers in a deal before making a decision, even though in the end he trusts his intuition more than the cold axioms of figures. "Perenchio is an indisputable leader who is always there when it's time to make important decisions," says an executive in the Cisneros Group.

Perenchio, Azcárraga, and Cisneros met in Los Angeles. Cisneros worked patiently to convince both men to join in the purchase of Univision. The Mexican and the American respected each other, but when these two strong personalities clashed, the atmosphere grew heated. Yet the negotiations bore fruit, with Gustavo Cisneros emphasizing the points they had in common above and beyond their differences.

Despite his occasional doubts, Azcárraga had a flexible spirit, and he did not want to collide again with the FCC as he had in 1986. Early in 1992 a small group of lawyers drew up documents to reflect what had been agreed upon. Cisneros had an agreement that was, in his own words, "hedge against the bad tempers of the partners."

Univision could make use of all the programming it wanted from Televisa and Venevisión, paying them 15 percent of its sales. The arrangement was beneficial to Univision, since American channels generally spent almost twice as much on programming. It was also excellent for Venevisión and Televisa, because they were recycling material whose costs had already been recouped in their markets of origin.

To avoid any objections from the FCC, Azcárraga and Cisneros ceded to Perenchio 75 percent ownership of the stations—the old SICC—and 50 percent of the SIN network. The rest was owned by Azcárraga and Cisneros in equal parts. Basically, Perenchio would control management and own a substantial portion of the company, even though the three had contributed the same amount of money to acquire Univision.

There was, however, a quid pro quo. Azcárraga and Cisneros inserted minority rights into the shareholders' agreement that would protect their interest over time. Perenchio, for instance, could not sell the operation without the approval of Gustavo Cisneros and Emilio Azcárraga. They also inserted, among other things, limits on the debt the company could incur. While the terms of the agreement might be viewed as cumbersome, for Cisneros they guaranteed that Univision would be administered "managerially and not emotionally."

Once the issues relating to the structure of the partnership had been resolved, Perenchio, Cisneros, and Azcárraga sent their executives to Kansas City, Missouri, to negotiate a price with Hallmark.

After much back and forth and several phone calls, the price agreed upon was $505 million. Only $100 million of the purchase price was paid in cash. The remainder constituted debt that the new partners assumed. The agreement was announced on April 8, 1992, almost a year after Barba had contacted Perenchio. It had been a very complicated process, but Cisneros was accustomed to difficult negotiations.

Emilio Azcárraga was satisfied with the result. All that was pending was the FCC's approval of the transaction. The United States was the most promising Hispanic market outside Mexico, and studies indicated that in ten years Hispanics would be the largest minority in the United States. In fifteen years, there would be more Spanish-speakers in the United States than in Spain, and they would have high purchasing power. Most of them had Mexican forebears, and Azcárraga was making certain that his company would provide the programming for them.

Cisneros also had reason to celebrate: he had entered a market full of opportunities, with an initial outlay of only $33 million (the portion that corresponded to the Cisneros Group). He was realizing a long-term dream.

The gamble, however, was not risk-free, because at that time there was more disappointment than hope for Hispanic television. No one doubted that demographic tendencies favored the segment, but investors had lost a good deal of money in Hispanic television. "We assumed that if we showed the advertisers that we had 3 or 4 percent of the viewers in the country, we could collect 2 or 3 percent of the advertising dollars," Henry Silverman, the founder and ex-president of Telemundo, told the *Los Angeles Times*. "But we're getting 1 percent [of advertising income]. The advertisers are telling us that Latinos don't matter to them."

Late in September of 1992, the FCC gave its blessing to the purchase. The new management cancelled most of the programs acquired by Blaya, among them one in which Xuxa, the well-known animator of programs for children, took part. But it kept *Sábado Gigante*, a variety program with live music that represented 15 percent of the channel's income. The infectious good humor of its Chilean host, Mario Kreutzberger, known as "Don Francisco," moved viewers to enthusiastically sing the advertising jingles of the program's sponsors. Nothing like it had been seen on American screens since the 1950s. Don Francisco's broad face and playful smile became an icon in the Hispanic community, and his program would be exported to nineteen countries. Kreutzberger knew very well who the new owners were. He went to visit Televisa's San Angel complex and was impressed by the immense size of the installations, which had 18,000 people working like ants in a space that could hold six football fields. "So big!" he exclaimed. "So many opportunities!" Then he visited Venevisión, met with Gustavo Cisneros, and took advantage of the opportunity to act as co-host with Gilberto Correa for an episode of *Sábado Sensacional,* a Venezuelan program of the same genre as *Sábado Gigante.*

In addition to *Sábado Gigante,* Univision's management kept *Cristina,* a somewhat suggestive live-interview show that shocked the reserved Mexican market but was loved in the United States. It also decided to keep the news department.

In fact, Univision quickly began to reap the benefits of its programming arrangement with Televisa and Venevisión. The viewers were happy and audience shares returned to what they had been in the days of SIN-SICC. From time to time the Mexicans threatened to take their programs elsewhere if their rights were not increased. In 1996, Venevisión implemented some changes in its operations in Venezuela in order to produce programming that was more attractive to the American market. One of its studios was adapted especially for a talk show hosted by Maite Delgado. Participants in the program were chosen carefully to reflect the multiethnic background that characterized the Hispanic community in the United States. In 1998, Venevision International began to tape soap operas in Florida, beginning with *La Mujer de mi Vida,* which achieved a record viewership in the United States, Venezuela, and other countries in Latin America and Europe. In fact, Venevision International has created six soap operas in Miami, more than any other producer.

For its part, Univision reversed its poor showing immediately. The EBITDA jumped from $34 million in 1992 to $60 million in 1993, and continued to climb until it reached $140 million in 1996, the year in which the company went public on the New York Stock Exchange. The EBITDA and sales for 2003 were estimated to reach $425 million and $1.5 billion, respectively.

Univision also proved to the three partners that the Hispanic market would not be a passing phenomenon, as many critics had predicted. In the 1960s, when Azcárraga started out with his stations, it was thought that the same thing that happened to Irish or Italian immigrants would happen to Hispanic Americans: in a few generations they would leave behind their language and, in some cases, their customs. Although some analysts believe that future generations of Hispanics will eventually assimilate fully into the style and traditions of the United States, for the time-being modern communications and proximity to their countries of origin mean that Hispanic immigrants tend to hold onto their customs and their language, as reflected in Univision's audience statistics. For example, KMEX, a station in Los Angeles, an area densely populated with Mexican immigrants, competes neck and neck with English-language networks such as Fox or CBS. Throughout the country, more Hispanics watch Univision than Telemundo and all the other English-language channels combined. Today, Univision is the nation's most-watched Spanish-language broadcast television network and the fifth most-watched, full-time network overall, competing head-to-head with the English-language television networks.

Within its growing segment, Univision became a great communications force. Of the twenty programs most watched by the Hispanic community in 1996, fifteen were on Univision. "Nobody approaches the control of 80 percent of the market that Univision enjoys," an analyst from Merrill Lynch & Co. said that year. "Not even in the English-speaking market."

What most attracted investors was that Univision had great economic potential. A report from the Salomon Brothers investment bank indicated that 4 percent of the population watched television in Spanish, but it received only 1.7 of the advertising pie. Others said that Hispanics consumers had more brand loyalty than other ethnic groups in the United States and were less likely to channel surf during commercials.

Investors pounced on Univision's stock when the company offered shares to the public in September 1996 at a price of $23 per share. In a single day the price per share shot up to $30. With 18 million shares in the Cisneros Group's possession, Gustavo Cisneros had multiplied the Group's initial investment in Univision several times over. Since Univision's initial public offering,

Alejandro Rivera has been the executive in charge of following the company for the Cisneros Group, reporting directly to Gustavo Cisneros. Today, as will be seen in detail, Univision's holdings include radio, music, and Internet businesses.

The idea of using Univision as a platform for distribution had worked beautifully. If it could be done in the United States, why couldn't it be done equally well in other countries? Mexico and Brazil were in a separate league since they were under the absolute rule of Televisa and Globo, respectively, but in the rest of Latin America the industry was much more fragmented and amenable to a process of consolidation. One could buy a channel in each country and then connect them in order to share costs, such as the costs of programs aired in common.

At the beginning of the 1990s, both Emilio Azcárraga Milmo and Gustavo Cisneros set out to buy television networks. Azcárraga moved first, with the acquisition in 1992 of 49 percent of Megavisión, the first privately owned channel in Chile, for $7 million. He was about to buy the Argentine state channel ATC, but privatization never occurred. A few months later, the Mexican paid $7.7 million for 76 percent of América TV, Channel 4 in Peru. Expanding into Chile and Peru was not accidental, since both countries had less restrictive laws with regard to foreign investment in the media.

Cisneros began to construct his Latin American network in October 1993 with the purchase of a 49 percent interest in Channel 11, owned by the University of Chile. The channel barely covered the central portion of the country and was losing a good deal of money. Cisneros' people worked hard to expand its coverage, but the conquest of Chile would not be easy.

In the television industry, each country has its own peculiarities. Chile was dominated by two channels, Televisión Nacional de Chile (TVN), and the Universidad Católica TV (UCTV). The first belongs to the state, the second to the Catholic Church. What was very unusual was that TVN ranked number one in audience preferences, since in the rest of Latin America channels associated with the government are typically in last place. Moreover, TVN and UCTV competed with each other, spending a large amount of money in the process. For TVN and UCTV, not losing money meant a good financial result.

Gustavo Cisneros renamed Channel 11 Chilevisión. The operation continued to report losses, and in 1995 the University of Chile announced that it wanted to sell the 49 percent it still owned. The Cisneros Group agreed to buy the rest of the channel. This raised the investment in the station to $30 million. The first thing Cisneros did was to expand the channel's geographical coverage from 43 to 98 percent, and at the same time modernize its technical installations.

Under the supervision of Carlos Bardasano, Chilevisión reduced its production costs as much as possible, importing half of its programming and focusing the rest on niches that were not excessively costly. The channel produced programs for the young, with youthful hosts, while other programs were directed toward women. It had no expensive productions that were aimed at finding a place on the list of most popular shows. In 1999, Chilevisión was at breakeven. The following year it reported a small profit. In 2001, Chilevisión gained 14 percent of the viewing market, as opposed to the 9 percent it had in 1995, and was the only channel to earn a profit that year in Chile. Bardasano, however, maintains, "Chile is the most complicated television market in Latin America."

Cisneros also analyzed the possibility of acquiring a channel in Ecuador and another in Puerto Rico. He was interested in the Colombian market, but that country had a curious system in which private stations had to lease bands of time in the schedule to insert their programs, a format that did not lend itself to long soap operas. When Colombia privatized television at the beginning of 1999, Cisneros joined his friend, the brewer Julio Mario Santo Domingo, in purchasing a license and launching Caracol TV, the first private channel in Colombia. The Cisneros Group owns 15 percent of the channel, which gives it a seat on the board of directors, and on the channel's programming council.

From the outset, Caracol TV has maintained a firm lead in Colombia's viewership. The Cisneros Group was also interested in channels 2 and 9 in Argentina; however, in both cases, the deals had been signed, but the transactions were not closed due to material issues that surfaced during the financial due diligence process, according to Steven Bandel, the executive president of the Group.

In 1994 the new technology of satellite television came on the market, rendering obsolete the idea of generating a network of free TV channels in Latin America. Cisneros would direct all his energy in that direction at the proper moment. The time for direct-to- home television via satellite was approaching.

11. With Our Heads Held High

> We made a mistake because we did not explain our point of view in a clear and timely way. Today we are beginning to do that. We will do it frequently. To explain our actions. To orient the country, with our heads held high.
>
> GUSTAVO CISNEROS

In the early 1990s, Spalding, Evenflo, and Univision, the Cisneros Group's principal investments in the United States, were very profitable. In Venezuela the situation was different, because the country was experiencing difficult times and was about to undergo a massive financial crisis. One of the most confusing, shocking, and painful episodes, which at the time affected not only the operations of the Cisneros Group but also Gustavo Cisneros' own family, had its origins in the Venezuelan banking crisis of 1993–94.

The collapse of half the Venezuelan banks was a reflection of an economy in a state of exhaustion; moreover, a highly polarized political climate was experiencing the death rattle of the democratic period initiated in 1958, a moment of agony marked by social divisions, political confusion, and radicalism. The environment was ripe for battling political actors to find scapegoats as a way to win power.

In 1989, in that unstable environment, Venezuela's Banco Central decided to give more freedom to private banks to charge the interest rates they wished. It was a sensible measure but was not accompanied by strengthened supervision of the sector, even though in Latin America there were countless examples of liberalization giving way to a banking crisis. Chile opened its financial sector in 1974 and experienced a banking collapse in 1981. Argentina did the same in 1976, and its financial crisis occurred in 1980. Bolivia deregulated banking in 1985 and its collapse came in 1987. Venezuela would not be the exception.

The management of Banco Latino was aggressive when the time came to take advantage of the new situation. It had bought a number of smaller institutions and had scattered high-tech branch banks throughout the country. It flooded the media with an attractive publicity campaign to bring in deposits. It paid interest rates higher than those of its competitors. At that time, interest rates in Venezuela were already high as a consequence of the monetary policy of Venezuela's Banco Central, which was trying to defend the *bolívar* and put a brake on inflation. The number of deposits began to increase, and in 1993 Banco Latino had 1.2 million accounts, ranging from small savers to the United States Embassy. It put the deposits to work in projects that were promising but less liquid, not a good formula for an economy that lived from heart attack to heart attack. It lent money to enterprises related to the bank, including agricultural and tourism projects, and had almost 500 branches throughout the country.

The strategy moved Banco Latino from eighth place in deposits in 1989 to first place in 1993.

For Banco Latino, and other banks that followed the same policy, the only way to maintain the high interest rates they promised their depositors was to invest in increasingly speculative assets. The small stock market in Caracas received enormous sums of money from the banks, and its capitalization (the sum total of the value of the paper transacted there) shot up to 11.2 billion dollars in 1991, almost ten times the figure for 1989.

The Cisneros Group owned 3.5 percent of Banco Latino, the result of its long association with Pedro Tinoco. At the beginning of 1993, Tinoco, who months before had left the presidency of Banco Latino to accept the same position at Banco Central, asked Ricardo Cisneros to join Banco Latino's board of directors. Tinoco valued the contribution that a person with Ricardo Cisneros' experience and financial savvy could make to the bank, but Ricardo initially turned down the offer after consulting with his brother Gustavo.

The Cisneros brothers had always been investors who maintained a distance from banks. They never sought to control a financial institution in Venezuela. Gustavo Cisneros liked to maintain good relations with all financial institutions, which was more complicated if one controlled a competing institution. He understood, too, that if the owner of a bank also had business interests in other sectors, he might succumb to the temptation of using the depositors' money to finance his enterprises at preferential rates or terms.

"No bank should be controlled by an industrial group, because it wouldn't enjoy the confidence of its depositors," he had told the *Miami Herald* in 1980.

However, Pedro Tinoco finally persuaded Ricardo Cisneros to accept his offer during a trip they took together to the United States. The banker suffered from cancer, and the trip was made for medical reasons. Ricardo was accompanying a friend in difficulty, and years of friendship influenced his decision to accept Tinoco's request with the understanding that his participation would be for a relatively short period of time.

As fortune had it, a series of economic, political, and financial events would collide while Ricardo was on the board of one of the banks most severely attacked by conflicting sectors and interests, in a turbulent Venezuela advancing toward the abyss.

Soon after his U.S. trip, Pedro Tinoco died at the age of sixty-five. In his varied and notable career he had been a deputy in the Venezuelan Congress for ten years, a presidential candidate, the minister of finance, the president of Banco Central, and the head of one of the most prestigious law firms in the country, as well as founder and promoter of ACUDE, the educational project very close to the hearts and goals of Gustavo and Patty Cisneros. Sadly for Banco Latino, and for almost the entire structure of the private financial system in Venezuela, when Tinoco died a leader of recognized intelligence and political ability was lost at the very moment that an astute and experienced captain was needed, one capable of keeping afloat a troubled banking system in the midst of an approaching storm.

In December 1993, a bitterly contested presidential election in Venezuela was won by Rafael Caldera, who had already held the office of first magistrate from 1968 to 1973. With a deeply divided electorate and abstention from the polls reaching 50 percent, Caldera triumphed, this time at the head of a heterogeneous coalition of political parties and movements.

Caldera took office at a complicated moment for the banks. At the beginning of that same December, Banco Central of Venezuela had sent the government a report warning that a group of seven banks—Banco Latino among them—was in difficulty. There was an "imminent risk of instability in the financial system." On December 23, 1993, in a confusion of rumors rippling up and down the backbone of the country's public and private finances, the Superintendency of Banks suggested to the shareholders of Banco Latino that they increase their capital by some 6 billion *bolívares* ($57.4 million) to cover the deterioration of the institution's loan portfolio. Gustavo Cisneros was aware of the danger that Venezuela, Banco Latino, and the rest of the private banks would face if the government did not act with the prudence that circumstances demanded. If Banco Latino failed, the crisis would reach monumental proportions because most other banks would be dragged down with it.

The Cisneros brothers immediately decided to design a rescue plan. Ricardo offered to value his own shares in the bank at zero, that is, he surrendered them; and he convinced other stockholders to contribute more capital—in other words, fresh money. At the same time, he made shares available as a promissory note to obtain a line of credit from Banco Central. He also contacted foreign bankers to invite them to invest in Banco Latino. Several of them expressed interest.

For the rescue plan to succeed, a constructive decision on the part of the Venezuelan government was required, but its reception of Ricardo Cisneros' plan was discouraging. Gustavo Cisneros himself appealed to President Caldera not to take over Banco Latino, but to give management the opportunity to find a way to heal the institution.

"Look," the entrepreneur insisted to the president, "I'm not doing this because of Ricardo, who's a director of Banco Latino, but because a takeover of the bank will generate a tremendous crisis of confidence."

The brothers' efforts to rescue the bank were in vain. Caldera identified the management of Banco Latino as a faction politically opposed to his own. Intrigues and struggles for political and economic power so darkened the Venezuelan horizon that decisions were made on the basis of retaliation and revenge, without an adequate sense of the immense risk involved in permitting the collapse of an important national financial institution, a bank that held an enormous amount of the public's savings.

On January 13, 1994, Banco Latino was taken over by the government.

The public received the news with disbelief. The prevailing impression was that Banco Latino was the Citibank of Venezuela, too large and too important to crash. The petroleum workers and the Armed Forces had their retirement funds deposited there. The bank also had affiliates in Miami and Curaçao that would be affected.

Presumably, savings were protected up to a total of $9.3 billion by Fogade, a fund that guaranteed deposits. But 34 percent of Fogade's assets were in Banco Latino and another 13 percent were in companies related to the bank. This in turn signified that the failure of Banco Latino took with it almost half of Fogade's assets. Furthermore, many instruments, such as checking accounts, lay outside state coverage.

Unlike similar situations in other countries, for example the crisis of Banesto in Spain, the takeover of Banco Latino was not executed with open doors, a process whereby Banco Central would take over management but permit the entity in question—Banco Latino, in this case—to operate normally, guaranteeing all deposits. The doors of Banco Latino were closed to the public. This produced a chain reaction that ruined a good part of Venezuelan banking, severely damaged the prospects of the new government that had just been installed, and paved the way for the eventual privatization of the national banking system.

On January 14, Gustavo Cisneros met with his closest associates to evaluate the scope of the banking crisis; the opinion of some was that it could be contained, although Cisneros sensed the imminence of the domino effect, which in fact did not take long to occur. The Cisneros Group had loans with Banco Latino in the amount of $23 million, the equivalent of roughly 13 percent of the Group's total liabilities in Venezuela. It was current in its payments. Cisneros' instructions were very precise: cancel all obligations with Banco Latino.

The accusations against the bank's board of directors went beyond public opinion. Directly or indirectly, legal responsibility fell on eighty-three directors and executives of the bank. Technically, under Venezuelan law, the mere act of signing off on year-end financial statements could imply legal responsibility for directors. Gustavo Cisneros was affected by his brother's situation. He even appeared on the screens of Venevisión to speak directly to Venezuelans.

"I want to talk to you about the crisis of Banco Latino," he said. "About the crisis that has paralyzed Venezuela. About the accusations made against my brother, and about the malicious campaign unjustly trying to blame him, and our Group, for the problems that afflict so many," he told the viewers.

Gustavo Cisneros said he understood the pain suffered by those who placed their faith in the bank and now had no way to pay for their rent, their food, their medicines. He also spoke about his personal pain.

"I want to talk to you about my brother, because that also causes pain. It hurts me deeply because he is my brother, and because I, more than anyone, know how hard he has worked to build a worldwide organization that has raised the names Venezuela, and Venezuelans, very high.

"It hurts because it is not just. Who can even think that a man who established companies in many countries without the help of any government could destroy a bank in Venezuela simply by attending seven board meetings during a fourteen-month period?" he asked.

He reiterated his commitment to paying all the loans his group had with Banco Latino, and he urged everyone else to do the same in order to allow the rapid reopening of the institution. "We are doing this for the clients with savings accounts, because it is important that all of them recover their money, so that confidence in the country's banking system can remain intact."

"We are to blame for one thing," he said at the end of his address. "And that is not having explained our point of view in a clear and timely way. Today we are beginning to do that. We will do it frequently. To explain our actions. To orient the country, with our heads held high."

From then on, the crisis was no longer an entrepreneurial concern; it became personal for Gustavo Cisneros. Sandra Zanoletti, his personal assistant and the person who manages the president's office, recalls the crisis of Banco Latino, along with the tragic deaths of Gustavo's brothers, as one of the most difficult moments for her boss. Carlos Enrique drowned in 1983, and Antonio José died in a plane crash in 1981. It was a time of serious difficulties and challenges, and a painful experience for the Cisneros family.

Some people blamed the Cisneros Group for the collapse of Banco Latino. Others said that the brothers had benefited for years from a close collaboration with Banco Latino, and especially with Pedro Tinoco, its leader, to increase their influence in the country. "What we wanted was to reduce our Venezuelan operations, to be smaller in a larger Venezuela," says Cisneros, recalling the Banco Latino case and its consequences for the Group. "A Venezuela that was more prosperous, much more open, focused, and within the international framework: a Venezuela that was competitive.

"I believe the years have proved me correct."

The attacks against them made them see that success has its price.

Cisneros instructed Zanoletti to clear his calendar so that he could immerse himself in defending his brother. He set up a crisis committee with four executives who were very close to him, all of them graduates of the same crushing course of study—serving as chiefs of staff to the president of the Group: Steven Bandel, Carlos Bardasano, Luis Emilio Gómez, and José Antonio Ríos. Bandel was a natural with numbers and a quiet motivator of people, and he would take care of the financial side and the negotiations with banks; José Antonio Ríos would supervise operations; Bardasano would tend to the institutional aspects and public relations; and Gómez would see to the legal aspects of the case.

Here began an institutional campaign on a worldwide scale to explain the Group's position. In the months that followed, many newspaper publishers and editors would receive long letters accompanied by ample documentation refuting the allegations that Cisneros considered obviously erroneous, as well as those that could lead to deceptive conclusions. He visited editorial offices—including those of the *Miami Herald,* the *Wall Street Journal,* and the *New York Times*—and gave his version of the facts to reporters.

Because of its importance and its ability to reach public opinion, Gustavo Cisneros designated Venevisión as a support in the defense of Ricardo, and the Cisneros Group ordered all its other companies to lower their profiles. Managers were instructed not to talk to the press unless it would benefit Venevisión and Ricardo Cisneros.

Cisneros' arguments were simple: the essential point was that the family's position stemmed from fifty years of hard work and persevering effort. As for Ricardo Cisneros, he had played absolutely no executive role in the ill-fated Banco Latino, and the Group's relationship with that financial institution was limited to a small percentage of ownership. The loans received from the institution were granted under conditions similar to, or even less favorable than those offered by other banks. In fact, at the time of the banking crisis, the Cisneros Group had normal business relationships with twenty-five financial institutions in the country, among them Banco Latino, which had been one of the five most important entities for the Group, but not the principal one. The Group's operations with Banco Latino were up-to-date and properly guaranteed, and Cisneros decided to pay, in cash and at 100 percent of their value, all the Group's obligations to the bank.

The crisis also contributed to the Cisneros Group's acceleration of its strategic plans for international expansion designed between 1991 and 1992. Gustavo Cisneros and his advisers were confident they could obtain a significant sum of money from the sale of companies that did not fit in with the Group's new focus. The banking crisis in Venezuela meant that plans had to be accelerated. A Daihatsu concession and representation of the Samsung brand were sold, along with the Group's shares in Televen.

In Venezuela, problems were multiplying. The government, by freezing prices, restricting imports, and increasing scarcity, had deprived CADA of oxygen. The supermarket could no longer provide the customer service that was its hallmark, or bring prices up to date without generating public relations and institutional headaches.

Cisneros was still betting on the supermarket sector, and in July 1993, before the Banco Latino crisis exploded, he paid $426 million to buy Pueblo Xtra supermarkets, in the United States, with the idea of providing the management of CADA with a vehicle for expansion abroad. Pueblo had five supermarkets in the Virgin Islands, twenty-one in Puerto Rico, where it also owned the Blockbuster franchise, and ten Xtra supermarkets in Florida. The group generated sales of 1.2 billion dollars, almost twice the amount of CADA at its best.

To the sorrow of some in the Cisneros Group, who felt that CADA was theirs, in March 1995 the operation was sold, along with Maxy's, to the Colombian group Cadenalco for more than 80 million dollars. After the contract was signed, one executive recalls, Ricardo Cisneros remarked that the feeling was like being separated from a child.

The financial crisis in Venezuela had a violent and dramatic impact on the country. It dragged down half of the private banks, with losses of some $9 billion.

As time passed, the episode of the Venezuelan banking crisis of 1994 allowed Gustavo Cisneros and the Cisneros Group to consolidate their commitment to Venezuela. "In spite of the ups and downs, in spite of the permanent economic instability in the country, and its sometimes exacerbated political controversies, I will always bet on Venezuela," Cisneros says, and he adds: "There is much to do and we are doing it; we are still investing in Venezuela." For Cisneros, it is a question of patriotism, of attachment to his native land and commitment to its destiny. It is something that goes far beyond business.

On March 20, 1997, the Superior Court for Safeguarding the Public Patrimony, in a report submitted by presiding judge Edith Cabello de Requena and with the unanimous vote of its three members, cleared Ricardo Cisneros of all accusations or responsibility with regard to the collapse of Banco Latino. The verdict put an end to three years of persecution and exile. Though it had been a very trying time, the Cisneros brothers were satisfied because, as Gustavo said, "The truth finally prevailed." The cost of the crisis was high, materially and spiritually, for the country and for its financial sector.

The experience, however, did not diminish the enthusiasm that Gustavo professes for Latin America. For Cisneros, in spite of the difficulties that still exist, the region is currently the stage for important changes that foretell a better future. His commitment to democracy and a strong civil society persists. Economic policies are generally favorable to private enterprise and the free market, consolidation and globalization, processes that imply an unavoidable reality: rapid interconnection in an increasingly communicative world, a world in which knowledge has become a key factor in productivity and in improving the quality of life.

Gustavo Cisneros saw that by means of telecommunications and entertainment, he would be a participant in these transformations, an active player and not a mere spectator.

Cisneros was convinced that his confidence would be compensated over the years. The time had come, in a continent-wide television project, for reinforcing Gustavo Cisneros' commitment to the hemisphere.

12. Globalized Television

> In the new globalized world, communications are the blood and television the heart.
>
> GUSTAVO CISNEROS

In August 1993, Gustavo Cisneros flew to Los Angeles to meet with Michael Armstrong, executive president of Hughes Electronics, the unit of General Motors that dealt with satellite television.

Hughes had the technology to offer pay television of impeccable quality to an entire continent at once, and Cisneros wanted to form a partnership with the American company in order to fulfill his vision of a single platform for distributing content to all of Latin America. An alliance with Hughes would mark a decisive step toward the internationalization of the Group in the field of communications. Cisneros was about to embark on one of the most challenging adventures in his entrepreneurial life, which would involve intricate negotiations with skilled media magnates.

The history of DirecTV Latin America began to develop several years before its definitive launch. In 1986, Cisneros attempted to place in orbit a satellite that would transmit a dozen television channels and telecommunications services to companies in the Andean region and the Caribbean. The satellite was named *Simón Bolívar*. "The opening of the market on a global scale is coming," Cisneros told his executives, "and when the telecommunications market opens, I want us to have a foot in the door."

At that time the numbers did not support the Venezuelan entrepreneur's vision. Placing a satellite in orbit cost some $100 million, and after a useful life of barely seven years, it had to be replaced. The estimated traffic of *Simón Bolívar* would not cover that investment, and certain legal obstacles killed the project.

Cisneros had moved ahead of the technology and the regulatory framework. During the 1980s, satellite television consisted of a receiver that seemed appropriate for detecting extraterrestrial life, having a diameter of 10 feet and a selling price of $3,000. Although it received a good number of channels, the quality of the image was mediocre. At that time, cable television was dominant. In 1980, 35 million households in the United States subscribed to cable. By the end of the decade, the figure had climbed to 65 million. The United States, along with Argentina, became one of the countries where this technology had greatest penetration. Its success proved that the public was willing to pay in order to have more programming options than those offered by traditional broadcast channels.

By 1991, Gustavo Cisneros had decided that his future was in telecommunications, and he asked his executives to study the feasibility of setting up a cable television network in Venezuela. The project would never be realized because it was an alternative with several points against it: networks were costly, piracy was rampant, and it did not meet Cisneros' requirement that all projects be capable of replication on a continental scale.

In reality the entrepreneur was betting on satellites, a technology that continued to develop throughout the 1980s. A small group of engineers and researchers in the United States were experimenting with a new technology of digital compression—based on the one used by the Pentagon for military purposes—to reduce the size of the land receiver and improve the quality of image and sound. They gave it the technical name of DBS, for Direct Broadcast Satellite, though skeptics said that DBS really meant Don't Be Stupid.

At a corporate seminar held in Caracas in 1989, Cisneros explained to his executives what he foresaw for the communications industry:

"Computers and satellites are opening a marvelous universe for future generations, with the possibility of access to the most extraordinary treasures of knowledge in one's own home," said Cisneros.

"Let us imagine what it will mean for young Venezuelans, Peruvians, or Argentineans to access through a computer terminal or a TV monitor the great information centers of the world, and to read books, see photographs and films on the screen, with an audio explanation, possibly in their own language if they wish. This is not as distant as we might suppose." He was right. In less than five years the first Internet browsers would make their appearance: Mosaic, Netscape, and, later on, Microsoft Explorer.

While technicians were improving satellite technology, Cisneros continued to make small inroads in the world of telecommunications. Aside from his investment in Telcel, the leading cell phone company in Venezuela, in the early 1990s he signed an agreement with Sprint, the American telephone company, to offer private data network services to companies. He also took on the representation of Motorola in Venezuela. There was not much more that Cisneros could do in a market regulated in favor of CANTV, the local monopoly of basic telephone service.

Technical doubts regarding DBS began to disappear, and the platform attracted the chiefs of the industry. Hughes (General Motors), NBC (General Electric), News Corp. (Rupert Murdoch), and Cablevision Systems Corp. (owned by the pioneer of cable television, Charles F. Dolan) decided to join forces in 1990 to undertake a DBS project costing $1 billion. The alliance did not prosper because the four partners could not agree on who would control the new company. Hughes, the firm that had been founded by the eccentric multimillionaire Howard Hughes, decided to continue with the project alone: it needed to develop a new market to compensate for cutbacks in its defense contracts after the end of the Cold War. In 1992, General Motors hired Michael Armstrong to head Hughes; he laid off a fourth of the labor force and went into high gear with DBS, which had been renamed DTH (Direct-To-Home). A product for mass consumption was just what Armstrong wanted for the satellite manufacturer. He signed an agreement with the French company Thomson to develop and fabricate the decoder boxes, the electronic units that convert the flood of "1s" and "0s" pouring down from the satellite to create a high-quality image.

The principal obstacle, however, was not technical: the large cable television companies in the United States were also the owners of the best pay-TV channels—Time Warner and HBO, for example—and they charged high fees to anyone they considered a dangerous competitor. The conflict moved to Washington, and Armstrong won the lobbying struggle: in October 1992, the United States Congress required the owners of cable channels to offer their content to all technological platforms without price discrimination. Six months later, Armstrong was displaying the first tests of his service at specialized trade shows. He was promising an incredible world of more than five hundred channels—compared to the sixty on cable television—with a clarity of image and sound comparable only to that on a videodisc and a CD. He could also include an on-screen interactive menu and the possibility of acquiring films by pressing a button on the remote control, an option called pay-per-view.

For the television industry, these innovations constituted a revolution. Time Warner had attempted to do something similar with cable TV, but its tests failed because the users were not willing to pay very much for those services. But the Hughes project would have an accessible price: some $800 for initial installation, and a monthly fee comparable to that for cable.

Armstrong had not been the first to introduce this technology to the market. Rupert Murdoch was launching something similar in the United Kingdom with BskyB, and he wanted to do the same with his Star project in Asia. Armstrong did not want to cede spaces to the Australian-born magnate, and he looked for partners for his project in Europe, Asia, and Latin America. In this last-named region, Cisneros was a good candidate since Hughes' partners remembered him because of the *Simón Bolívar* project.

As a consequence, when Cisneros decided to talk to Armstrong in Los Angeles, he felt that everything was ready for launching a totally new service in Latin America. Countries were beginning to open their satellite transmission markets, and the price of the technology had come down to reasonable levels.

Cisneros and Armstrong agreed to divide the project into two operational levels: a regional company—Galaxy Latin America

(GLA)—would act as an umbrella organization for a series of local operators that would be in charge of marketing the service in each country, under the name DirecTV. Armstrong reserved 60 percent ownership of GLA for Hughes. The remaining 40 percent could be shared by Cisneros and other partners he might recruit. In terms of the local operations, on the other hand, Armstrong had no problem with local investors being majority shareholders. Armstrong informed Cisneros that his demand for 60 percent had been a problem in the earlier approaches the Hughes people had made to Emilio Azcárraga, of Televisa, and Roberto Marinho, of Globo. These two moguls wanted more control over their operations, and Armstrong was not prepared to give it to them.

Cisneros also offered to create new channels that would be attractive for the new medium. Management would be divided among Hughes, Cisneros, and future partners. Cisneros put two of his best people at the disposal of the new venture: José Antonio Ríos, his chief of operations, and Consuelo Sánchez, the former manager of the telecommunications area in the Cisneros Group, and the person who had established the first contacts with Hughes. He also said he would do everything possible to have Azcárraga and Marinho come together under Hughes' wing, though he suspected that Rupert Murdoch, who was promoting his own DTH project for Latin America, had already lured them away. For that reason it was necessary to have other alternatives at hand. The race had begun.

Globo and Televisa were fundamental pieces for assuring the success of DirecTV. Two out of three Latin Americans lived in the zone of influence of these mega-enterprises. No one had better content or channels that were better known locally. With them, the DTH platform would surely win out over cable, which Cisneros perceived as the real competitor in the world of pay television.

Early in June 1994, Gustavo Cisneros met in Río de Janeiro with Roberto Marinho and two of his sons: João, who managed the radio stations, and José, who was in charge of the group's newspaper. Another son, Roberto, who managed the television business, was in Europe. The Marinhos received Cisneros with a great deal of warmth. They had known one another for years, and each party respected the accomplishments of the other. Cisneros explained his project. He said he was about to sign a letter of intent with Hughes, stipulating that the American firm would own 60 percent of the business and the rest could be divided among the Latin American partners. Cisneros offered them 10 percent of GLA and the majority of the local operation in Brazil.

Marinho said that the project seemed interesting but that he had to discuss it first with his son Roberto. Then he dropped the feared bomb: he thought that Roberto had already signed a memorandum of understanding (MOU) with Murdoch. This document is often a simple letter in which two parties declare their intention to negotiate in good faith a transaction whose specific terms have to be agreed upon within a predetermined period, typically six months. Its central points are confidentiality and an exclusivity provision: the parties cannot engage in parallel negotiations with another group while the memorandum is in effect.

"When Roberto comes back from Europe, he'll call you," said the older Marinho. "I don't want to go over the heads of my children."

In effect, at the end of the month the younger Roberto Marinho spoke to Cisneros on the phone. He said he could not sign anything with Hughes because he had made a commitment to Murdoch. He justified his decision on two counts. First, the Hughes satellite, he said, had an angle of elevation of barely twenty-nine degrees over the crucial market of São Paulo, which meant that many households in that densely populated city would not receive the service. Second, he did not think it was appropriate for the Americans to own 60 percent of the business because Hughes was a technology firm, not an entertainment company.

Cisneros knew about the Brazilians' reservations concerning the technology. Consuelo Sánchez had already tried, to no avail, to convince the Globo technical people that the angle of elevation was enough to avoid the tops of the buildings. Later, Cisneros would congratulate Murdoch on the success of his negotiation with the Marinhos.

Then there was Azcárraga. It was difficult to meet with him because he was struggling with cancer. At the end of 1994, almost six months after the Marinhos' negative response, Cisneros traveled to Mexico to attend the inauguration of President Ernesto Zedillo, and Azcárraga received him in his office, in San Angelín. In a courteous and amiable tone—very far from his reputation for arrogance—Azcárraga made it clear that he did not like the Hughes project:

"I know I have to go into satellite television, that's my next challenge, but not in *that* project, because this is entertainment and not satellite management," said the Mexican. "These people from Hughes want to have majority ownership without knowing anything about the entertainment industry."

"Well, Emilio, that was at first," responded the Venezuelan. "But in its first six months, DirecTV enrolled 500,000 subscribers in the United States, and that's a phenomenal number, a greater penetration than when VHS technology was launched. If you decide to come in now, we have the possibility of revolutionizing television on a continental scale."

Azcárraga was not convinced:

"No, no, no, they're technicians, they sell equipment," said Azcárraga. "I want to do this with Sky."

"Emilio, you can't do business with Sky. You and Rupert [Murdoch] are exactly the same, one in English and the other in Spanish. It's impossible for the two of you to agree."

"This is a Latin American project, and we Latin Americans should have the 60 percent."

In the end, Gustavo Cisneros agreed with Azcárraga, but he knew he could never persuade Armstrong to cede control of ownership. For better or worse, since 1987, Hughes had invested $750 million to develop DTH. Thanks to Hughes, a digital tool existed that was capable of revolutionizing the world of entertainment and television. That, in Michael Armstrong's eyes, was worth 60 percent, no more and no less.

"Let's join forces and get together in DirecTV; perhaps we can convince Hughes," Cisneros insisted.

But Azcárraga maintained his position.

The future would prove both of them right. Relations among Azcárraga, Marinho, and Murdoch grew worse almost immediately after the agreement was signed, while Cisneros would have his own problems with Hughes.

The refusal by these two magnates was not based solely on a few percentage points of ownership. The DTH project revealed "differences in the concept of power," as a former executive explains, between Marinho and Azcárraga on the one hand, and Cisneros on the other. The three men dominated their national markets, that is, Brazil, Mexico, and Venezuela. Cisneros needed DTH to achieve continental coverage. Azcárraga and Marinho, on the other hand, found DTH necessary as part of a defensive plan to prevent anyone else from employing the medium to threaten their properties, built up over decades in their own large, captive markets. For that reason Cisneros placed his vision of coverage on a Latin American scale, even knowing that he risked a flight of viewers with the arrival of a rich offering of soap operas from Colombia, Brazil, and Mexico. He could compensate for that loss with the possibility of transmitting Venevisión, and other programming it could produce, to 500 million Hispanics. Venevisión, he thought, will have to find the way to compete in a new setting of continent-wide television. For Cisneros, globalization demanded the integration of the world's markets. Azcárraga and Marinho, on the other hand, thought they could manipulate globalization to protect their domestic markets.

In practice, their divergent concepts of power translated into differences regarding who controlled the partnerships. Cisneros, a new arrival in continent-wide communications, was disposed to share and even to cede control, even to Hughes. His father had done the same thing when Pepsi-Cola grew in Venezuela under the leadership of other partners. And Cisneros had an affinity with Armstrong. Hughes had designed its platform so that it was genuinely regional. A single satellite could cover the entire continent, which would have a great support center in Fort Lauderdale, Florida, where subscriptions could be activated or deactivated. But Marinho and Azcárraga saw this as a threat to their territories. They wanted to control who subscribed and what they saw, and each man wanted a satellite for his own country.

The association of Murdoch-Azcárraga-Marinho looked formidable on paper, but in reality it was a matter of strategic convenience, a terrain in which the Australian magnate had to give in to the demands for autonomy from the two Latin American moguls in order not to leave the field to Hughes in Latin America, a market of 75 million households. Murdoch, in reality, shared Cisneros' open philosophy, but the Australian had failed in his attempts to work with Hughes in the early 1990s. His only option was to join forces with the two great media powers already established there. Marinho and Azcárraga passed a costly bill to Murdoch. Essentially, Sky became a feudal operation with three separate enterprises: one Mexican, the other Brazilian, and the third comprising the rest of the region. Each could make autonomous decisions without consulting the others. The barons had made certain that King Murdoch would respect their territories.

The trenches between DirecTV and Sky had been dug. On one side the arsenal of DirecTV was deployed, with its superior technological and regional conception. On the other was the army of Sky, whose superior weapon was its offering of local channels, not only those of Globo and Televisa but also those of Murdoch (principally the Fox channels: Sports, Kids, and News). It was technology versus programming.

Despite not having local channels in Brazil and Mexico, Cisneros was confident his project would pull ahead. Hughes was adding 3,000 new subscribers a day to DirecTV USA, a good omen for the potential of the technology in Latin America. A month after Roberto Marinho's negative response, the Venezuelan had an agreement with Roberto Civita. Well educated and very astute in business, the Brazilian had been an intern at Time Warner in the 1960s, and when he was back in his own country he convinced his father—who had made a small fortune selling Disney cartoons—to publish Brazilian equivalents of *Playboy*, *Time*, and *Fortune*, which gave rise to *Playboy Brasil*, *Veja*, and *Exame* respectively. In contrast to the Marinhos, his magazines were able to maintain a degree of independence during the dictatorship, giving him credibility and a high profile, especially among the country's elite. Civita had a good eye for going into businesses that could be promoted by his magazines, such as the distribution of compact discs and videos. During those years, Civita wanted to plant a flag in pay television. In 1992 he had launched TV Abril, which distributed some thirty channels with a microwave technology, the land-based ancestor of DTH.

In Mexico he turned to the Vargas group, a family that operated in the market of radio stations, hotels, and telecommunications. They also owned MVS Multivisión, a successful pay-television operation in competition with Televisa.

Televisa's efforts and distribution in Mexico, and Globo's in Brazil, gave Sky a considerable advantage over DirecTV in those two countries, which was why the Argentine market became critical for Cisneros. If he did not find a good local partner, DirecTV would be overwhelmed by Sky in all the large Latin American countries. He chose the Clarín Group, the Argentine enterprise that belonged to a widow, Ernestina Noble, and was managed by a world-class executive, Héctor Magnetto. The media group was as powerful in Argentina as Globo was in Brazil. The newspaper that bears its name competes for the largest circulation in the Hispanic world; the group also owns an open TV channel—founded by Goar Mestre in the 1960s—but at that time it was facing the same dilemma as the Cisneros Group: its original market did not give it sufficient scope to become entrenched there, as Globo had. Magnetto wanted to distribute abroad, and he asked that Clarín not only be a partner in the local operation in Argentina but also that it manage Chile, Paraguay, and Uruguay. The first, with its open telecommunications market and a pay-television industry still in diapers, was of special interest to him. But in Chile a MOU had already been signed with the Luksic Group, owner of a pay-television operation in that country; Clarín, finally, would stay with Argentina. In Colombia, Cisneros and Hughes chose the Carvajal and Santo Domingo groups. In Peru they began talks with Delgado Parker, of Panamericana TV, but he died in the middle of negotiations and an agreement could not be reached with his successor.

isneros and President Ronald Reagan, who "buried" the Soviet empire, at Walter Annenberg's residence uly 1989). The Cisneros couple maintained a close friendship with the late President Reagan and his ife, Nancy.

meeting of the International Advisory Council of the Power Corporation of Canada (November 1989). p row, from left to right: F. Ross Johnson, William M. Fuller, Pierre Haas, Gustavo Cisneros, Lord nstrong of llminster, Gérard Eskenazi, Pierre Scohier, and The Right Honorable The Viscount thermere. Bottom row, from left to right: Mr. Rong Yiren, Sheikh Ahmed Zaki Yamani, former West rman Chancellor Helmut Schmidt, The Honorable Paul Desmarais, The Right Honorable Pierre Elliott deau, The Honorable Paul Volcker, and Baron Albert Frere.

Cisneros at the White House with Lord Peter Carrington, former British minister of foreign relations and leader of the House of Lords, David Rockefeller, President George Bush, and Henry Kissinger, former U.S. secretary of state, discussing the goal of free trade in Latin America (1990). The North American Free Trade Agreement was enacted during Bill Clinton's first term as president.

Gustavo Cisneros in Managua with the recently elected president of Nicaragua, Violeta Chamorro, who was a beacon of hope for democracy in the Central American nation (April 25, 1990).

...h Walesa, former president of Poland, a symbol of freedom for our times, is deeply respected by ...neros, who met with him in Caracas (November 1990).

...anni Agnelli, head of Fiat, was ...ways a good friend and adviser to ...sneros. A long-standing friend-...ip was consolidated with mutual ...cking for their respective projects ...both America and the Old ...orld (La Ribereña, the Cisneros ...miliy residence, Caracas, Feb-...ary 1991).

King Juan Carlos of Spain during a private visit to the Cisneros residence in "Los Roques," Venezue[la]. Cisneros shows the king a map of the archipelago (April 1992).

The Cisneroses sponsored a visit by the Dalai Lama to Venezuela. Pictured with the Dalai Lama from [left] to right: Gustavo, Guillermo, Carolina, Patty, and Adriana Cisneros. This notable emissary of internatio[nal] peace and harmony spent a week at "La Ribereña," the Cisneros family home in Caracas (June 1992).

atty and Gustavo Cisneros with Brian Mulroney, the Canadian prime minister, one of the architects of e North American Free Trade Agreement, at his official residence in Ottawa (September 1992).

Cisneros with Caspar Weinberger, ormer U.S. secretary of defense, nd Christopher Forbes, owner of Forbes magazine and former presdential candidate, guests at "La iebereña," the Cisneros family resience, during their visit to Caracas n a mission to explore new busiess opportunities (October 1992).

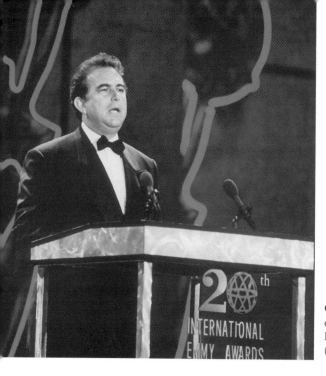

Cisneros addresses the audience as ho
of the 20th Anniversary Internation
Emmy Awards ceremony, in New Yor
(November 23, 1992).

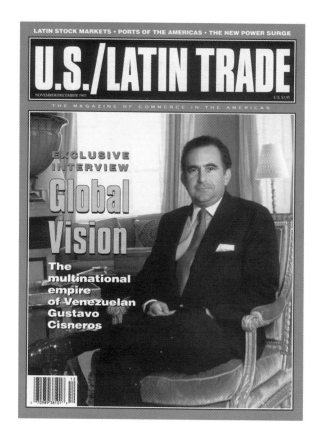

Cover of *U.S./Latin Trade* magazi
(1993). The article referred to Ci
neros' "instinct for business" and "su
cess in forming managerial teams."

Gustavo and Patty Cisneros with British Prime Minister Margaret and Dennis Thatcher, in New York (November 1994). Cisneros respects the "Iron Lady" and recognizes the effort she made to modernize the British economy.

Gustavo Cisneros listens to Mexico's President Ernesto Zedillo at a reception held for international figures at the "Los Pinos" residence, in Mexico City (December 1, 1994). On that day Zedillo had assumed the presidency, and Cisneros would take advantage of the trip to meet with Emilio Azcárraga Milmo and propose a partnership in a satellite-television project.

Brazilian President Fernando Henriqu[e] Cardoso, whom Cisneros considers one [of] the key figures in modern Brazil, at [a] meeting of the Americas Society at Planal[to] Palace, seat of the Brazilian presidenc[y] (Brasília 1995).

Gustavo and Guillermo Cisneros during their visit to Brazil for the Galaxy Latin America road show, at [a] dinner given by entrepreneur Don Roberto Marinho (March 23, 1995). Marinho was the founder of th[e] Globo Network and a longtime friend of Cisneros. President Lula da Silva decreed three days of nationa[l] mourning when the Brazilian entrepreneur died.

elaxing with good friend Michael Eisner, chairman of Disney Corp., at Eisner's residence in Aspen, olorado (April 1995).

ernational Advisory Council of Chase Manhattan Bank: Thompson M. Swayne, E. Michael Kruse, bert G. Murphy, Rahmi M. Koc, James Zeigon, Michael A. Miles, Koichiro Ejiri, Charles Bauccio, an Naval Tata, Giovanni Agnelli, Timothy McGinnis, Jean-Luc Lagardère, Hans W. Becherer, Edzard uter, Allen E. Murray, Jack C. Tang, Lord Peter Carrington, Sir Arvi Parbo, Gustavo Cisneros, Antonio dero, Dennis M. Goggin, José Joaquín de Ysasi-Ysamendi, Paulo D. Villares, A. Wright Elliott, Pebr G. lenhammar, Willard C. Butcher, Henry Kissinger, David Rockefeller, and Thomas G. Labrecque tober 1995).

Launch of the Galaxy III-R satellite for DirecTV Latin America, in which Gustavo Cisneros is a partner, from Cape Canaveral, Florida (December 14, 1995). It is noteworthy that DirecTV is one of the few companies with its own satellites, which at that time projected more than 150 channels to Latin America. Cisneros maintains that this was "one of the most emotional moments of my life."

New Year's Eve at "Casa Bonita," the Cisneros family home in La Romana, Dominican Republic (December 31, 1995). Top row: Linda Wachner, Prime Minister Brian Mulroney, Katherine Graham, Shirley Rosenthal, Abe Rosenthal, Mila Mulroney, Senator John Warner, Annette de la Renta, and Barbara Walters. Bottom row: Gustavo Cisneros, Oscar de la Renta, Alex Mulroney, Patty Cisneros, and Guillermo Cisneros.

enry Kissinger and Gustavo Cisneros during a meeting of the Council on Foreign Relations in New York 996). Cisneros is a founding member of the Council's International Advisory Committee, and he and ssinger share a long friendship and an ongoing exchange of opinions.

ie of the many gatherings between Patty and Gustavo Cisneros and Emilio Azcárraga, the Mexican dia baron, known as "the Tiger," and his wife, Adriana Abascal. They are pictured here at "Casa Bonita," Cisneros residence in the Dominican Republic. Cisneros' relationship with Azcárraga was very active 1 close, and became more solid with their joint acquisition of Univision (March 1996).

Gustavo, Ricardo, and Oswaldo Cisneros with the late Roberto Goizueta, president of the board of directo of the Coca-Cola Company, and Douglas Ivester, president of the company, in Atlanta, at the culminatir moment of the negotiations with Coca-Cola (August 14, 1996).

News of the change in t franchise from Pepsi-Cola Coca-Cola traveled around t world. The Cisneros Grou negotiations with Coca-C are still discussed as a case stu in various business schools.

With legendary Cuban diva and friend Celia Cruz at "Casa Bonita," the Cisneros family residence in the Dominican Republic (September 1996).

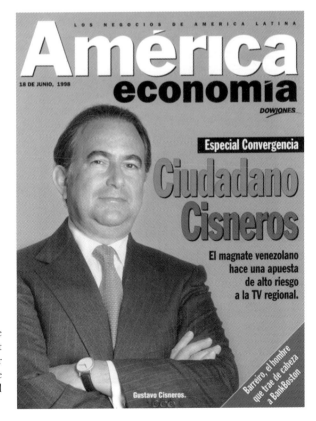

Cover of *AméricaEconomía* magazine (1998). The article maintained that "Cisneros sees television at the center of everything. His ambition is to be present, through this medium, in all the homes in Latin America."

Cisneros with Prime Minister Benjamin Netanyahu of Israel and his wife, Sara, at a reception at the Kir David Hotel in Israel (May 17, 1998). This visit gave rise to two strategic alliances with Israeli groups the area of cutting-edge technology.

Patty and Gustavo Cisneros with Nelson Mandela at the residence of the great South African leader Johannesburg (August 15, 1999). Cisneros calls Mandela "the great man of reconciliation."

Venezuelan President Hugo Chávez Frías with Gustavo Cisneros visiting an exhibition of the Fundación Cisneros' Colección Orinoco, a collection of Amazonian ethnographic objects, in Bonn, Germany (October 1, 1999). Other exhibitions drawn from the Colección Orinoco have also been seen in France, Switzerland, the Czech Republic, and Finland, and will soon be presented in Sweden.

Gustavo Cisneros at the headquarters of DirecTV Latin America, in Caracas (2000). DirecTV transmits 150 digital channels and 100 music channels in twenty-eight countries, to a million-and-a-half subscribers. (Photograph courtesy *BusinessWeek*.)

Patty and Gustavo Cisneros greet President Bill Clinton at the gala dinner held in honor of the king and queen of Spain at the White House (February 2000). "Gustavo Cisneros," said the Spanish ambassador in Washington, Antonio de Oyarzábal, "has complete faith in the idea that there is no more than a lake between Spain and the rest of America."

The work of reaching agreements with partners was a laborious process. Executives presented a business plan to a potential partner, which, if approved, would form the basis for elaborating co-participation in income among the regional partners (Hughes, Cisneros, Civita, and Vargas) and the local partners (Luksic, Carvajal-Santo Domingo, Clarín and Cisneros, and Civita and Vargas, in Brazil and Mexico, respectively). Consuelo Sánchez had to elaborate a menu of needs and a working budget for each market, ranging from the special licenses required to the number of salespeople and installation teams needed to launch the service. The process was repeated in more than twenty countries.

While his people were completing this arduous difficult work, Cisneros decided the time had come to make the DirecTV project for Latin America public.

A press conference was held in New York on March 9, 1995. Cisneros was accompanied by Kevin McGrath, the CEO of Hughes Communications (the division of Hughes that managed DirecTV), Ernesto Vargas, and Roberto Civita. DirecTV Latin America, they said, planned to invest $500 million to launch the service. The subscribers would have to pay $600 to acquire the decoding boxes and the receptor antenna, but McGrath promised that in a year the price could drop by half.

Calculations as to the probable number of subscribers were encouraging. The project would break even when it reached a figure of 1.3 million subscribers, which would probably happen in less than a year following the launch, planned for February 1996. By 2002, the Hughes people estimated that 10 million subscribers would be hooked into their satellite, buying pay-per-view films or tuning in to one of their 150 video and music channels.

The number of subscribers was the critical variable for determining the success or failure of DTH, even more than for its cable TV counterpart. A cable network can expand to accommodate the number of people who subscribe to it. In theory, at least, a very small cable television network, even one with fewer than a thousand subscribers, could be profitable. On the other hand, the satellite business is one of critical mass. A large number of subscribers is needed to cover the initial costly investment in the satellite.

The projection seemed reasonable. The only country in all of Latin America that had a broad penetration of pay-TV was Argentina, which meant there was an entire continent to conquer, one in which the majority of households did not see more than five or six channels. It was logical to think that many of them would be willing to pay the equivalent of the price of a color television set to improve their entertainment offerings.

The partners highlighted the fact that DirecTV was something really new in its pan-regional conception. "We are creating our own version of the FTA," said a radiant Civita, referring to the Free Trade Agreement sponsored by the United States to unite thirty-four countries in the American hemisphere.

In April 1995, Gustavo Cisneros began a trip to promote the DirecTV project accompanied by his international team and his children. For the latter, this was an interesting opportunity to join their father on a business trip intended to prepare the terrain for the arrival of DirecTV. The first stop was Brazil, where Cisneros explained the scope of the DTH project to President Fernando Enrique Cardoso. Then they left for Uruguay, where they spoke to President Julio Sanguinetti.

The journey continued on to Buenos Aires. They talked with President Carlos Menem and had lunch with Héctor Magnetto. From there they went on to Chile, where they had an appointment with the mining entrepreneur and banker Guillermo Luksic. President Eduardo Frei was interested in the educational applications of the new technology. Then they flew to Peru, where they made a brief stop to visit Machu Picchu, to the delight of Guillermo and Adriana. They stopped in Ecuador and Colombia, and finally landed in New York. During the trip, Gustavo Cisneros met with six presidents and an equal number of partner-entrepreneurs. In recent years the growth and expansion of the Cisneros Group have made the life of the Cisneros family practically one ongoing trip, in which there is a mix of business, culture, and exchanges with friends from all over the world.

DirecTV Latin America was launched in mid-1996, a few months behind schedule but ahead of Sky, which had more delays because it lost a satellite during a launch.

The problems began to surface almost immediately. The channels' suppliers were hard on DTH, just as they had been with DirecTV USA. Program directors have a rate card that they charge cable television companies for registered users. Depending on the popularity of the channel, this ranges from some 10 cents per subscriber to 50 cents for the channels that show recent movies or adult programming. The cable television companies did not always report all their subscribers. Even if the numbers did not make sense to the program directors, they had no way to prove any deception, which weakened their incentives for lowering fees.

Still, Cisneros was confident that the Latin Americans' desire to see more channels of impeccable quality would overcome the problem of price. The strategy was to transform DirecTV into an object of desire. Its first trial by fire was the Venezuelan market, where the service was inaugurated, as well as in Mexico and Brazil.

Gustavo Cisneros controlled 80 percent of the Venezuelan operation and Hughes the remaining 20 percent, but local managers made decisions by mutual agreement with executives in the United States with regard, for example, to marketing plans and the prices that could be charged.

It was on the management level that the differences in style between the Cisneros Group and Hughes became apparent. For decades the American company had led a happy existence as a supplier to the Pentagon, making its living by fulfilling a few juicy annual contracts. The Hughes directors, most of them engineers highly skilled in electronics but less capable in the dynamic world of marketing, became embroiled in details, such as satisfying the desires of clients or meeting deadlines at any cost. The atmosphere at Hughes was hierarchical. Work was carried out according to previously designed processes. People knew what they had to do and how to do it. It was not an atmosphere that valued individual initiative or rewarded risk-taking. It was rigidity incarnate. If one wanted to make changes, procedure dictated that one had to have the endorsement of a consultant, recalls an executive in the organization.

This was a world separate and distinct from the managerial style of the Cisneros brothers, with their ad hoc groups, versatile executives, and the speed with which they made decisions in the demanding business environment of Venezuela.

The procedure at Hughes dictated that the equipment for DirecTV had to be sold in specialized stores such as RadioShack or Circuit City. That worked in the United States, where there is a prevailing "do-it-yourself" culture and customers snapped up decoders and receptors. People who did not feel like climbing up on the roof to install the antenna paid good money to have a technician come to the house to install it. This formula was also convenient for DirecTV because it allowed DirecTV to dispense with the need for a sales force and to shift the cost of inventory to RadioShack. The truth is that this formula suited a rich country that had vast rural areas with a fair amount of purchasing power and no other option in pay television.

DirecTV's sales strategy worked in Vermont, but in Venezuela trying to sell digital television through a specialized store, which either did not exist or was weakened by smuggling, was hardly practical: the sales channel was inappropriate. There was a problem even more fundamental: many Venezuelans did not understand the concept of pay television because the penetration of traditional cable barely reached 3 percent of the viewing public. It was therefore even more difficult for them to digest concepts such as "direct-to-the-home," "digital," and "pay-per-view." In order to overcome these difficulties one had to have a demonstration, and for that one needed salespeople. But Hughes insisted on its U.S. model of business. The result was that only "300 subscriptions a month were sold while the business plan had called for 3,000," recalls Victor Ferreres, the man designated by Cisneros to head DirecTV in Venezuela.

Ferreres had been the president of Apple in Venezuela and knew how to sell a high-end product. He designed a new plan for distribution and marketing, but approval by the heads of Hughes was slow in coming. His plan migrated from one desk to another without finding anyone who would dare to give it his blessing. "The executives at Hughes never made risky decisions," Ferreres recalls.

He took his plan to Gustavo Cisneros, who took care of the matter directly with the Hughes people, who then gave Ferreres their approval. The company hired more salespeople and put them in small kiosks located in affluent commercial centers and surrounded by television sets proclaiming the advantages of DirecTV. People who signed a contract had a receptor antenna and decoder box installed in a few days. Ferreres organized small operations to deploy his salespeople in wealthy neighborhoods. He would place them on a busy corner and there, with a good deal of fanfare, they would invite residents to try out the new service *in situ*. If they subscribed, an installer was sent to their house immediately. Special financing for the decoder boxes permitted a rental fee of eight dollars a month for the equipment.

Sales skyrocketed. In eighteen months they had 50,000 subscribers, and the executives at Hughes were obliged to recognize the merits of the methods employed by the Cisneros Group. In fact, these would become part of the procedure for launching the service in other countries. First, they looked for captive clients, those who had money, lived in an area without cable television, and would be prepared to pay a premium. The service had to be offered to them. Once that segment had been exhausted, special promotions could be held to attract more difficult clients and compete directly with cable. The goal was to take customers away from cable on the premise that DirecTV was offering a better product using the latest technology. At all costs they avoided a price war with Sky, fearing this would devalue the product.

Certainly, it was a more complicated way of going into countries like Mexico and Brazil, where Sky was powerful. Why pay more if Sky had the local channels? The temptation for Vargas and Civita was to compete on the basis of price. As expected, it was an uphill battle for DirecTV to become established in Mexico and Brazil.

Beyond the tactical successes and mistakes, it was clear that Gustavo Cisneros had been overly optimistic about the immediate potential of DTH in Latin America. Both Sky and DirecTV poured 1 billion dollars into their respective projects, and at the beginning of 1999 each had 600,000 subscribers. There were no surprises in the distribution of clients: DirecTV was quickly outstripped by Sky in Brazil and Mexico. Except for Chile, DirecTV was ahead in the rest of the region.

There was an impasse. Neither company was close to reaching the target of one million subscribers needed to cover costs. Each was spending significant amounts of money on marketing in order not to lose ground to the other (and to the cable television companies, which were beginning to respond to the arrival of DTH), which further increased the target number of subscribers needed to reach profitability. Some analysts predicted that DirecTV and Sky would begin to make money in 2002. The cost of satellite television components—decoding boxes and receptor antennas—on the one hand, and the blow of the currency devaluation in Brazil on the other, would force Vargas and Civita to sell their respective interests to Hughes, who now controlled 80 percent of the business while Cisneros had the remaining 20 percent.

In the midst of the vicissitudes typical of a new and risky business, certain successes began to be achieved. Subscribers to DirecTV Latin America bought almost three times the number of movies on pay-per-view as their counterparts in the United States, which increased the money that the operator received from each account. Moreover, almost half the subscribers took what were called premium packages—which include movie and premium channels such as HBO, Movie City, and Playboy—a higher ratio than had been anticipated.

The situation in Argentina, where DirecTV was led by the powerful Clarín Group, became favorable. DirecTV signed an exclusivity contract with the popular program-supplier HBO, and Sky, which lost a good deal of time looking for a suitable partner, delayed its entrance into that market until the end of 2000, when DirecTV was already well positioned with 300,000 accounts (in

2002, Sky would withdraw definitively from Argentina). DirecTV surpassed Sky in Colombia, and it reached twenty countries, compared to Sky's seven. In Venezuela there was no competition since Sky did not enter the local market.

The success of DirecTV was bittersweet for Cisneros. The company began the new century with more than a million subscribers. The Hughes-Cisneros partnership was now one of the large operators of pay television in Latin America, something that had been unthinkable at the beginning of the decade. It still needed to earn money, and to do that it had to join forces with Sky. It was a subject that was still pending with Azcárraga, Marinho, and Murdoch.

With six hundred channels radiating from a satellite, there was room for Gustavo Cisneros to carry out projects that were dear to him. One was the continuation of the educational plan he had begun on the Mata de Bárbara hacienda in the late 1970s.

With ACUDE, Patty Cisneros had demonstrated how technology could be put to good use in the service of education, through audio aids, reaching the most remote places and adapting to the needs of the users. ACUDE was a program directed at a population with low educational levels, which began with literacy and continued with activities to reinforce and complement new skills. The idea was to develop users in an integral way, motivating them by means of self-esteem, with the final goal of contributing to the defeat of poverty.

After twenty years of activity, and having achieved important goals—teaching literacy to as many as 150,000 people a year when ACUDE was at its height (1984–94), recruiting up to 100,000 volunteers and 557 sponsors and patrons from the public and private sectors—Cisneros decided to propose a new challenge in terms of education. These were two projects based on his own business units: the channel Cl@se (Latin American Corporation for Educational Services),and AME (*Actualización de Maestros en Educación*, or Professional Development for Educators). Both projects are today administered by the Fundación Cisneros. They cover a wide territory in Latin America, simultaneously reaching thousands of communities, schools, teachers, and students by employing the satellite platform of DirecTV.

Cl@se is a commercial-free educational channel that is also entertaining, and it serves in many cases as a complement to classes taught in schools. Its programs include shows like *El Mundo de Beauman, El Autobús Mágico,* and *Testigo Ocular,* and classes in English and French, among other languages. The principal cost is renting space on the satellite, some $600,000 a year, which is shared with Hughes. Currently Cl@se is offered both to subscribers to DirecTV, as an integral part of the basic package, and to subscribers to cable television. The objective of the channel is to reach the greatest possible number of people in Latin America with high-quality educational programming. In many cases, based on earlier alliances, DirecTV and other entities donate a computer, a receptor antenna, and a decoder in order to offer the service to schools. The package is complemented by games and informative and instructional material for certain television programs, which in turn are designed to integrate with the curricula in various Latin American countries. Information about this service can be accessed on the Web site www.clase.net.

AME is a program aimed at teachers of basic education, providing dynamic professional-development courses to help improve teacher performance in the classroom. Its educational content is focused on the use of new technologies and the teaching of reading, writing, mathematics, and other topics, as well as general civic values.

"Latin Americans have on average a sixth-grade education, which is linked to our poverty and quality of life," says Peter Tinoco, the executive chairman of the Fundación Cisneros. "It is a problem of education. There were frustrated people. They knew how to read but did not understand what they were reading, or they knew how to write but not compose."

AME initiated its activities with a pilot program in October 1998, encompassing seven countries, 150 schools, and 1,500 teachers. This initial base was endorsed by UNESCO and a private consulting firm. Following this evaluation, the creation of a committee of specialists in basic education, and consultations with the participants, a series of adjustments were made in the content offered and the follow-up process.

The program is aimed at the school as a work unit; participating teachers are grouped into teams, receiving their instruction on television, and at the same time carrying out activities in the classroom with information provided on the Web, along with guides provided to each teacher.

"We are going to strengthen the teachers of basic education," Tinoco explains. "It is showing the teachers how to be better teachers. And the ripple effect is fabulous."

Each course consists of eight fifty-minute classes on television; four hours of preparation are required for each class, in addition to participating through the AME Web site in chat rooms that allow an exchange among different countries and schools. The program culminates in the presentation of a project for the particular school or classroom. The courses are developed by universities selected by AME, including the Universidad Autónoma de Barcelona and the Pontífica Javeriana.

DirecTV put the vision and tenacity of Gustavo Cisneros as a businessman to the test. He saw the potential of the new satellite technology, and observed at an early stage that efforts ought to be oriented toward establishing a single platform for Latin America. He had waited decades to complete his vision of one television for an entire continent. Now it was closer than ever.

13. The Swan's Triumph

One morning, at the end of July 1994, two investment bankers, Violy McCausland and Javier Macaya, flew to Aspen, Colorado—8,858 feet above sea-level—to keep an appointment with Gustavo and Ricardo Cisneros. Without the snow and bustle typical of the ski trails, the town, which is idyllically serene in summer, was the place chosen to outline the strategy for one of the most spectacular corporate coups in Latin American history.

The bankers had been asked to brainstorm with the Cisneros brothers about the Pepsi-Cola company as a follow-up to a meeting that Gustavo Cisneros had with James D. Wolfensohn on the same topic.

At the beginning of the year, Cisneros had invited McCausland and Wolfensohn, who assumed the presidency of World Bank in 1995 and was a brilliant player in the field of international finance, to have breakfast at his home in New York. The entrepreneur told them of his desire to focus primarily on his businesses in communications and entertainment.

The Venezuelan's words made it clear to Wolfensohn and McCausland that an excellent business opportunity had opened up for them.

Cisneros wanted to sell Pepsi-Cola-Hit Bottlers of Venezuela. The firm bottled Pepsi-Cola and other soft drinks of its own, including Chinotto, Hit, and Frescolita, as well as the Schweppes line of products. A simple question was posed: who is the logical buyer for this enterprise? The answer would be key for determining what investment bankers call the "value" of a company—that is, its "price." Some transactions lend themselves to simple financial formulas that bring estimates of the company's cash flow and future earnings to a present value. Pepsi-Cola-Hit Bottlers reported a solid profit of $50 million a year (of which $10 million went to PepsiCo for the right to use its brand name and formula) on sales of $400 million. The company could perhaps fetch a price of some $800 million. But there were complications. The soft drink business is essentially a franchise, which does not lend itself to standard bidding. This reduces the list of potential buyers to those approved by PepsiCo.

There was an additional problem: Coca-Cola dominated the market in Latin America, with the exception of Venezuela. In fact, Coca-Cola outsold Pepsi worldwide by a margin of three to one. That meant that bottling Pepsi had less value than bottling Coca-Cola, even in Venezuela where the Cisneros operation outsold Coke by a margin of five to one. Moreover, there were no guarantees that this margin could be sustained over time, because rumors were circulating that Coca-Cola wanted to launch a counter-offensive in Venezuela to regain the market that Diego and Antonio Cisneros had won from them half a century earlier.

Gustavo Cisneros knew firsthand what Coca-Cola was capable of: Coca-Cola Femsa launched so intensive a campaign in Mexico in the 1990s that Pepsi-Cola practically folded in that country. Douglas Ivester, Coke's new president and the designated successor to the legendary Cuban Roberto Goizueta, was "very competitive and aggressive." The speculation was that Ivester would give the franchise in Venezuela to one of his favored Latin American bottlers, probably Panamerican Beverages Inc. (Panamco), a company founded in Panama by Staton Woods, an American who had operations in several countries in the region. If Panamco came to Venezuela, competition with the Cisneros operation would turn fierce. "Coca-Cola can spend $100 million to flood the soft-drink market," said Cisneros, "and for them that's not much money."

All these factors, combined with the increasingly gloomy economic landscape in Venezuela, led to the conclusion that there was only one buyer prepared to pay an adequate price for Pepsi-Cola-Hit Bottlers of Venezuela: the Coca-Cola Company.

Switching from Pepsi to Coke was not a question of simply repainting the outside of a factory. There were numerous complex questions that did not have clear answers. Who would pay a possible penalty for terminating the contract with Pepsi-Cola that was in effect until 2003? What percentage of the market would Pepsi-Cola recover when it was in the hands of another bottler, considering that for better or worse, Pepsi had many loyal consumers? And what would be the position of the Venezuelan authorities when faced with the prospect of a bottler with 82 percent of the market (of which Pepsi-Cola accounted for 42 percent and Hit's other non-cola drinks the remaining 40 percent) suddenly joining with the competitor that had the other 12 percent? Together, Cisneros and Coca-Cola would control 94 percent of the soft-drink market in Venezuela. This combination would certainly involve serious regulatory issues.

The questions were so complex and the margin of uncertainty so wide that the idea never got past the starting gate.

Everyone understood that the transaction, which would be called by the English name Swan—equivalent to the Spanish *cisne*, and also an abbreviation for Cisneros—had to be kept absolutely secret. If PepsiCo ever suspected the Cisneroses' intention, it would mount an aggressive legal campaign to stop it.

Immediately following his meeting in Aspen with McCausland and Macaya, Gustavo Cisneros picked up the phone and dialed the number of his friend Roberto Goizueta, the president of the board and highest-ranking officer at Coca-Cola, to outline an important proposal.

Gustavo Cisneros' disenchantment with PepsiCo had begun decades earlier, when he detected a certain indifference on the part of the multinational toward the Cisneroses' business dispute with the Monsanto family, which had concerned his father at the time. He considered this attitude disloyal to the man who had made the Pepsi brand name great in Venezuela. He interpreted PepsiCo's neutrality as a tactic to keep the bottling company's top leadership divided.

"It was very strange that PepsiCo did not intervene somehow to remedy the situation, when Diego Cisneros was its most successful bottler in the world," says Gustavo Cisneros.

Further, the American firm had not supported the Cisneros Group during its difficult ventures into Brazil and Colombia. Coca-Cola had brought in all its artillery to ruin the landing of the Venezuelans, and PepsiCo had ignored it. This happened not only in Colombia and Brazil, but in other places as well. For example, in 1972, in Málaga, Spain, PepsiCo displayed similar indifference when the Cisneros Group bought a bottling factory that made La Casera a very popular drink in that country. "We were accustomed to business going smoothly for us in Venezuela, but when we entered other countries, it was very difficult to start from zero against a powerful Coca-Cola," says an executive in the Cisneros Group who worked in Málaga for a time. Finally, in 1976, the Cisneros Group sold its participation in the Spanish project.

Despite the disagreements, the idea of abandoning PepsiCo did not enter Gustavo Cisneros' mind until many years had passed. The ties to the multinational were deep. Cisneros, like his father, was a friend of Donald Kendall, the head of PepsiCo until 1986. Cisneros would invite him to go fishing in the Dominican Republic, and Kendall would reciprocate by taking the entrepreneur salmon-fishing in Alaska.

A further disagreement with PepsiCo resulted from another international venture by the heirs of Diego Cisneros: the acquisition of All-American Bottling (AAB) in 1984. AAB bottled everything except Coca-Cola and Pepsi-Cola, and Cisneros wanted PepsiCo to allow him to bottle its cola. Kendall understood Cisneros' concerns, but he was in a difficult situation. On the one hand, he liked the Venezuelan and respected him as a businessman, but on the other, PepsiCo's policy was clear: it was necessary to keep the bottlers weak and territorially divided so that they would comply with PepsiCo's orders.

"The system at PepsiCo dictated that we would not be welcome, because they believed we were demanding too much authority," Cisneros recalls.

PepsiCo never gave its approval, and Gustavo Cisneros, at the prospect of becoming a second-division player, preferred to sell AAB when he saw that the consolidation of the industry was approaching.

Kendall asked Cisneros for patience. He offered him a bottling plant in New York and another in Tennessee, but both were losing vast amounts of money. "In Venezuela we called those plants 'junk' because their financials were so bad," recalls a member of the Cisneros Group who was responsible for reviewing the numbers of the bottling plants.

The dominance of Pepsi-Cola in Venezuela, which lasted more than three decades, was orchestrated by Diego Cisneros and continued by his nephew, Oswaldo, who was four years older than Gustavo. Nothing happened at Pepsi-Cola-Hit Bottlers of Venezuela without Oswaldo knowing how, when, and where it had occurred. In his inspections he was meticulous; not content with looking over the plant, he would even go to the warehouses where managers stored material that was later thrown out, because he knew that a good deal of money was lost this way.

Gustavo and Ricardo Cisneros shared, in equal parts with their cousin, the controlling stock in Pepsi-Cola-Hit Bottlers of Venezuela. An operational dividing line always existed between the Cisneros Fajardo and the Cisneros Rendiles families. Oswaldo, at the head of the Fajardo branch of the family, operated Pepsi-Cola-Hit; Gustavo and Ricardo, the leaders of the Rendiles group, managed Venevisión and CADA. There were also significant businesses that both sides shared, for example the cell-phone enterprise Telcel, managed by Oswaldo, and Cervecería Regional, managed by Gustavo and Ricardo.

No matter how able and dedicated Oswaldo was as an operator, Gustavo Cisneros feared the effects of an eventual offensive by Coca-Cola in Venezuela. In the mid-1990s, Venezuela was one of the few countries in the world where Pepsi-Cola sold more colas than its staunch rival. Even in the Soviet Union—where Pepsi-Cola had entered as the company favored by the Communist bureaucracy—Coca-Cola had surpassed it. Venezuela was "a stone in the shoe" of Coca-Cola—as Cisneros says—and he knew that Roberto Goizueta was longing to remove it.

Goizueta pressed his executives and bottlers with apparently impossible objectives. For him there was no such thing as a saturated or mature market. If the goal was to increase market participation, he argued that the competition was not just among carbonated soft drinks, but included any and all beverages. From that point of view, market participation was not some 40 percent but more like 3 percent, because all beverages counted, even coffee and tap water.

Faced with the prospect of a revitalized Coca-Cola, Gustavo Cisneros wanted to sell Pepsi-Cola-Hit Bottlers of Venezuela to Goizueta. He wanted to be a mega-bottler, and if he could not be one with PepsiCo, he would have to opt for Coca-Cola. The idea of selling to Coca-Cola was born in 1985, conceived by Cisneros and his bankers. Cisneros presented his plan to Oswaldo. Cautious and very loyal to Pepsi-Cola, his cousin did not want to leave the brand name he had developed with so much perseverance ever since his adolescence. He wanted to give Pepsi-Cola more time.

"I'm hopeful that things are going to improve with Pepsi-Cola," said Oswaldo.

"When you have no more hope, we'll go to Coca-Cola, because PepsiCo is *never* going to solve our problems," Gustavo Cisneros told him.

In fact, after Kendall's retirement, matters grew worse. Wayne Calloway, the executive president of PepsiCo since 1984, was more committed to the idea of diversifying the company's business, and he had little interest in international operations. Cisneros asked PepsiCo's directors to copy Goizueta's strategy, giving more territories to its concession holders and forming partnerships in which both would have greater strength for confronting Coca-Cola.

"Coke is surrounding us, and eventually they'll do something better than we do," he told them. "Invest more in the business. Like it or not, the brand name is yours, not ours. Help us!"

Once again, his demands were ignored.

In the mid-1990s, Coca-Cola succeeded in reversing the success that Pepsi-Cola had enjoyed in the United States in the 1980s, and it outsold its competitor. Outside the United States, where Pepsi-Cola was vulnerable, things were also going very well for Coke. Goizueta wanted his soft drinks to be everywhere, from Kremlin Square to South Africa. They were, and three-fourths of Coca-Cola's income came from outside the United States. Surveys indicated that Coca-Cola was the most admired brand name in the world, a true icon of successful marketing and the globalization of business. The value of Coke on the stock market rose from $4 billion when Goizueta assumed control to $145 billion fifteen years later. Sales in 1995 reached $18 billion in contrast to $30 billion for Pepsi-Cola, but Coca-Cola's $3 billion earnings were almost twice the $1.6 billion recorded by Pepsi-Cola. In what was called the Cola Wars, the momentum once again favored Goizueta.

Goizueta loved the idea of buying the Venezuelan operation. Gustavo Cisneros developed a warm relationship with him, and also established a friendship with Donald Keough, who for many years was Goizueta's closest lieutenant.

"Keough and Goizueta have an incredible human side," Gustavo Cisneros recalls.

He made certain that Ricardo and Oswaldo would also establish personal relationships with Goizueta, so that "we would all be very connected."

In the early 1990s, Oswaldo began to experience his own frustrations with Pepsi-Cola. In 1990 he turned fifty, and he wanted to sell the company to devote himself to other things. Out of loyalty to PepsiCo, Oswaldo, in the name of the family, went to discuss the matter with the man who was then head of international operations, Roger Enrico. A true marketing star, Enrico was also the author of the book *The Distraction of the Other: How Pepsi Won the Cola Wars* (1986), in which he analyzed, among other subjects, Coca-Cola's failure with the introduction of "New Coke." This charismatic individual was a very good friend of Oswaldo, whom he called "Ozzie." The conversation did not produce the desired results. Oswaldo had already suggested that Enrico buy his shares in Pepsi-Cola of Venezuela, but the American had not shown much enthusiasm: perhaps he could acquire a minority share, he said. It was not what Oswaldo wanted to hear, and in 1990 he agreed to explore a sale to Goizueta.

This time, however, it was the Atlanta company that put up obstacles.

"Gustavo, I'm going to pass this on to my lawyers so they can study an alliance between us," Goizueta told Cisneros.

Cisneros thought that was a mistake.

"That's impossible, Roberto, because the lawyers and the auditors are going to raise so many obstacles to the deal that you're going to call me personally to find a better time."

Goizueta called him three months later.

"Listen, Gustavo, you were right...I'll call you when we're ready."

Consequently the idea of selling the bottling plants to Coca-Cola was not revived until the summer of 1994, in Aspen.

When it was time to start negotiations, the team soon realized there was a huge difference in valuation. Cisneros wanted $800 million. The Coca-Cola people said they were prepared to pay only $300 million. Even if Goizueta wanted to make the deal, the lawyers and auditors of Coca-Cola were against it. Months went by, and the talks were going nowhere.

Early in 1996 the parties decided to bring in new advisers to help in the valuation of Pepsi-Cola-Hit Bottlers of Venezuela and in drafting the agreements. Up until then, there had been only verbal agreements among Goizueta, Douglas Ivester (executive president of Coca-Cola), and the families of Cisneros Fajardo and Cisneros Rendiles.

Negotiations were conducted with absolute secrecy. When the negotiators spoke of Operation Swan, they used code terms. Pepsi-Cola and Coca-Cola were "Blue" and "Red" because of their respective corporate colors. The team working on the deal was forbidden to fly in planes belonging to the Cisneros Group. It could not use the services of SAECA, the travel agency that belonged to the Group, to make plane or hotel reservations. It never used the offices of Coca-Cola in Atlanta to negotiate. Meetings were usually held in airports.

A small operational group from Pepsi-Cola-Hit Bottlers of Venezuela, carefully supervised by Oswaldo Cisneros, began to plan the complex logistics behind the radical change in brand name. Twenty-five hundred trucks had to be repainted without interrupting distribution (the key to the soft-drink business), and thousands of new Coca-Cola bottles had to be brought in, all with the utmost secrecy.

Finally, a deal was structured that would be carried out in phases. First, half of the firm would be handed over to Coca-Cola for $500 million; $300 million would be paid in cash (the initial valuation that the Americans had made of the Venezuelan operation), and another 200 million dollars in assets belonging to Coca-Cola, basically the six bottling plans it owned in Venezuela and its fleet of five hundred trucks. In the second phase, to be completed a few months later, Coca-Cola and Cisneros would sell everything to Panamco for $1.1 billion, payable in cash and in shares. The Cisneros family group would then own 11 percent of Panamco. Once the valuation and purchase price had been resolved, final signatures seemed imminent. Goizueta finally agreed that Coca-Cola would pay the penalty for the early termination of the contract with PepsiCo, if in fact there was one.

During the summer of 1996, the teams worked on drafting agreements, shuttling between Caracas, New York, and Atlanta. They had to convince the stockholders of Hit Bottlers—some of them dating back to the time of Diego Cisneros—to sell their shares. The transaction was used to define the respective participation of the Cisneros Fajardo and Cisneros Rendiles branches. Oswaldo gave his shares of Cervecería Regional—the brewery they had bought together in 1992—to his cousins Ricardo and Gustavo, and in exchange they gave him the shares they owned in Telcel.

In April, the executive presidency of PepsiCo passed to Roger Enrico, Oswaldo's old friend. As soon as he assumed office, Enrico called Ozzie, who did not return the call. Enrico called again, but Ozzie did not respond. This made Enrico suspect that his friend was conspiring with the "enemy." He spoke to his subordinates in Latin America, and they assured him that the stories of a sale to Coca-Cola were only rumors. That, of course, was what Oswaldo Cisneros was telling them.

Still, Oswaldo wanted to give Enrico a last chance. In June 1996 he instructed Violy McCausland to explore the situation one more time to see if PepsiCo was interested in buying Hit Bottlers. By making contact through McCausland, an investment banker, Oswaldo wanted PepsiCo to understand that his desire to sell was serious. McCausland did not say that Cisneros was about to sign with Coca-Cola, but she did ask if PepsiCo wanted to buy Pepsi-Cola of Venezuela. She obtained the usual response: perhaps they would buy minority participation, 20 or 25 percent, at a price that would not satisfy the Cisneros family. The fate of Pepsi-Cola in Venezuela was sealed.

The agreements were signed at ten in the morning on Friday, August 16, 1996, in Panama City, the legal residence of the international division of Coca-Cola, which was going to buy Pepsi-Cola-Hit Bottlers of Venezuela. The faces of those present reflected a mixture of exhaustion and relief. At last, after so many attempts through the years, they had managed to close a deal that had seemed impossible to achieve. For the Venezuelan team in particular, the episode had an emotional charge, as one executive recalls: "We knew it had been attempted earlier, and the effort had failed. We knew that the family was divesting itself of an asset it loved, one that represented the important origins of the Group. We also knew that the partnership between the Cisneros Fajardo and the Cisneros Rendiles families, a relationship that had been unbelievably fruitful for many years, was coming to an end."

For Gustavo Cisneros, reflecting some time later on this extraordinary corporate saga, the transaction was largely in response to PepsiCo's rejection of the Cisneros framework of plans appropriate to a legitimate and creative way of doing business: "Pepsi-

Co was suffocating us, for no good reason, and we had to breathe," he told his people. "I believe it learned from the experience, and from now on it certainly will be more flexible. We acted with calculated boldness. We passed the test."

On that day in August 1996, the negotiators moved to the branch offices of Chase Manhattan Bank, which issued the payment orders for the shareholders in Hit Bottlers. With the deal concluded, it was time to celebrate.. A group left for the official celebration at Coca-Cola headquarters in Atlanta. It was an event that captured the masterful way in which Goizueta had managed the affair from the human point of view. He had known how to touch the precise emotional hot buttons that would lead to the heart of each member of the two Cisneros families, and of the other shareholders, in order to smooth rough ground, calm misgivings, and have each party finally give its blessing to the transaction. Goizueta spoke to them as a Latin American. Without this element, perhaps Operation Swan would never have taken place. "This is a business of human relations," the president of Coca-Cola would later explain. As a consequence, the atmosphere was intimate, almost familial. Goizueta showed them the desk where the founder of Coca-Cola had worked. Gustavo Cisneros was very pleased. Three Cisneros generations were present, including Doña Carmen, Oswaldo's mother. Goizueta accompanied them to the main dining room where they shared the moment.

While the successful conclusion of Operation Swan was being celebrated in Atlanta, Oswaldo's people were setting Operation Switch in motion. This consisted in erasing every vestige of PepsiCo in Venezuela. All the red paint in the country was used up and more had to be specially imported from Colombia. An Agence France-Presse photograph showed a truck newly converted to the colors and logos of Coca-Cola but still carrying bottles of Pepsi-Cola. By Monday, August 19, all the vehicles were displaying their new colors and distributing their bottles of Coca-Cola, which had been flown in from the United States on a Boeing 727. The astonished employees who came to work on Saturday the 17th had to turn in their Pepsi-Cola uniforms and put on the ones from Coca-Cola.

The press reports came out the afternoon of the 16th. They explained the basic outline of the deal but did not go into details. The reports included a triumphant statement from Ivester: "For decades Venezuela was like a black spot on the global map of Coca-Cola. Today it is one of its most brilliant spots." All the spokespeople for Coca-Cola, the Cisneros Group, and the Cisneros Fajardos were carefully instructed with regard to what they could say in public in order not to compromise their defense in the difficult legal battle that lay ahead.

The size of the new Coca-Cola-Cisneros venture was relatively modest compared to other giants born of corporate mergers, such as Daimler Chrysler or AOL Time Warner. The Venezuelan market consumed 220 million cases of soft drinks a year, barely a tenth of what people drank in Mexico. Before the merger, the sales of Pepsi-Cola-Hit Bottlers of Venezuela were a little more than 2 percent of the Coca-Cola Co. Still, what happened in Venezuela on August 16 had a symbolic relevance that went far beyond its real economic impact. Operation Swan revealed how well things were going for Roberto Goizueta's Coca-Cola and how badly they were going for Roger Enrico's PepsiCo. The two companies were engaged in one of the most public rivalries in the corporate history of the United States. Furthermore, the fact that Coca-Cola had taken a bottling company away from PepsiCo in so unexpected a manner gave all the color the media needed to underscore the impact of the situation.

From the *Times of India* to the *Frankfurter Allgemeine Zeitung*, the news media was fixated on the Cisneroses' triumph. Reporters dusted off their address books to search for analysts and experts in the soft-drink industry who would give them juicy quotes to liven up their articles. "Everybody in the industry is talking about only one thing: how could Pepsi-Cola allow this to happen?" Jesse Meyers, founder of the specialized publication *Beverage Digest*, told the *New York Times*. "In thirty-five years I can't recall a single case of a Coca-Cola bottler switching to PepsiCo. People in the industry are asking themselves how it is possible that Venezuela, the greatest Pepsi-Cola success in the world, could be snatched away by their archenemy in the full light of a sunny day."

"There are many alarms going off [at Pepsi-Cola] right now," the analyst Tom Pirko, president of Bevmark Inc., told Bloomberg News. If you eliminate distribution, reentering the market becomes very complicated."

The people at PepsiCo felt as if a stake had been driven through their hearts. Enrico tried in vain to call his friend Ozzie and vent his rage.

"I hope he can understand the reasons that led me to do this," Oswaldo Cisneros would say afterward.

The moment could not have been worse for PepsiCo. The firm had attempted to counteract the strategy of Goizueta's megabottlers, but results had been negative with Buenos Aires Bottler S.A.(BAESA), which had too much debt to make inroads in Brazil, a market where Coca-Cola was very powerful. BAESA—of which Pepsi-Cola owned 24 percent—declared losses of some 251 million dollars in the three-month period April–June 1996. A few days before Operation Swan, BAESA declared a cessation of payments to its creditors. At the same time, the Pepsi-Cola bottling company in Puerto Rico was also facing accounting problems. Now, added to all this, there was the defection of Cisneros to the enemy. The international management of Pepsi-Cola was shaken. Its head, Christopher Sinclair, resigned "for personal reasons" after barely four months in the position. In September of that year, Pepsi-Cola would declare a loss of some $525 million.

PepsiCo followed the only defense it had left: it became the victim. Its spokespeople insisted that the company had been sensitive to signals from Oswaldo Cisneros regarding the option of leaving the business or forming a partnership with PepsiCo, but it was he—not Pepsi—who presumably never responded to its offers. PepsiCo published full-page advertisements in Venezuelan newspapers attacking the deal. It sent a small army of lawyers to file a complaint before ProCompetencia, the governmental entity that handles antitrust cases in Venezuela.

To show that it had no monopolistic ambitions, Coca-Cola offered to sell its five hundred trucks and six bottling plants in Venezuela, among other assets, to whoever might wish to bottle Pepsi-Cola. The offended directors of Pepsi-Cola said it was all "garbage." "They couldn't even be sold at a trash recycling center in the United States," said Alberto Uribe, PepsiCo's president of Andean operations, a man who considered himself an old friend of Oswaldo's. Pepsi-Cola demanded payment of $100 million as a penalty for breaking the contract.

In December, ProCompetencia issued a fairly balanced ruling: it fined Coca-Cola $2 million for monopolistic practices. It also demanded that in cases in which the combined Coca-Cola-Cisneros venture produced soft drinks with similar flavors under different brands, the venture had to sell one of the brands. Both Coca-Cola and PepsiCo agreed. In September 1997, when the operation had been sold to Panamco, a judgment came down from the International Court of Arbitration, located in Paris. Coca-Cola and Cisneros had to pay $94 million to PepsiCo as indemnification for early termination of their contract. The amount seemed high, and some analysts said that PepsiCo came out of it very well since it earned only $10 million a year from its Venezuelan operation. However, the people at Coca-Cola insisted that this amount had always been included in their calculations. Once again, all those involved declared themselves winners.

Roberto Goizueta could not appreciate the outcome of his work, for he died in October 1997, consumed by lung cancer. But he did have the satisfaction of removing the "stone in his shoe" that the case of Venezuela had represented for so long, and precisely at the high point of the company to which he had dedicated so much effort.

Finally, PepsiCo reappeared in Caracas in 1997 with the Polar Group, the traditional and powerful beer manufacturer. The new partnership spent a fortune on rebuilding infrastructure and by means of a price war recaptured 30 percent of the soft-drink market in 1998. Two years later this market share rose to 40 percent, when, as will be seen, the great battle of the beers began in Venezuela, with Gustavo Cisneros as a key protagonist. In 2003, Coca-Cola regained its position with 70 percent of the dark-colas market.

The Cola Wars followed their cyclical course. Now Gustavo Cisneros could allow himself the luxury of watching it from a

prudent distance. As part of the deal with Coca-Cola, the Cisneros family became stockholders in Panamco, the largest soft-
drink bottling company in Latin America, with two seats on the
board of directors, followed by the Statons—the founding family—and the general public. From the beginning of the negotiations, there had been speculation regarding a future in which, in
the end, only one great bottling company would survive in the
Americas: either Panamco would buy Femsa—the largest bottler
in Mexico—or vice versa (as Roberto predicted). The latter occurred in May 2003, due in no small measure to Gustavo Cisneros' determination and contributions as a member of the board
of Panamco. The Femsa-Panamco merger has turned the new
company into the second largest bottler in the world, measured
by the volume of its production.

In the midst of all the publicity generated by the negotiations with Coca-Cola, few people noticed that Gustavo Cisneros
had closed the book on another of his anchor enterprises: Spalding and Evenflo. This sale in no way resembled the complex process that had marked the deal with Coca-Cola. The sale process
took barely five months. There were no meetings in hotels or
conversations in code. Cisneros engaged two investment banks
to auction the company to the highest bidder. There were many
interested parties among the investment funds and what are called
"strategic buyers," that is, competitors. A logical buyer was a financier, because it was simpler for Cisneros to sell the sporting-
goods company and the manufacturer of furniture and accessories
for babies in a single package. The recommendation to sell had
come from Ricardo Cisneros and Alejandro Rivera. They argued
that the competitive horizon was looking stormy because new
players wanted to enter the lucrative golf-ball market, among them
Callaway, a manufacturer of golf clubs, and Nike.

Gustavo Cisneros agreed with Ricardo and Alejandro. Spalding and Evenflo formed part of the list of companies identified to
be sold at the beginning of the 1990s. They were one of the smartest investments he had made. Its annual profits approximated

$50 million, and the resources the company generated not only canceled the entire debt that Cisneros had assumed in order to buy it, but it brought in foreign currency that proved very useful when operations in Venezuela needed assistance.

In twelve years, Cisneros had tripled Spalding's sales, half of them outside the United States.

Although Spalding was the largest manufacturer of basketballs in the world, golf balls always provided its main support. When the company was sold, it was producing a million golf balls a day at its plant in Chicopee, Massachusetts. It was a tap from which money flowed. The operational margin for the most expensive balls reached 70 percent, equaling what Coca-Cola obtained from the sale of its concentrate to its captive customers, the bottling plants.

Of course, the technology behind those golf balls was increasingly sophisticated. Spalding had always been a great innovator in this area. In the 1960s it was Spalding that had introduced the dimples on the surface that characterize present-day golf balls. At that time, Spalding specialized in the popular segment, manufacturing balls for occasional golfers who play with a high handicap. They did not need very sophisticated golf balls; they needed balls that were sturdy. The volume in the popular segment was good, but the most attractive margins were found in the high-performance balls bought by professionals, amateurs with a low handicap, and the misguided players who believed they could improve their score if they acquired a more expensive ball, while in reality they only lost more of them—to the benefit of the manufacturer. A box of a dozen premium balls could cost $40, double the price of the standard ones. But the premium market was in the hands of Titleist, which scored a tremendous success with its HVC line, a favorite of professional golfers. Protected by eleven patents, an HVC golf ball has a balata gum covering and a hard coiled-rubber core. The soft covering gives the golfer more control since it "flattens" against the club when it is hit, while the hard center gives it distance. And the dimples, if they are well designed and distributed, give the ball balance for a straighter shot.

This 350-year-old sport had entered the era of high technology. The directors at Spalding searched for a product that could compete with Titleist's HVC balls. Instead of using a rolled band, which is costly to manufacture, the technicians at Spalding invented plastics of different hardnesses, which resemble the soft exterior of balata gum and the hard center of rubber. The result was the first ball with three pieces or layers. After various failed prototypes, the professional golfers consulted by Spalding gave the thumbs-up, and the Strata line was launched in June 1996. Even though each ball cost three dollars, it was a great sales success and the icing on the cake that eventually persuaded the directors of Kohlberg Kravis Roberts & Co. (KKR) to pay a good price for Spalding. For several years they had been telling Gustavo Cisneros of their desire to buy the operation, perhaps because they owned other assets related to the world of golf.

In recent years, the strong growth in sales came not so much from Spalding as from Evenflo. Golf was reaching a point of maturation that could not guarantee high rates of growth. Evenflo, on the other hand, increased its sales by exporting to new markets. The irony is that Evenflo was considered a dead weight in 1984 and reduced the purchase price of Spalding.

KKR paid $900 million for 94 percent of Spalding and Evenflo. The Cisneros Group retained 6 percent and a seat on the company's board of directors. The deal was closed while Cisneros spent a weekend at Henry Kravis' ranch in Colorado.

Cisneros had made a good deal. With Spalding and Evenflo he had multiplied his investment fifteen times.

Once again, as he had with Coca-Cola, he showed that he had a good sense of the time to sell a business, when it was at the height of its evolutionary curve. "Gustavo knows how to buy and sell, and that duality is unusual," says a businessman who is a friend of his.

Later, the competitive environment for Spalding, which split off from Evenflo in August 1998, became more difficult, adversely affecting its results. Even so, the company continued to develop innovative products (including a self-inflatable basketball), and Strata achieved an excellent reputation among the golfing elite of the world. Nevertheless, Spalding was restructured in bankruptcy, and KKR lost its investment.

The month of August 1996 was a milestone in the career of Gustavo Cisneros. It was the culmination of a series of transactions that would deliver cash flow to the Group, so that it could continue its move into communications.

The sale of Spalding also carried a symbolic message: Cisneros had divested himself of the last of the great purchases he had made in the 1980s employing the mechanism of the leveraged buyout.

No firm better embodied that period of mergers and acquisitions than Kohlberg Kravis Roberts & Co. Its purchase of RJR Nabisco for $31 billion in 1989 is still one of the greatest deals of its type in history. But by the end of the 1990s, LBOs were no longer the driving force behind deals in the American corporate world. In the first nine months of 2000, less than 2 percent of all acquisitions were financed with LBOs, compared to 34 percent during the comparable period in 1988. Today, KKR is one of almost a hundred investment banks dedicated to the business of acquisitions, but it has been years since it had the annual returns of more than 40 percent that it enjoyed in the 1980s. Still, the influence of Henry Kravis and his partners was decisive in the change of mentality experienced by company executives in the United States. From then on they had to begin to think as owners, to focus on the price of shares and on the creation of value, just as Goizueta had done at Coca-Cola.

The corporate saga of Pepsi-Cola versus Coca-Cola in Venezuela is a case study in the business schools of various universities throughout the world, the object of analysis and discussion by experts who see in the process multiple points of interest for the education of new entrepreneurs.

The deal with Pepsi-Cola-Hit of Venezuela was an excellent illustration of coordinated work among three partners—Oswaldo, Gustavo, and Ricardo Cisneros—that brought benefits to both executives and workers.

Gustavo Cisneros summarizes the chapter in these words: "Business is not a game. That must be understood. Courage and vision are required, as well as prudence. We did what had to be done to conquer new territories, and we generated jobs and prosperity in these new regions. We were frustrated for very valid reasons, and our traditional partners did not want to understand this. Then it was their turn to be dissatisfied. That's the way things are. Life goes on."

14. The Internet

The summer of 1996 was coming to an end, and Gustavo Cisneros had a meeting with some of his closest colleagues at the Group's New York office, known as Highgate. The first item on the agenda was to analyze a plan for new investments following the sales of Spalding and Evenflo and Pepsi-Cola-Hit Bottlers of Venezuela. Eduardo Hauser, Cisneros' assistant at Highgate, asked to speak:

"Let's form an alliance with America Online (AOL) to offer Internet service in Latin America," he said.

Once again Hauser was returning to his Internet project. The Cisneros brothers like their executives to take a leadership role and defend a new project. Cisneros calls this kind of manager "the hero of a deal," because he or she has the difficult task of eliminating all the doubts of the financial heads of the Cisneros Group.

In 1996, Cisneros was fifty-one years old, and several of the same people who had joinedhim at the beginning were still with him, for example Carlos Bardasano (since 1966), Alejandro Rivera (1976), and Steven Bandel (1983). At this point all of them were older and undoubtedly more experienced in corporate battles. A longtime collaborator in the Cisneros Group says: "At thispoint, it's very hard for Gustavo and me to be surprised by anything." Hauser was part of the new, young talent, following the managerial philosophy of early identification of executives with high potential.

AOL had been in the market for seven years, and although it did not offer an Internet connection as such—since browsers like Microsoft Explorer and Netscape had not yet been invented, and the Internet was much slower than it is today—it still offered e-mail service, a good data base of content, and one of Hauser's favorites: chat rooms. The company provided essentially the same services available on the Internet today, but for a smaller number of fanatical users of the technology. AOL permitted Hauser to present to Cisneros a portfolio with relevant newspaper articles, the firm's latest financial reports, and his counterpart's CV. While this is standard today, at that time it was noteworthy.

At the end of 1994, Hauser proposed the installation of a private network that would connect all the computers in the organization. He knew of a firm, Cambridge Technology Partners (CTP), that could provide the Group with a budget and consultations.

"That sounds good," Cisneros told him. He was attracted by the possibility of having the latest that communications technology could offer.

CTP came up with a project for connecting a hundred computers in six countries, with their respective servers and dedicated connections. It even contemplated the possibility of holding video-conferences. The cost was $1.3 million. This meant that when a person in the Group connected to the private network, regardless of whether it was done from Madrid or Caracas, the screen showed the honeycomb logo of the Cisneros Group.

The CTP project was not new for the Cisneros Group. As a result of the association with Sprint in Venezuela, Gustavo Cisneros already had his first electronic address: gustavo.cisneros@sprintnet.sprint.com, but this time the initiative was worldwide, which meant that Hauser could more efficiently conduct the follow-ups to the meetings held by his dynamic boss. In this way, after a working meeting, all the participants could receive by e-mail the minutes of the meeting and the points that had been agreed upon.

Parallel to the installation of the CTP project, Eduardo Hauser began to explore the possibility of an association with America Online to offer Internet services in Latin America. The first browsers had already appeared, and the Internet was beginning to take on the shape and form it has at present. He looked into the American firm's interest in a possible expansion south. The reply was categorical: at that time AOL had no interest in Latin America, since its priority was the United States.

Still, the opportunity presented itself at the end of 1995, when AOL announced an agreement to launch its service in Germany in conjunction with Bertelsmann AG. Each party would have equal participation in the alliance; America Online would provide the technology and the Germans would contribute the money and their knowledge of the European market. For Hauser, the Cisneros Group was the "Bertelsmann" of Latin America. Both were private, family-owned multinationals, involved in communications. It made perfect sense for the Americans to choose the Cisneros Group to be their partners. Hauser asked his employer to authorize his making initial formal contact with America Online.

Cisneros told him that the Group's financial priority was launching DirecTV Latin America. Furthermore, the sales of Pepsi-Cola in Venezuela and Spalding and Evenflo in the United States were taking up a good deal of his time.

But the subject of an alliance with AOL reemerged at that meeting at Highgate in the summer of 1996. When Hauser presented his proposal regarding an alliance with AOL, no one objected. It was a topic that Gustavo Cisneros had been contemplating for a long time, waiting, as always, for the right moment, and so he briefed Hauser and gave him instructions.

A few months later, the young man was in the Malibu Room, next to the office of Steve Case, the president of AOL, in Dulles, Virginia, explaining to AOL executives the virtues of a group that had revenues of $4 billion a year. AOL not only had operations in Germany but was also expanding into France, England, and Australia. Hauser sensed that there was interest. He needed to make a good first impression, and he was prepared. He had brought a PowerPoint presentation that highlighted the Cisneros Group assets and the economies of Latin America, with basic macroeconomic data.

He concluded his presentation with a simple idea: he wanted AOL to be what Hughes had been for DirecTV Latin America. Furthermore, he told them that Cisneros was the Bertelsmann for Latin America. He left the executives with a portfolio containing more information about the Cisneros Group.

A short while later, a consultant made a presentation to the Cisneros brothers at Highgate. He explained the basic architecture of the technology used by AOL, including Internet Protocol, how data was transmitted in small packets by means of the servers and routers, and how these, in turn, communicated with telephone networks. The two brothers listened and asked questions.

"If I earn a dollar from a subscriber, how do I have to share it?" asked Ricardo Cisneros.

The consultant explained the economics of an Internet provider at the end of 1996: how much had to be paid to generate content, how much went to the telephone company for the international connection, and how much equipment cost. As he learned more about this technology, Ricardo became enthusiastic about the project.

AOL and the Cisneros Group did not take long to reach an agreement on the basic structure of the new partnership. To begin with, AOL would contribute technology and branding and Cisneros would provide $100 million. That would allow them to launch the project and establish a 50 percent interest for each side in the partnership. In subsequent financial rounds, both would have to inject the same amount of cash to maintain their ownership interest. There was talk of an offering on the stock market.

Then the discussions bogged down because of valuation differences. Pricing a technology is never easy, even less so at the very beginning of a service like the Internet. Besides, AOL was distracted by a series of purchases it began to make in the United States. It acquired CompuServe, an Internet service provider (ISP) that was smaller than AOL; ICQ ("I Seek You"), an innovative service for instant messages and chat rooms; and Netscape, a browser that was losing its battle with Microsoft's Explorer. With each acquisition, the Americans argued that their contribution was worth more, and they asked the Cisneros Group to increase its initial contribution of cash. Ricardo and Gustavo Cisneros refused. They already had an agreement and did not want to revise it with each acquisition made by AOL. The AOL negotiators offered to leave CompuServe outside the partnership. That was unacceptable because CompuServe—which AOL intended to use as the brand name to compete with cheaper Internet service providers—could enter into competition with the future AOL-Cisneros partnership (in fact, CompuServe was already operating in Mexico). "It was like an agreement with Coca-Cola without Sprite included in the package," says Hauser. "In the end, both compete for a share of your stomach. Here, both were competing for an Internet client."

The deadlock over valuation lasted all of 1997 and part of 1998. The failure to reach agreement proved costly to the venture because other competitors were strengthening in the region. The competitors included Brazilian Universo Online, UOL, which was in effect a kind of "copy" of the AOL model with regional ambitions, the Spanish Telefónica with plans to provide telephone connections to the Internet, and StarMedia, a portal that did not offer connectivity and relied on the support of several North American investment banks, which were arriving en masse to invest in Internet assets.

In the meantime, Gustavo Cisneros wanted to make his own inquiries into the Internet. He was not especially interested in technical details, but he did want to know the implications of this technology on people's lives. He located a friend, Robert Pittman, president and head of operations at AOL and second in command of the company after Steve Case.

His relationship with Pittman is an example of how Gustavo puts into practice his father's philosophy in the field of human relations: they should never be destroyed; they must always be built and cultivated. The gift of his good memory helps Cisneros when he meets a person again after a period of time. He usually lets slip a detail to indicate that he *really* remembers the person. If the contact is closer, he is sure to send the person a card or a small holiday gift, simply to express his gratitude for a good time or a congenial talk. Cisneros' friend, the businessman Plácido Arango, who lives in Madrid, says: "Gustavo tends to his network of relationships, but he does it naturally because Gustavo is a good friend."

Cisneros met Pittman in 1991, when the younger man was thirty-six years old and working for Steve Ross, the baron of Time Warner. Ross needed partners for a new division, Time Warner Entertainment, which would group together his cable TV assets, Home Box Office (HBO), and Warner Brothers. Cisneros was invited to take a look at the project, and Pittman was impressed. The Venezuelan seemed to know everybody. And Pittman, as Steven Bandel recalls, remarked on this during a later meeting: "I was introduced to the Group in 1991 in a meeting at Warner where Gustavo Cisneros articulated his vision and strategy for his group in the years to come. From that time on, I have been following him, and I have been struck by how that strategy has been impeccably executed. An AOL partnership in Latin America, should, in my opinion, be carried out with the Cisneros Group."

Cisneros did not join Time Warner Entertainment but he did maintain contact with Pittman. They had mutual friends and shared a love of television. Pittman appreciated the global perspective of the Venezuelan's businesses. At that time, the captains of the industry in the United States did not look much beyond Rockefeller Center in New York or Sunset Boulevard in Hollywood. There were exceptions, of course. Since Japanese firms had invested heavily in Hollywood, Japan, like Europe, was a well-understood factor because of historical connections. But Asia in general, and Latin America in particular, were known only superficially.

In the mid-1990s, the real potential of this new technology was not yet clear. Was it the equivalent of the telephone at the end of the nineteenth century, or was it a game console, like Nintendo in 1990? The first meant a revolution in communications. A game console was interesting and amusing, but in the long run only a toy. In which of the two categories did the Internet belong?

During this time, people began talking about "convergence." The idea was that the Internet would absorb traditional media— television, radio, the print media—and reconfigure them into "0s" and "1s," the language of computerized data. This new combination of digitalized entertainment would not only improve its quality and capacity, but would be interactive as well. The technology gurus fueled speculation about the potential of "convergence," but in 1996 and 1997 the implications of the Internet in convergence generated more questions than clear answers. What would be the best medium for channeling the promised interactivity of the Internet? Television, perhaps, because of its simplicity and ubiquity. Cisneros bet on television.

"We are not fortune-tellers who know *how* the convergence among telecommunications, computing, and communications media is going to develop, but we think it will take place around television," he would tell *AméricaEconomía* magazine in 1998.

In the 1950s and 1960s the great driving forces of the television industry had been men who came from radio, such as Goar Mestre and Emilio Azcárraga, "the Tiger." Who would have the leading role now in the new medium? The captains of the television industry? Was the Internet the domain of a company like Microsoft, or a telephone company, or a media conglomerate like Time Warner?

Cisneros spoke about convergence with Pittman. Their talks fluctuated between the philosophical and the practical-entrepreneurial, with more emphasis on the practical. Pittman had no doubt that the Internet was going to be huge. "The computer, connected to the Internet, makes people's lives easier, and I'm a person who thinks that when something simplifies your life, you adopt it eventually," says Pittman, recalling his conversations with Cisneros. The computer with the Internet is "the box that simplifies my life," while television is "the box that tells me a story." Television entertained, while the personal computer (PC), with AOL, helped children with their homework, eliminated the mountains of paper that constituted traditional mail, managed personal finances, and even simplified vacation planning. Advice as fantastic as this had to be valued by consumers, especially by parents who wanted the best for their children. "When you create something that people really want to have, you'll earn money," Pittman told Cisneros.

For these same reasons, Pittman was convinced that the Internet was going to be a phenomenon throughout the world, not only in the United States. The Internet was comparable to the advent of the telephone and television. The fact that the PC, was expensive did not concern Pittman. In time a market would emerge for used PCs, or some mechanism for accessing lower prices. "If you can pay for a television set," he says, "you can buy a computer." The two men concluded that while the Internet was growing in the United States, it was logical that other countries in the region would follow suit, especially Mexico, for more telecommunications traffic crossed its border with the United States than in any other part of the world. There were also large, dynamic economies like Brazil. The territory was ready for the Internet.

Cisneros took what his friend said a step further. He was enthusiastic about what the Internet could do to improve the life of Latin Americans, especially in initiating a revolution in education. Improving education was Cisneros' philanthropic passion. He was convinced that Latin America could overcome underdevelopment if it upgraded the education of its children and young people, and the Internet was the perfect tool for achieving this.

"I call the Internet a tool for equalization," he would say in a speech a few years later, "because from the moment someone has access to a computer, a good program, and good services, that person can work, develop, become educated by means of the services we offer, as rapidly as any person in the United States, Europe, or Asia. We have the possibility of creating a personal and social tool for development."

He would go on to say: "I am confident that the technological gap between the United States and Latin America will continue to shrink as services become more accessible and the purchasing power of the Latin American consumer increases."

Cisneros spoke of "a transformation in Latin America," in which "each child and each teacher with access to the Internet would have the possibility of bringing the entire world into the classroom."

Cisneros and Pittman fed on each other's enthusiasm for the Internet project in Latin America. The benefits they could derive from the deal were well worth the effort of overcoming the valuation difficulties that kept their people in checkmate for months. In mid-1998, a delegation headed by Gustavo and Ricardo visited the headquarters of America Online in Dulles, Virginia, intending to close negotiations once and for all. When they left, all the problems had been resolved. Pittman and Case instructed their executives to sign the agreement with the terms proposed by Cisneros. "In the end, you have to decide if you want to close a deal with that partner or not," says Pittman. A member of the Cisneros Group says that AOL lowered its bid by "more than half." CompuServe and ICQ would be available to the new Latin American partnership, which they called America Online Latin America (AOLA). The browser Netscape, however, was not included. First, AOLA would launch into Brazil, Mexico, and Argentina and then later into the rest of the region. Cisneros wanted to include Spain and Portugal as well, but Pittman and Case already had a commitment with Emilio Botín, the head of Banco Santander, to work with him on the Iberian Peninsula.

The alliance with AOL also meant the coming together of Gustavo Cisneros and Steve Case. Cisneros considers Case the "great visionary" that "every group needs." "He is one of the few people with whom you can sit and discuss what is going on in the world, the reason for things." For Gustavo Cisneros, the alliance also meant the opportunity to establish even closer ties of friendship with Richard Parsons, an outstanding lawyer and adviser to Nelson Rockefeller, and now chairman and CEO of AOL-Time Warner.

The partnership was announced to the public on December 15, 1998. The magazine *AméricaEconomía* published an issue with a photograph of Cisneros and Case on the cover and the caption: "The alliance that will change the Internet." The two men were bringing a proven functional technology into a region where, although other providers existed, only 2.5 million people had access to the Internet; it had an enormous potential for growth and increased penetration. Although there was a good deal of optimism, they opted not to make specific predictions, as had been done with DirecTV Latin America.

The AOL-Cisneros partnership had points in common with the Hughes-Cisneros partnership in DirecTV Latin America. In both cases, a Venezuelan company associated with an international partner in order to encompass an entire region. In both cases, the partner from the north contributed the technology, with Cisneros, bringing his knowledge of Latin America, plus cash.

AOL embodied the Internet in the United States. The company strove to make browsing simple and intuitive for the many users who had been frustrated by the PC's complexity in the era of DOS. Content was distributed in what were called thematic "channels," ranging from health to love to news; and a voice made famous in a film starring Meg Ryan and Tom Hanks would announce "You've got mail" when someone received an e-mail.

Furthermore, AOL was not a traditional company refitted to enter what was being called "the new economy." In fact, many traditional companies that attempted to conquer the new medium failed, as was the case with Disney and Time Warner. AOL, on the other hand, already had twelve million subscribers at the end of 1998, and it added almost a half million new clients every month. Even more important, AOL made money after it reached the ten-million-subscriber mark. It was enjoying an attractive business model: more users also meant more people interacting in its chat rooms, which made them seem more attractive, which in turn drew new users. AOL had become the de facto operating system for the Internet in the United States, and it was surpassing Microsoft, its most significant competitor, the promoter of MSN.

Cisneros had acquired a first-class partner.

The Cisneros Group and AOL opted for a small managerial structure and a partnership in which Cisneros and AOL would be equal partners (50-50). The partners also agreed that management at AOLA would be independent.

However, to avoid excesses of independence, a control mechanism was chosen: a "steering committee" consisting of one person from AOL (Jack Davies) and another from the Cisneros Group (Cristina Pieretti, executive vice president of operations in Venezuela).

America Online Latin America (AOLA) began operating in São Paulo on November 15, 1999, eleven months after the announcement of the partnership of AOL and Cisneros. The launch of this exciting venture demanded a spectacular event generating so much excitement that everyone in the country would know that AOL had arrived in Brazil. The organizers devised a three-day agenda.

The launch would begin with a dinner at the United States embassy, with a group of special guests. Then Gustavo Cisneros and Robert Pittman would pay a protocol visit to the president of the country. Charles Herington, the CEO of AOLA, would visit the minister of education or of technology, or both. The press conference, the key event on the agenda, would be meticulously choreographed and rehearsed. When it was over, the directors would attend a round of individual interviews, giving preference to the local media.

The partners of AOLA who had contributed local content would have a special luncheon. The conclusion would be a gala supper, to which individuals from the local business world, functionaries, politicians, and the print media would be invited. The last named would have restricted access to the celebrities invited especially for the event. In the case of Brazil, they were counting on the presence of Michael Douglas.

The room selected for the press conference in the Renaissance Hotel in São Paulo was packed. In the midst of the fervor for the Internet, the arrival of AOL was an event that generated great expectations. At that time, a business plan with hints of the new economy and a smattering of words like Internet, networks, and breakeven attracted the attention of investors, analysts, and journalists. Besides, AOL was not just any dot.com. The largest Internet company in the world had come to Brazil. Cisneros' face revealed the enormous pride he felt. AOL had announced its merger with Time Warner. This meant that the Cisneros Group had formed a partnership not only with the leading Internet company in the world, but also with the largest group of entertainment companies on the planet.

It was a special moment. Cisneros wanted to remember his father. He told the reporters that he had made his first visit to Brazil when he was eighteen, and since then he had been impressed by the beauty of the country. Four years later, he added, his father had begun to bottle Pepsi-Cola in Rio de Janeiro.

"From that moment on, the investments and faith of the Cisneros family in the great destiny of Brazil were joined," Cisneros said.

That night there was a huge party in a newly fashionable, historic train station, with more than 3,000 guests attending. It was spectacular, and Cisneros was happy.

The launch was a success. However, there were difficulties inherent in an intensely competitive environment, which is what Brazil was at that time, above all with respect to the Internet. AOLA's installation CD, when employed by users, caused a "new" screen to appear on their computers, something that in no way affected the functionality of the PCs, but which disconcerted the clients. This, however, was used by others to create uncertainty and produce confusing propaganda about the process. Still, in the end, the problem was resolved satisfactorily.

In July 2000 it was Mexico's turn. This time Cisneros wanted to supervise the launch more closely to make certain there were no errors or oversights like the "new screen" issue in Brazil. The agenda, programmed down to the last second, followed a plan comparable to the Brazilian one. Of course, no one knew that Vicente Fox would be elected president eleven days before the arrival of AOLA.

Cisneros decided to request an interview with President Fox.

The carefully orchestrated agenda had to be changed in order to allow time for the meeting between Cisneros, Pittman, and the newly elected president. The Venezuelan entrepreneur thought it an opportune moment to meet again with Fox, whom he had known when the politician was working at Coca-Cola. He understood the symbolic meaning of the election of someone who had ended the PRI's seven decades of control. The country was experiencing a moment of euphoria. Furthermore, Cisneros saw in the new president a manifestation of the modern politician he had hoped for on the Latin American continent: one committed to democracy, openness, and education.

"Our primary task is not to interfere with businesspeople, to let them do their work," Fox told Cisneros. "We welcome AOLA to Mexico."

Cisneros, in turn, had praise for the elected leader.

"We find ourselves before a head of state who understands that we wish to contribute to political transparency, education, and growth in Mexico."

The arrival of the Internet and its impact on democracy and education was one of the issues that most engaged Cisneros, a sure topic of conversation for the Venezuelan and the leaders he visited. As he had with DirecTV, Cisneros saw in the Internet a valuable tool for improving education in Latin America.

Gustavo Cisneros also met with former President Ernesto Zedillo. At the press conference in the Four Seasons Hotel, Gustavo Cisneros mounted the podium and did something that won him the goodwill of the more than one hundred reporters gathered. It was difficult for him to gain their attention because Cisneros was flanked by the Mexican actress Salma Hayek as well as by Antonio Banderas, Boris Becker, and Magic Johnson. Most of the reporters had only a vague idea of who Gustavo Cisneros was, since his corporate presence in Mexico was limited, and, of course, it was logical that they would be much more interested in Hayek. Cisneros began by abandoning his script and saying: "I've just had a conversation with President Fox..."

He could not finish the sentence because the room burst into spontaneous applause. Normally, an opening like that could sound pretentious: someone boasting of his contacts with important politicians. But at that unusual moment, it won over the room.

"For us Mexico is the future, it is change, and we want to be part of that change," he said.

After the press conference, Cisneros, Hayek, Becker, Banderas, and Johnson gathered around a gigantic computer mouse and made a symbolic click to indicate the opening of AOLA México. Later a gala supper was held at the traditional Mexican Hacienda de Los Morales. The next day AOLA was everywhere in the press.

A month later, the AOLA retinue traveled to Buenos Aires. Cisneros told the local press, gathered in the Alvear Palace Hotel: "AOLA will be the greatest Internet company on the continent."

Once again the ritual of the giant mouse was carried out, again, with Salma Hayek and Magic Johnson present as well as Ruth, a popular Argentine disc jockey on MTV.

The directors of AOLA stressed the worldwide success of AOL, with its 24 million subscribers, and declared that they would invest aggressively in publicity to introduce the service to the market that consisted of the richest population in Latin America. In fact, they flooded the streets with 1.3 million installation CDs.

For the gala supper they chose the elegant Teatro Colón, symbol of the resplendent past of the Argentine capital, and hired a well-known local designer, Juan Rossi, to decorate the room. The celebration had musicians, dancers, and enormous banners that hung from the ceiling and lent a European air to the celebration.

AOLA's arrival in Argentina coincided with its appearance on NASDAQ, the U.S. stock exchange primarily comprised of technology companies. It was an act of daring, considering that U.S. investors had already lost their appetite for everything that smelled of the Internet or the new economy. The opening price was eight dollars a share, half the amount they had expected.

The bursting of the Internet bubble meant a belt-tightening at AOLA; the partners needed to dig into their pockets to finance the start-up of the Internet provider. The business burned money, more toward the end of 2001 when AOLA found itself in the front ranks with Terra Lycos, Prodigy (of Teléfonos de México), and UOL (almost exclusively in Brazil). The number of subscribers signing up for the AOLA service was good, but the company could not uncork the champagne yet.

The dot-com debacle was only part of the problem; the devaluation of the Brazilian *real* in January 1999, combined with stiff competition from UOL and the free Internet providers, meant that AOLA was earning a little more than ten dollars a month per subscriber, less than half of what its Mexican counterpart earned. In an attempt to gain a stronger position in Brazil, AOLA signed an agreement with Banco Itaú, the second largest private financial entity in the country. The bank had seven million clients, of whom 1.4 million used its on-line services, which could be shifted to AOLA. AOLA ceded 12 percent ownership to the bank in exchange for $20 million and the commitment to bring in 250,000 subscribers before Christmas 2001, and an equal number the following year.

At least in Brazil, with the cooperation of Itaú, a recovery was beginning. The economic recession in Argentina, at its height when Cisneros came to Buenos Aires, would grow worse until AOLA was forced to adopt a lower profile and a strategy of slow, organic growth.

In Mexico, on the other hand, things were going well for AOLA. It would be the company's market with the highest billings, even better than Brazil.

For Gustavo Cisneros, the best news of all was how Latin Americans were embracing the Internet, confirming his predictions of 1996 and 1997. The year 2001 ended with fifteen million Internet users in the region. This figure was six times the number of subscribers at the end of 1998, when AOLA was announced. The overwhelming progress of the new medium was so great that even in Argentina, despite the economic devastation of the 2001 crisis, the number of Internet users that year jumped from 1.9 million in April to 3.1 million in December, according to the consulting firm D'Alessio/Irol.

The Internet, in fact, had surpassed the initial penetration of the telephone and television. And AOL continued to expand. At the beginning of 2002, AOL—which had merged with Time Warner—had 33 million subscribers worldwide. Half of the people in the United States who accessed the Internet did so with AOL software. Each AOL subscriber was connected for an average of seventy minutes a day, as compared to forty-seven minutes in 1998. The Internet had become part of people's daily lives.

The alliance with the Parsons-Pittman duo created a difficult problem in the Cisneros Group: the appearance of possible conflicts of interest between AOLA and DirecTV with regard to the pojected future technological convergence.

And this was precisely one of the many reasons why, in mid-2000, Gustavo and Ricardo made a decision formalizing a de facto situation: they selected the man who would be the new head of operations of the Cisneros Group, the one they knew was best suited for facing these kinds of challenges.

The appointment of Steven Bandel as executive president of the Cisneros Group was the culmination of the managerial restructuring started at the beginning of the 1990s. Ricardo Cisneros wanted to distance himself from day-to-day concerns and concentrate more on strategic issues, while Gustavo Cisneros wanted to focus on envisioning and planning new businesses. But they could not adequately perform these tasks, which demand time and dedication, with so many people reporting directly to them about countless operational matters. Now Bandel would assume all the operational responsibilities for the Group. This was not a matter of simply adding another title to Bandel's business card. Gustavo Cisneros tends to give a good deal of autonomy to his executives, on the condition that they produce good results and always keep him informed. The delegation of power to Bandel was real and broad. Operations in every country, as well as every vice president, would have to report to him.

An ex-colleague describes Bandel as a "balanced person who combines calm with efficiency." He has a serene, analytical manner that reflects his training in finance, and he prefers to inspire others by example rather than by imposing his authority. A man of few words, he enjoys listening. Perhaps his greatest strength is his ability to negotiate in difficult situations.

Bandel had been working with Cisneros for eighteen years and had passed the demanding test of being the director of the office of the presidency, the chief-of-staff position created by

Cisneros. He knew how Ricardo and Gustavo thought, and what they wanted for the Group. A few words from the brothers are all Bandel needs to implement a line of action. "They understand that if I make a decision, it's in line with what they themselves would do," Bandel says, referring to the Cisneros brothers.

In the final analysis, for Gustavo Cisneros apparent conflicts of interest can be rationalized if one steps back and takes a wider view of the situation. As Victor Ferreres, former president of DirecTV and current head of Venevisión, points out: "Gustavo has taught us to develop an ability to respond that allows us to maximize a favorable situation and reverse a negative one." After all is said and done, both AOL and DirecTV are technological tools for entertaining people and for doing what Cisneros considers his true reason for being—to help education and development in Latin America.

"This technology is the great equalizer of society. Everyone has a right to Internet access. We should turn it into a tremendous tool for helping the region in the field of education without losing sight of the fact that this should be implemented in terms of the human being, our customs and our needs."

For Cisneros, the Internet implied "a true transformation of Latin America" and an opportunity to integrate small, innovative entrepreneurs into the global economy.

DirecTV also played its part in his vision. In order for the dream of a digitally unified Latin America to be realized, he needed Pittman, Parsons, and Rupert Murdoch to be under a single Latin American umbrella held up by Cisneros. In 2000, the Venezuelan felt that the moment was near. By then it was clear that DirecTV and Sky could not continue their bloody battle and had to join together, just as Cisneros had wanted at the beginning. But first he had to convince two people to set aside possible differences for the sake of a more promising future. That was one of the tasks he assigned his recently appointed executive president and negotiator par excellence, Steven Bandel. The other was to put in order the investments he had made with his friend Thomas Hicks.

As Cisneros pointed out at the end of 1999: "We wanted to be pan-regional and we wanted to be in the Internet. We wanted to approach the Spanish and Portuguese market. Integrate Spain, Portugal, and the rest of the Americas."

15. King of Content

On April 17, 1997, Emilio Azcárraga Milmo, the Mexican media magnate, died of a brain tumor. Gustavo Cisneros felt the loss deeply. The Venezuelan appreciated and respected Azcárraga, who had kept him on the board of directors of Televisa until 1996, when Cisneros himself decided to resign because of the conflict of interests entailed in the launching of Sky by the Mexican group.

This outstanding businessman left to his son, Emilio Azcárraga Jean, an empire that produced more programming than the NBC, ABC, and CBS networks combined, and exported it to seventy-five countries. The Televisa Group included three music labels, seventeen radio stations, the largest cable TV system in the country, a majority stake in the Sky digital television company DTH in Mexico, and fifty magazines, including the Spanish-language versions of *Cosmopolitan* and *Good Housekeeping*.

But Azcárraga Milmo left his son, who was not yet thirty, only a sixth of the voting shares, and transferred to his shoulders the heavy burden of a debt of $1.8 billion. Azcárraga Jean had to confront a complicated series of power struggles among diverse groups with interests in Televisa, while he tried to keep the rest of the heirs united. Azcárraga Jean carried out a painful program of cost-cutting in order to gain the backing of Wall Street. He purged upper management of directors who did not approve his measures.

The young man faced serious obstacles to fulfilling his father's dream of projecting the enterprise into the world.

To reduce the group's debts, Azcárraga Jean ordered the sale of most of the shares Televisa owned in Univision, keeping only 13.6 million shares—5.7 percent of ownership—to maintain the special voting and veto privileges his father had negotiated with Cisneros and Jerry Perenchio in 1992. Since Perenchio had also been selling shares, the Cisneros Group, with 45 million shares—roughly 19 percent of the total—became the largest shareholder of Univision, whose business today includes two broadcast television networks (Univision and TeleFutura), and a cable TV network (Galavisión), whose numbers were excellent, along with other businesses in radio, music, and the Internet.

The second consequence was that, since Azcárraga was withdrawing, Cisneros would no longer compete with the Mexicans to buy a broadcast channel in Spain, one of the Venezuelan's longstanding dreams.

He wanted a channel in Spain because one of the constant pressures on the Group was the generation of sufficient content for TV. Latin American tycoons like Azcárraga and Marinho, and the large media corporations in the United States, considered the content they placed on their screens central to their own maintenance and growth. With DirecTV, Cisneros did have a valuable distribution tool, but that was comparable to a network of canals to irrigate an area in the desert: without water—the equivalent to content—the land lacks value. "Cisneros understands that distribution is important, but he knows that content is king," says a former collaborator.

True, the *telenovela* format traveled well from country to country. But *telenovelas* could not be the only fuel to move Cisneros forward, and it would be difficult to surpass Televisa and Globo in a field that was also attracting new players, like the Colombians. In the United States, his nephew Carlos Enrique was beginning to revitalize a group of channels that would enrich the programming the Cisneros Group was offering for pay television and could be useful for feeding Univision, but he needed even more. Spain and Argentina, the other great markets after Mexico that generated entertainment in Spanish, would form a good complement to his menu of channels, leaving only Brazil as unfinished business.

With Madrid and Buenos Aires in his sights, at the end of the 1990s, Cisneros' destiny became entwined with that of two individuals who burst onto the scene with ambitions as large as the amounts of money they had in their pockets. Juan Villalonga and Thomas Hicks were investment bankers, and Villalonga was also the first president of Telefónica in Spain after it had been privatized. Although they had very different personalities, both were infected with the enthusiasm still generated on Wall Street at that time by any stock that involved communications, entertainment, or the Internet. The entertainment industry in Latin America, according to the consulting firm Booz Allen & Hamilton, had sales of $32 billion a year, and 82 percent of that came from television. Cisneros' favorite medium continued to be the king of entertainment, but its ownership was still fragmented throughout the region and limited to local entrepreneurs. Many thought the sector was ripe for consolidation, but this, inevitably, depended on the actions of financiers like Villalonga and Hicks, who recognized that Latin America is a region as fraught with difficulties as it is promising.

Gustavo Cisneros viewed Spain as a bridge between Latin America and Europe, and the Group, in turn, as a platform for deepening and extending the Spanish language in the United States, with an interesting new source of content. His objective at the end of the 1990s was to become a major stockholder in an important Spanish channel. In April 1993, Cisneros had negotiated the acquisition of 18 percent of Antena 3 with Don Javier de Godó y Muntañola, the Count of Godó, but on that occasion Banco Central Hispano moved ahead of him. Subsequently, when Antena 3 was put up for sale early in 1997, Cisneros again explored the possibility of acquiring a percentage of the network, but he could not realize his aspiration.

During this time a new Spanish corporate star was born: Juan Villalonga. Known for having a dominating personality, the Spaniard brought to the business scene in Madrid the sharpness and bite of a Wall Street investment banker (he had worked at Bankers Trust). He realized very early on the appetite of investors for a project of convergence involving the telephone system, the Internet, and the media. If Telefónica, rich in resources thanks to its monopoly of local and international calls in Spain, was aiming at those hot industries, the price of its stock—something that obsessed him—could skyrocket, and what he saw as an inevitable flurry of consolidations in the telephone-system industry would begin. He began buying assets in telecommunications and the media, especially in Latin America.

Juan Villalonga and Gustavo Cisneros met for the first time in Caracas, in 1997, during Villalonga's visits to various Latin American capitals. They exchanged ideas regarding the direction of the communications industry. Villalonga invited the Venezuelan to participate in Vía Digital, the DTH project he was establishing to compete with Canal Satélite Digital, an equal partnership between the Prisa Group (owner of the newspaper *El País*) and Pierre Lescure, the French television baron who controlled Canal Plus, a kind of European HBO. Cisneros found the idea interesting. He needed a platform to place the new channels he intended to produce in Miami for DirecTV Latin America, though he knew that the existence of two satellite television companies for Spain made no economic sense. If Latin America, with 75 million homes that had television, had problems in accommodating both DirecTV and Sky, Spain with 12 million would do even worse.

Cisneros was betting that sooner or later Vía Digital and Canal Satélite Digital, the digital platforms for television direct to the home in Spain, would unite, just as he expected Sky and DirecTV to join eventually, which meant he would have participation in a large Spanish digital platform.

Evidently that was the dream. The problem was that Villalonga wanted to manage the DTH project in Spain, and the Prisa Group wanted to do exactly the same thing with Canal Satélite Digital. The impasse that existed in Latin America between DirecTV and Sky was being duplicated in Spain, though with different actors.

Cisneros proposed a solution: they should compete in programming but share the satellite in order to save money. A single satellite transmitting different feeds of programming, depending on the provider selected, made more sense.

"The idea of two satellites competing is obsolete," Cisneros said at the beginning of 1997, but Villalonga insisted on his own satellite.

At the beginning of 1998, the shareholders of Hughes and the Cisneros Group acquired 6.9 percent of Vía Digital with the option of raising their stake to 17 percent, equaling Televisa's percentage. Cisneros and Azcárraga, who could not reconcile their interests in order to act together in Latin America, now found themselves united under the roof of Vía Digital in Spain.

In the course of the next three years there would be a series of failures in the efforts to unite Vía Digital with Canal Satélite Digital. Both companies spent fortunes on exclusive programming. Tired of Vía Digital's losses, Televisa would withdraw from Villalonga's project. For his part, in the late 1990s Villalonga was at the height of his power, as he prepared his Internet project—Terra Networks SA—for an offering on the stock market, while investors and analysts applauded his vision of a great convergent empire consisting of television channels, distribution networks, and the Internet. With 2.3 million cable subscribers in Chile, Argentina, and Peru, he was the principal provider of pay television and the largest operator of telephone systems in all of Latin America. His television channels were leaders in viewership in Spain and Argentina. Not a month went by that Telefónica did not announce some spectacular deal or acquisition.

But in July 2000, brought down by a scandal of options for executives of his company, including himself, to buy shares, Villalonga resigned. He left with the distinction of having multiplied by seven the price of Telefónica shares, and changing the face of the company. The great beneficiary of the media battle between Prisa and Telefónica was the Spanish television viewer, who for thirty euros could obtain a complete package of seventy channels and several pay-per-view films. Satellite technology had demonstrated its strength. By Christmas 2001, out of a total of three million Spanish subscribers who paid to watch television, almost 1.9 million had bought their small satellite dishes.

While Cisneros was attempting to expand his influence in Spain, he also needed a strong partner for Latin America. On December 12, 1997, he thought he had found one, and he had a large bottle of champagne brought in for a group of executives with whom he was meeting in La Romana. Among them was a tall, soft-spoken Texan, a far cry from the well-known stereotype of the oil-business cowboy. It was Thomas Hicks, another financier who was about to make a spectacular entrance in Latin America. The atmosphere was very optimistic. Cisneros had his picture taken with Hicks and the bottle of champagne, and then they both signed a small symbolic contract. Hicks, Muse, Tate & Furst (HMT&F), the private equity firm headed by the Texan, was going to join with the Cisneros Group to create a fund whose "principal objective was the acquisition of interests in the transmission or programming of television or radio in Latin America and the Iberian Peninsula."

John Gavin, the former United States ambassador to Mexico, and a well-connected man, had brought the two together.

"I believe you ought to meet him," he told Cisneros, "to see what you can do together."

Their first meeting was held in Caracas, and they immediately established a warm relationship. Hicks appreciated the Venezuelan's perspective, which combined the astuteness of an investment banker—the result of so many years of interacting with Wall Street—with that of an entrepreneur knowledgeable in television.

Besides, they both liked to ski in Colorado.

Until the beginning of the 1990s, Hicks had been a financier not very well known outside his native Dallas, but he executed some brilliant maneuvers that earned him the recognition of his peers and the respect of a very loyal group of investors—principally large pension funds. In 1986 he bought the brands Dr. Pepper and Seven Up separately, merged them, and then sold the operation to Cadbury Schweppes. The deal sextupled the money for his investors. At the beginning of the 1990s, the Texan began to diversify his holdings in mass consumption toward the entertainment industry. It was the topic of the day and what investors wanted. Who was Hicks to swim against the current? As he told *AméricaEconomía* in 1998: "We are not in the sports business or the radio business; we are in the investment business."

At a television channel it is easy to squander money and lose a fortune. Hicks needed a local operator and found him in Cisneros. Cisneros, in turn, was joining a true star of investment banking. At the end of 1997, Hicks was managing $10 billion more in assets than consolidation players like Kohlberg, Kravis Roberts, & Co. Hicks formed part of what in the 1990s came to be called a private equity investor.

The term "private equity" refers to an outside investor who takes possession of a company—partially or totally—with the aim of subsequently selling that interest at a higher price. The rise in the price of assets and the impossibility of financing deals with "junk bonds" did away with the old LBO funds. Private equity funds tend to incur less debt for their acquisitions and prefer private and family-owned businesses, to which they bring capital and management in order to sell them later, either to the public on the stock market or directly to a strategic buyer. They rarely opt for a hostile takeover.

Until the end of the 1990s, the historic annual return that Hicks had achieved for his investors approached 40 percent.

Hicks wanted to invest $1.2 billion in a communications empire in Latin America. If things went well, he would add another $800 million.

The Texan, who combined cowboy boots with Armani suits, conquered the Latin American businessmen with his open, direct personality. He would take them to the stadium to see his baseball team, the Texas Rangers, play.

According to Hicks, a "relationship of mutual trust" was established between him and the Venezuelan entrepreneur. He invited Cisneros to join his "strategy council" for Latin America. There he would be part of a select group of advisers to Hicks, among whom were three former ministers of finance (including Hernán Büchi, the architect of the so-called "economic miracle" in Chile). Hicks paid them "the equivalent of the remuneration received by a member of the board of directors of a Fortune 100 company" for attending a couple of summit meetings a year to review the investment portfolio and debate potential purchases.

In November 1995, Hicks made an exploratory trip to Buenos Aires and was delighted when he returned. "The business culture in Argentina is very similar to the one in Texas," said the banker. "Both share a rural inheritance, they like ranches, and they believe in a handshake, not in lawyers." His first inroads seemed to confirm his positive impressions. At the beginning of 1997 he bought a small cable television company in the province of Buenos Aires for $104 million. Almost ten months later he sold it again at a profit of $125 million. By the time of the December meeting in La Romana, Hicks wanted more, much more.

Cisneros and Hicks each contributed approximately $250 million of value to the new fund born at La Romana. Named Ibero-American Media Partners, it would be known as IAMP. In another gesture of confidence, for which Hicks would be grateful, Cisneros put $75 million into another fund the Texan was amassing for his Latin American project, focused on Argentina.

IAMP was the content component that Gustavo Cisneros was missing to establish a solid platform on which to consolidate his communications organization. He knew that with $500 million he would not go very far at a time when the purchase prices of television channels were inflated. But it was a beginning. The idea was to bring the fund to $2 billion. Carlos Enrique Cisneros, Gustavo's nephew, would head the pay-channels division, and Carlos Bardasano, who was then head of Venevisión, would manage the broadcast channels and radio division.

Gustavo Cisneros had a good number of assets to bring to IAMP, such as the broadcast channel and the radio stations he owned in Chile. Hicks did the same with other radio stations he had bought separately in that country, and they formed a network that comprised 40 percent of market share in Chile.

Cisneros' other contribution to IAMP was the Cisneros Television Group (CTG). This business had been created to generate segmented content for the growing pay-television industry, as well as to make an attractive addition to DirecTV. It was a creation of the efficient and charismatic Carlos Enrique, who knew how to impart to CTG the magic that Miami Beach brought to all things Latino. His offices on Washington Avenue were spacious, open, youthful, and functional. He asked his creative people and his executives to participate in community activities, and he would lend CTG facilities for receptions and events organized by the city. Thanks to him, the name Cisneros began to have more exposure in Miami media and philanthropic circles.

Carlos Enrique knew it was a mistake to generate programs to compete with the large American channels. Not even the Europeans had been able to displace a powerful Hollywood. Instead, he attempted to join with other companies to create thematic channels. Many niches were full, such as programming for children (Nickelodeon, Cartoon Network), news (CNN in Spanish), or films (HBO, Movie City). In the segments where there was no offering, CTG presented a partner to act as distributor and add a Latino touch to programming. In September 1996, an agreement was signed with Playboy Enterprises Inc. to distribute Playboy's content throughout Latin America, Spain, Portugal and the U.S. Hispanic market. (A similar joint venture with Playboy Enterprises was entered into in 1999 to launch adult-entertainment channels globally outside the United States and Canada.) Two months later they signed with Hearst Entertainment to launch Locomotion, an animated channel for young adults with series like *South Park* (it would be sold in June 2002).

Miami, with all its activity, was an important location, but to be a serious player it was necessary to make inroads in Argentina, the country that at the end of the 1990s had half the cable subscribers in Latin America. Whoever became strong in Argentina had an excellent base for expanding elsewhere. In mid-1997, the opportunity arose to buy Imagen Satelital, a programming provider with a portfolio of six channels: I-Sat and Space (films), Venus (adult), Júpiter (comedies), Uniseries (old television se-

ries), and Infinito (documentaries). The owner of Imagen Satelital, the local entrepreneur Alberto González, set his price: $114
million. It was high, and there was intense debate over whether it
was worth paying this price. But Cisneros was prepared to close
the deal because of its strategic advantages.

Imagen Satelital actually was a minor complication compared to the great imbroglio in which Tom Hicks was becoming involved.

The Texan had become enthusiastic about Raúl Moneta, a
banker who seemed to open all the doors to economic and political power in Argentina, yet turned out to be a very bad partner.
When the president of the United States, Bill Clinton, visited
Argentina in 1997, he went to Moneta's ranch with President
Carlos Menem to have wild boar barbecue and enjoy the banker's valuable dancing horses.

Hicks became associated with Moneta when the Argentine
was president of CEI Citicorp Holdings Inc., a vehicle created by
Citicorp at the beginning of the 1990s to exchange certificates of
debt for shares in companies that were being privatized by Carlos
Menem. Behind CEI was a small group of influential figures, all
of them graduates of the same secondary school in Quilmes, on the
outskirts of the capital: Moneta, Ricardo Handley, and the former
president of Citicorp, John Reed. In a very short time CEI had
purchased shares in nine telecommunications companies, seven
cable operating companies, three dedicated to the Internet business, and twelve involved in television, radio, magazines, and program production. Together, this group of investments generated
revenues of $5.5 billion in 1997, attributable primarily to the 50
percent interest that CEI had in a partnership that controlled—
along with Telefónica of Spain—the principal telephone company in the country. It owned shares in Telefé, a company that bought
the rights to the local soccer championship, an entertainment
magazine with a wide circulation, and Cablevisión, the largest
cable company in Latin America, with 1.5 million subscribers.
Not bad for someone who began with Banco República, a small
investment bank. By the time Hicks came on the scene, Moneta,
with 32 percent, was the largest shareholder in CEI.

In April 1998, the Texan traveled to Buenos Aires to see Moneta, who arranged a meeting with Menem. The president was delighted that an investor of Hicks' stature wanted to invest in Argentina. Hicks enjoyed a barbecue at Moneta's ranch. There they reached a verbal agreement according to which neither man would do anything at CEI without the consent of the other.

The ink on the check for Hicks' $500-million investment in CEI had not yet dried when Banco República suspended payments. Moneta was in serious difficulty. Hicks bought more shares in order to help him, and HMT&F eventually invested almost $750 million in CEI.

Argentina would deteriorate until it reached the traumatic devaluation at the beginning of 2002, which put an end to ten years of monetary stability. The crash dragged down another of Hicks' gambles, the sports channel PSN, which had spent a fortune on rights to events like the Copa Libertadores and Fórmula Uno. In February 2002, PSN declared bankruptcy.

In August 2001, Hicks dismantled his operation in New York that supervised Latin America—an attempt to raise between $700 million and $1 billion from institutional investors had met with a very cold reception—and he decided to return to his roots: the purchase of mass-consumption companies that were rich in cash flow (in May he had bought the company that prepared the Yellow Pages for British Telecom).

Hicks was looking for a way out of IAMP. Cisneros found the solution in Roberto Vivo and an Internet project called El Sitio.

In August 2000, when Gustavo Cisneros was launching AOLA in Buenos Aires, he attended a party in the pleasant offices of the channel Much Music, on Calle Humberto Primo in the picturesque district of San Telmo. It was a building that had the melancholy charm of old Buenos Aires, with huge windows, creaking floors, and very high ceilings. Everyone in Argentina who had any connection to Cisneros was there, including the people from Imagen Satelital and El Sitio, an Internet portal.

Much Music was a happy inheritance from the acquisition of Imagen Satelital. Ralph Haiek, an Argentine entrepreneur, took the Much Music franchise from Canada and brought it to Buenos Aires with the idea of competing with MTV, which at the time was operated from Florida, and did not have any content that was too local. The announcers spoke in Caribbean Spanish about what was happening on Ocean Drive in Miami Beach, while young Argentines were more interested in Avenida Santa Fe and the Buenos Aires neighborhood of Palermo. Haiek created a dynamic and inexpensive operation, with Argentine creative people and announcers who rarely were more than twenty-five years old. In the studios they had a cubicle where visitors could record a message that was aired later; or they placed a chair and a couple of microphones in the middle of Calle Florida, in the center of Buenos Aires, to encourage people to strum a few notes on the guitar, which the channel would later broadcast. The viewership of Much Music skyrocketed, forcing MTV to make its content more local.

Imagen Satelital was a distributor of Much Music, and Carlos Enrique Cisneros, Gustavo Cisneros' nephew, fell in love with the concept. He bought the operation from Haiek, who went on to become creative director for Imagen Satelital's six pay channels. The idea was to repeat Much Music in the rest of Latin America, always following the same philosophy of localization. Gustavo Cisneros also liked Much Music, which somehow balanced the concept of a regional channel (the same trademark for all of Latin America) with content adapted to each country.

But on that August afternoon in 2000, the entrepreneur had other things on his mind besides the launching of AOLA and the festivities taking place at Much Music. He located the Uruguayan-Argentin businessman Roberto Vivo, president of the board of directors of El Sitio, 18 percent of which belonged to the Cisneros-Hicks partnership, and the two men met.

Gustavo Cisneros proposed a merger of IAMP and El Sitio. The Cisneros-Hicks partnership would bring in thirteen television channels (twelve of them channels for pay television) and eight radio stations, a formidable operation in the Southern Cone countries, but with significance for the rest of the continent thanks to the Playboy joint venture and Locomotion. Vivo's contribution consisted of the traffic that El Sitio attracted and part of the proceeds raised from its initial public offering at the end of 1999.

The Venezuelan explained the logic of the merger. By combining IAMP's television and radio assets with El Sitio's Internet assets, they could create a pan-regional entertainment company capable of creating, gathering, packaging, and delivering differentiated content across multiple media platforms. Such a company would be appealing to advertisers that wanted to target specific audiences with strong purchasing power throughout the region. Vivo, who had already been approached several weeks earlier by Carlos Enrique regarding the merger, said he loved the idea and had also been thinking for some time along those same lines. Vivo, reflecting on this conversation with Cisneros, says: "That is what distinguishes the multimedia approach, because one really aims at segmented audiences, but by reaching massive individualization of those segments. As a consequence, one can offer the client a much more clearly identified target audience and campaigns with much more precise results for each dollar he invests."

For example, if a promoter needs to sell tickets for a U2 concert in Santiago, he places advertisements on El Sitio's pages on the Internet aimed at young fans of rock music, as well as in chat rooms on the subject and channels with news about rock music within the site. The message is reinforced on radio stations and on a Chilevisión program oriented toward young people. IAMP-El Sitio charges the client only if a minimum number of tickets are sold. Vivo called this "anticipating technological convergence with entrepreneurial convergence."

It was the philosophy that motivated the merger of America Online and Time Warner in the United States, where the old communications media were incorporating the latest technologies of interactivity and segmentation. The operation of Hicks, Cisneros, and Vivo would be something similar, but smaller and carried out with Latino creativity.

Cisneros offered Roberto Vivo the position of chairman of the board and chief executive officer of the operation, with Carlos Bardasano and Rick Newman as vice chairmen of the board; the latter was Hicks' idea. The combination would have revenues of close to $100 million a year. The Argentine accepted. "Now the investment banks will come to evaluate how much each one's contribution is worth," the Venezuelan entrepreneur concluded.

But in the interim a problem emerged: by now investors were losing patience with the promise of the Internet. Vivo had launched El Sitio at the height of investors' enthusiasm for portals, when details like earnings or cash flow did not matter very much. When El Sitio appeared on the stock market in December 1999, its price was $16 a share. It immediately shot up to $33 Twenty days later it reached its high: $39.30.

The story of what came next is well known. The United States Federal Reserve began to raise interest rates in order to cool off an economy that had seen continual growth for nine years. The brake on investments was a blow to technology providers, and increasing doubt regarding the Internet business model began to emerge. Portals suffered a double blow because their income came from advertising, which decreased because of fears of a recession in the United States. Uncertainty regarding Latin America increased investors' uneasiness, and the price of stock in El Sitio, whose losses were high, as were those in the rest of the sector, nosedived. El Sitio's share price fell below the minimum one dollar per share required for listing on NASDAQ. The fluctuations in the price of El Sitio stock meant that it would be difficult to determine the percentage corresponding to each partner in the new company devised by Cisneros. There were times when the deal was about to fall through, but Steven Bandel, chief of operations for the Cisneros Group, used his skills as a negotiator to convince Vivo to give his blessing to the agreement. In November 2001, Claxson Interactive Group made its formal debut. The old shareholders in El Sitio held 20 percent, the Cisneros Group owned 45 percent, and Hicks had 35 percent.

The years 1999 to 2002 were particularly difficult ones for Latin America. Added to the collapse of the stock market on Wall Street were the recession in the United States, the attacks on the Twin Towers and the Pentagon on September 11, 2001, the war in Afghanistan, and massive devaluations in Brazil, Ecuador, Argentina, and Venezuela. Latin America continued to fluctuate between excess and scarcity, famine and feast.

Gustavo Cisneros also felt the blow of the crisis in technology stocks and the recession in the United States, as well as the depression in Argentina, but he had the foresight to protect the downside. The challenge, entrusted to Roberto Vivo, was for Claxson to show the way to convergence in an environment of extreme austerity. The staff at El Sitio, in fact, was reduced from four hundred employees to forty. Claxson began to explore new forms of interactivity between television and viewers. Today, its Internet business provides broadband content to AOLA (Cisneros' joint venture with AOL), Cablevisión (belonging to Hicks), and all the channels in the group. Much Music, a channel that shows fewer and fewer video clips and more and more varied programming for young people, airs a program— *Te Gusta, No Te Gusta*—that places video clips on one part of the screen and a live chat session on the other, access to which is through El Sitio. Viewers who have a Webcam can also send an image and a greeting.

The documentary channel Infinito was relaunched as a channel specializing in topics having to do with the new millennium. UFOs, ghosts, and other supernatural matters, with a number of its own productions, comprise its offerings. The channel, which already has more than ten million subscribers, is the only one originating outside the United States to reach that mark in Latin America. The next challenge is to place Infinito in the Hispanic market in the United States.

Claxson's traditional and new media assets are a media mini-empire. In addition to *Much Music*, which is strong in the Southern Cone countries, Claxson owns HTV, a Latino music channel with good distribution in northern Latin America and in the U.S. Hispanic market. A techno beat usually accompanies the models on the runway on Fashion TV. Then there is DMX Latin America, a provider of digital music channels grouped according to music genres and distinct audio landscapes.

Claxson's portfolio does not stop there, and the offerings and distribution of new channels are expanding. Among these are

Space, a film channel; I.Sat, a channel of entertainment for viewers between eighteen and thirty-five; Retro, a classic film channel; Playboy, Spice Clips, and Venus, adult entertainment; Crónica TV, 24-hours-a-day news; Venevision Continental, family entertainment; and Chilevisión, one of the five television networks with national coverage in Chile, which is a general channel that reaches thirty-five major cities and 98 percent of the population.

In addition, there are 120 radio stations in the networks Pudahuel FM, Corazón, Rock & Pop, FM Dos, FM Hit, Futuro, Imagina, and Concierto, with 40 percent of the Chilean audience. In Uruguay, Claxson operates the Sarandí radio network, which controls both AM and FM circuits.

Through its state-of-the-art facility in Miami, Claxson also provides network origination, dubbing, subtitling, and post-production services.

Claxson's formation came in the midst of a total financial drought, when investors were bolting Latin America after the Argentine devaluation in January 2002. Brazilian certificates of debt were being devalued as a union leader with a populist background, Luiz Inácio Lula da Silva, was rising in the presidential polls. Venezuela experienced moments of extreme political tension, and there was no letup in the internal conflict in Colombia. Success stories like Chile and Mexico seemed to be solitary exceptions. Outside Latin America, the winds of war were blowing through the Middle East, and the economy in the United States had not yet recovered from the blow it received on September 11, 2001.

In order to achieve figures in the black, the management of Claxson moved cable-channel operations from Miami to Buenos Aires, where labor costs were low following the devaluation. Staff in the United States was reduced from 150 to 12. In the Argentine capital, offices were concentrated into a single facility instead of two. Claxson reversed its negative EBITDA earnings before interest, tax, depreciation, and amortization of almost $4 million in 2001 on a pro forma basis to a positive one of $10 million in 2002. In 2003, when Argentina was beginning to show economic recovery, the EBITDA reached $14 million.

DirecTV and Claxson reflect how faithful Cisneros continues to be to his goal of vertically integrating distribution with content. This has been the guiding principle of the Cisneros Group since the days of Diego Cisneros and Pepsi-Cola.

"We have withdrawn from sectors that did not have an international future and integrated into others that do, by means of our ties with Canada, the United States, and South America," says Cisneros. "For this reason, we endure and grow, even more so when times are bad. The group maintains a strategy of vertical integration, of controlling everything from manufacture or creation to distribution, which is what yields the greatest dividends in the long term."

Cisneros' commitment to the region during difficult times, something he considers his continual challenge, has made him an even more valuable partner in the eyes of large international business groups. In November 2001, when the magazine *Forbes Global* published a piece on Cisneros entitled "The Visionary," Marjorie Scardino, CEO of Pearson—the company that controls the *Financial Times*, among other media—wrote to him: "Congratulations...I haven't lost hope that our paths will cross one day." One of the heads of Vivendi Universal wrote: "A great article and great potential. I'd love to discuss it with you the next time you're in NY."

But Cisneros would not consider his vision complete until he could join Murdoch, Marinho, and Azcárraga under a single large satellite umbrella. That was his new challenge.

16.   An Obstacle Course

It was almost inevitable that the paths of Gustavo Cisneros and Rupert Murdoch would eventually cross. Cisneros was attracted by the concept of employing satellites to offer television on a regional scale; Murdoch was doing it throughout the world with his SkyGlobal project. The two men had been about to make a deal together in Spain, but it had fallen through.

The rise of Rupert Murdoch is one of the most notable achievements in the communications industry. At the age of twenty-three he took over a newspaper given to him by his father. Young Murdoch's guiding principle was clear: to give people the news in a way that was pleasing, entertaining, and—why not?—scandalous. He was not overly concerned by critics who accused him of distributing content of very low quality that appealed to the baser instincts of human beings. For him, these criticisms were the reactions of his competition, which did not know how to please and attract audiences. He defined himself as an iconoclast who was shaking up industries traditionally dominated by oligopolies.

Cisneros was heedful of the steps Murdoch was taking to structure his DTH platform—that is, his satellite-television business. Murdoch already understood in 1987 that in order for digital television via satellite to be acceptable to Hollywood, it needed a practically infallible encryption technology to avoid the piracy of signals. In less than a year he recruited a team to start a company in Israel that owned the patents to create the encryption technology that would reassure the movie studios. Even DirecTV uses Murdoch's encryption technology.

In the 1980s, Murdoch gave a new face to News Corp., his international media group, when he launched the Fox network in the United States. The channel was a success, and he subsequently added others: Fox Family, Fox Sports, and Fox News. At the start of the third millennium, Murdoch turned seventy and News Corp. was one of the great entertainment enterprises in the world, along with AOL Time Warner, Sony, Bertelsmann, Disney, Viacom, and Vivendi Universal.

Although the foundation of his empire is currently in television, Murdoch's heart is still in newspapers.

"Rupert has two passions, though I don't know exactly in what order," says Gustavo Cisneros. "He's very political, and he's a born publisher." And Cisneros confesses: "I identify a good deal with him, I'd like to be a publisher; it's what I'd like to do most."

Cisneros and Murdoch were communicating on the same frequency. Both had the capacity to look ahead and detect opportunities that lay beyond the horizon. Both, moreover, maintained the family stamp of their businesses. Despite the public character of News Corp., Murdoch tends to tackle new challenges guided by his instincts, not worrying too much about the opinions of Wall Street analysts, who are always obsessed by earnings in the current quarter. That same attitude had led Cisneros to leave the lulling security of Pepsi-Cola and Spalding for projects like DirecTV and AOLA, which had great potential value but initially needed capital and cash.

They both agreed on television's ability to channel the imminent digital revolution. BSkyB, the satellite television company that Murdoch owns in the United Kingdom, was already pointing the way with its five million registered subscribers at the end of 2001, most of whom regularly used the interactive services offered by the company. In Europe, Domino's Pizza sold more on interactive television than through its electronic business sites on the Internet.

Under the trademark Sky, Murdoch's satellites operated over Europe, Asia, and Latin America, but the United States was needed to complete the picture. Launching a new service in the United States would be too costly, which meant Murdoch would have to buy one of the two established players: Hughes Electronics, with 10.3 million subscribers at the end of 2001 (not counting the Latin American operation with Cisneros), and EchoStar Communications, with 6.4 million subscribers. He had already attempted to form a partnership with Charlie Ergen, the owner of EchoStar, but negotiations failed. The two men were too independent to work together.

Murdoch wanted Hughes. If he could buy it, DirecTV could finally join with Sky in Latin America, and Cisneros would have the single platform he had dreamed of. Murdoch had a strong stomach for tolerating the challenges of the world of communications and entertainment, but he was aware of his limitations. He understood the English-speaking world, but for the Spanish-speaking world he needed partners, and Cisneros knew it.

As soon as he learned that General Motors wanted to sell Hughes Electronics, Cisneros decided to make a couple of telephone calls. He located his friend Henry Kravis and asked him if he was interested in joining a group to buy Hughes. He said the business would be operated by the Cisneros Group, and that he was prepared to invest capital, though the bulk of the financing would have to come from a group of financiers. He explained that it would have to be a friendly acquisition because the Cisneros Group was not interested in a hostile takeover. Kravis said he was interested.

After a few more calls, Cisneros had a small list of potential financial partners, including Texas Pacific, and preliminary contacts with Citigroup.

Cisneros mentioned his idea to Michael Smith, the CEO of Hughes at the time, who indicated that he would consult with the directors of General Motors regarding the possibility of accepting an offer. If there was interest, Cisneros would sit down to study the numbers.

General Motors' response was that it was willing to sell Hughes as long as the buyer was the operator. The company was not interested in a financial group because there would be no synergies with other operations in the world. General Motors also stated that it had begun talks with Disney, General Electric (owner of NBC), Viacom, and News Corp., and Cisneros was asked to join one of those groups. Charlie Ergen's EchoStar was also interested but was having problems obtaining financing.

In the months that followed, interested parties fell by the wayside, and Murdoch ended up as the sole bidder. General Motors imposed a condition for selling Hughes to him: he would have to negotiate an alliance in Latin America between Sky and DirecTV. In this way, maximum synergies would be derived the from the acquisition, which was consistent with what GM had told Cisneros earlier.

GM asked Murdoch for a written agreement among the five principal partners involved in Sky-DirecTV: Hughes Communications, the Cisneros Group, Globo, Televisa, and News Corp.

In mid-2000, talks among the parties began. Representation of the Cisneros Group fell to Steven Bandel, who was aware that the talks would not be easy. The two groups had attempted to merge earlier but could not overcome obstacles related to the programming that could be transmitted from the DTH platform. Basically, Televisa and Globo wanted to retain the right to veto channels to protect the programming costs of their cable networks on the ground. In this way, if a program supplier like HBO threatened to raise prices, the Mexicans and Brazilians could have a very powerful negotiating chip, because they would control not only the content of their cable networks on the ground but what DTH, their principal competitor, would transmit.

Gustavo Cisneros, on the other hand, believed that each asset had to maximize its value, even at the expense of other assets in the same group. "They (Televisa and Globo) believe in policies of control, and they demanded rights that were very difficult to grant," Bandel explains. "We had been talking about a merger for years, and we could never come to an agreement because of the issue of control of programming. It's very difficult to close a deal when they control content at our expense."

Although Murdoch agreed with Cisneros on this issue, they had to find the middle ground that would leave everyone satisfied.

Bandel thought it would be a good idea to have a meeting in which the five shareholders would sit around a table until they had settled the problem of control. Perhaps more than one of them would lose patience at times, but eventually an agreement would be reached.

Instead of that, Chase Carey, the president of SkyGlobal and Bandel's counterpart in the negotiations, devised a negotiating plan that Bandel did not consider feasible. The Cisneros Group would not have the opportunity to talk face-to-face with Televisa and Globo. Any message that Bandel might have for Televisa would have to pass through Carey. Although he found the arrangement inefficient, he had no choice but to accept that rule of the game. The company buying DirecTV was Sky, and the common link among them all was Murdoch.

A skilled and experienced negotiator, Murdoch calculated—correctly—that Gustavo Cisneros was not going to be a problem because there was a perfect philosophical harmony between them. The owner of News Corp. foresaw more complications on the part of his own partners, Televisa and Globo. He was afraid that if he brought them together, the requirement of one of those partners would become a demand by all of them. On the other hand, if everyone negotiated through Carey, Rupert Murdoch could hold all the strings. Still, the negotiation did not turn out as Murdoch and his designated negotiator expected.

"What happened is that the Cisneros Group was not prepared to sign without first knowing the terms of the agreement with Televisa and Globo," says Bandel, "and Televisa and Globo said the same thing. In the end they had to show us the [bilateral] agreements, and everyone did the logical thing and said: 'Ah, you gave this to Televisa; fine, I want it too,' and 'You gave that to Cisneros; I want the same thing.' [Murdoch] had wanted the *least* common denominator, and what he got was the *largest*. He had to give everyone what he had conceded to each party individually."

In the end, the result was very similar to what would have been achieved if everyone had sat down to talk face-to-face. A serious problem was that months had been lost while Carey's office tried to coordinate an increasingly complex negotiation. Counting analysts, investment bankers, and corporate lawyers, Bandel had twenty people reporting to him. The papers of the bilateral agreement with Murdoch were piled high on the conference table, and the situation was repeated with each of the parties. Bandel calculates that in the final analysis, more than a hundred people were involved in the project.

By the time Carey realized that the system was not working, it was too late to begin again. During the year-and-a-half it took to try to reach an agreement, Bandel never sat face-to-face with his counterpart in Televisa or Globo.

Bandel and Carey could not convince Televisa and Globo to abandon their right to veto programming. They had to agree on a compromise: no partner could withdraw a signal without the consent of at least one of the other shareholders. Bandel says: "If they want to veto HBO or ESPN, they have to convince me or Murdoch. The decision cannot be unilateral." Of course, the door was open for the Brazilians and Mexicans to form an alliance to mutually support their programming decisions. "It wasn't the best situation," Bandel recognizes, "but in a negotiation everyone has to concede something."

In the agreement, rules were established for the valuation of each party's assets to determine what percentage would correspond to each of them in the new Sky-DirecTV partnership. First, they would hire an auditor to ensure that the financials were prepared in a consistent manner to guarantee that everyone was speaking the same language (when Sky entered a subscriber in its records, it used dates and criteria different from those employed by DirecTV).

Then, each of the five investment banks involved would prepare its own valuation for its respective client—Cisneros had contracted with Morgan Stanley Dean Witter—and there would be a session so that the five banks could try to reach an agreement on the basis for these valuations. If this failed, the process would be repeated with the shareholders, and if this was not successful either, then an independent mechanism for valuation acceptable to everyone would be created through a process of arbitration.

Bandel reported the progress of negotiations to Cisneros, who in turn met with Murdoch. It was a way to eliminate what Bandel calls "points of friction." Each time the two entrepreneurs reached an agreement, they would impart the relevant instructions to Carey and Bandel.

Negotiations continued slowly until August 5, 2001. On that day, Charlie Ergen of EchoStar decided to deliver his decisive blow. For more than a year Ergen had made public his interest in acquiring DirecTV, but the management of Hughes and the directors of General Motors had not paid much attention. They thought he did not have the resources to buy a company as large as Hughes, which at that time had a stock market valuation higher than General Motors'. Further, there was concern that the regulators might not approve a merger of that nature for fear of a satellite monopoly.

Tired of being ignored by Hughes, Ergen, who is known for his persistence, wrote a letter to the board of directors of General Motors in which he stated his readiness to pay $32 billion for the satellite subsidiary. The amount was higher than Murdoch's proposal. But the Ergen offer was exclusively in stock, while Murdoch was offering $7.2 billion in cash, thanks to the contributions of his multimillionaire allies Bill Gates and John Malone.

Two weeks after receiving Ergen's letter, General Motors agreed to negotiate seriously with the entrepreneur from Littleton, Colorado, but demanded at least $5.5 billion in cash. If he could offer that amount, DirecTV would be his.

Ergen had an advantage over Murdoch. If he joined his platform with that of Hughes, forming a single base of almost eighteen million subscribers in the United States, he would realize significant savings in the cost of programming and the satellite. The space freed up on the satellite would allow him to offer more local channels, which was one of the disadvantages of DTH compared to cable, and more interactive television services. Ergen calculated that in five years he could generate savings and/or additional income of up to $40 billion. Murdoch's intention, on the other hand, was oriented toward a vertical integration in the United States that would guarantee the distribution of the channels produced by News Corp. The real savings would come from Latin America, where Murdoch had estimated that the alliance of Sky and DirecTV would bring in $1 billion in two years. "It changes in a fundamental way the economies of this deal," he had told some analysts in June 2001.

With two bidders instead of one, the dynamics of the negotiations changed. It was no longer a cakewalk for Murdoch; the matter had turned into a race against the clock.

Ergen did not have the $5.5 billion that GM had demanded, but he worked very hard to secure it. In August even Cisneros had to recognize the entrepreneur's advantage: "Today, Ergen is in the lead." Murdoch had to conclude the agreement with his Latin American partners in order to make a formal offer to the General Motors board of directors.

Ergen's counteroffensive occurred when the partners of Sky and DirecTV Latin America were debating the difficult question of the valuation mechanism. Bandel and Carey agreed that they had reached a point where it would be useful for Cisneros and Murdoch to have another meeting to resolve their differences. Each party revised his calendar, and they set a tentative date: September 12, 2001.

That meeting became a question that has not stopped turning over in Steven Bandel's mind: what would have happened if it had been held a few days before the fall of the Twin Towers? Would the negotiations with General Motors have concluded differently?

The chaos that ensued after the events of September 11, 2001, found Cisneros in Los Angeles, where he had gone to attend the Latin Grammy Awards and a dinner being held for his friend Julio Iglesias. With the skies closed to commercial and private traffic, Cisneros was trapped in Hollywood for five days. Carlos Bardasano, who was also in Los Angeles, looked for all possible ways Cisneros could leave the city and keep his appointment with Murdoch; he even considered traveling by automobile, but this alternative was quickly abandoned because it would be impossible for a car to cover the 3,000 miles separating the two cities in time for the meeting. He also considered crossing the Mexican border , taking a plane to Canada, and then going by car to New York. Impossible. Gustavo Cisneros was stuck. At the same time, he was in anguish over the whereabouts of his daughter, Adriana, some of his children's friends in New York City, and his collaborators in the New York office. As Patty Cisneros recounts, he calmed down only hours later, when he spoke with them.

Murdoch, for his part, did not fare much better. The September 11 attacks found him in Washington. He traveled by car to New York but could not reach his house in Manhattan because the bridges were closed.

The meeting between Murdoch and Cisneros never took place. Bandel, who was in New York, appeared at Chase Carey's offices at the specified time, but neither man was in any condition to discuss the deal with the necessary calm. They could not believe that the nightmare was true, and they were concerned about the imminent threat of war. In their state of mind, they were not prepared to settle the valuation of assets.

On September 21, the directors of Hughes, General Motors, and News Corp. met to evaluate the situation. Murdoch's collaborators had to recognize that they were still far from reaching an agreement with their partners in Latin America. In the midst of general discouragement, and with the market in a nosedive, the directors of General Motors informed their counterparts at News Corp. that negotiations were suspended. The matter had to be ratified by their respective boards of directors the following week. Ergen, for his part, could not obtain financing after September 11. It was the worst moment in a process that already seemed eternal.

But Murdoch was not prepared to allow the deal of his life to slip through his hands so easily. He made a counteroffer, and General Motors, which needed cash to confront the imminent recession, decided to give the tycoon another opportunity.

Having absorbed the initial impact of September 11, the negotiators went back to the table to settle the question of valuation. By early October they had designed a three-step mechanism. First, an independent investment bank would valuate the five packages. If there was agreement, fine, but if anyone had an objection, a second investment bank would be asked for its opinion. If no agreement was reached in that instance, the opinion of a third bank would be requested. The value assigned by the last bank would be averaged with the result, provided by the previous two banks, that was closest to this amount. In other words, if a bank had valued a contribution at $2 billion, the second at $ 2.2 billion, and the third at $2.18 billion, the average would be derived from the last two, which are the ones closest to each other. This value would be binding on all parties. Cisneros, who owned a significant percentage of DirecTV Latin America, thanks to the success of the local operators in Venezuela and Puerto Rico, thought he ought to aspire to an ownership interest in the new Sky-DirecTV partnership, maintaining a position equal to that of his Latin American partners.

The plan was relatively complicated, but it was the only way to give a certain peace of mind to entrepreneurial groups like the Cisneros Group or Televisa, which had invested millions in their assets and now had to put them on a negotiating table and wait for the verdict of a third party to decide how much they were worth. It was like jumping into a pool blindfolded, not really knowing if there was any water in it. "It was difficult for all of us to digest that," says Bandel, "but at least we would finally reach an agreement."

On October 16, Gustavo Cisneros sat down in his office in Caracas and spent four hours listening to fifty lawyers and bankers expound and work on the details of the document that would shape the results of eighteen months of what surely had been the most difficult negotiation in the corporate history of Latin America. Once the representatives of Hughes, the Cisneros Group, Globo, Televisa, and News Corp. placed their signatures on that valuable document, they would take it to the board of directors of General Motors for its approval of the sale of Hughes to News Corp.

The teleconference ended with no upsets, to Cisneros' relief. For five long years he had worked to have a single DTH platform. Now the prize was close, very close. The General Motors board meeting was set for Monday, October 22. The only bidder was Murdoch. General Motors had to accept or reject his offer.

But Gustavo Cisneros had traveled this road too many times. He knew it had hidden obstacles and precipices. "This deal may be closed next week or in the next six months," he warned as soon as the telephone conference had ended.

And, in fact, a few hours after the conference, Bandel called his boss with bad news: there was a problem with the World Cup.

DirecTV Latin America had acquired the rights to two World Cups, Korea-Japan in 2002, and the next one, in Germany, in 2006. It was a $415-million stake that included five countries: Mexico, Colombia, Chile, Argentina, and Uruguay. The cost was high but Cisneros understood the incredible appeal of soccer in Latin America, and persuaded the board of directors to make the acquisition. The idea was to recoup the money by selling special packages to DirecTV subscribers, and by reselling the rights to broadcast channels for either cash or advertising space. If everything worked out, DirecTV Latin America would not only recover its investment, but it would have a powerful tool to distinguish them from Sky and the cable competition.

Televisa had argued that these rights were worth very little in Mexico because most of the games were transmitted in the middle of the night, and the network supposedly had an agreement with TV Azteca not to buy soccer rights except at market prices. That left DirecTV with few negotiating options. But in the meantime, Mexico qualified for Japan, and a third party approached DirecTV and offered a fair amount of money for the World Cup rights. Contrary to what Televisa had argued, the Korea-Japan World Cup had acquired significant value. Televisa, through the intermediary of News Corp., made its signature conditional on DirecTV guaranteeing that the World Cup would go to the company. That required Bandel to negotiate soccer transmission rights with Televisa, which was no easy matter. Once an agreement had been reached for the 2002 World Cup, Televisa added another demand: it wanted the 2006 World Cup in Germany to be reserved for it as well. Steven Bandel refused because with a guaranteed buyer, he was at the mercy of whatever price Televisa wanted to place on those rights. At that point, negotiations stalled.

Murdoch had to ask General Motors to postpone the meeting of the board of directors for a few hours in order to resolve the dispute over the World Cup. The board moved the meeting from Monday to Tuesday, and then to Saturday, October 27. General Motors told News Corp. it would not accept further delays.

Rupert Murdoch lost his patience. He told the Brazilians and the Mexicans that the agreement had to be signed as it was or he was pulling out of the deal with Hughes.

"Don't send lawyers; don't send anybody," the magnate warned, "because I'm not in the mood to negotiate with anyone."

It was the moment of truth: if the Mexicans really wanted to join the two platforms, they would have to accept Murdoch's ultimatum. Televisa gave in to the pressure.

A few hours after the decisive meeting at General Motors, Bandel could feel satisfied with what he had accomplished. The position of the Cisneros Group going in was not the best, because Globo and Televisa were already Murdoch's partners. It was logical to suppose they would obtain special advantages. Bandel felt that the agreement was equitable, and Cisneros agreed.

The board's delays due to international tension following September 11 suited Charlie Ergen perfectly. During that week he had convinced the management of Hughes Electronics of the merits of his proposal, and succeeded in calming the fears at General Motors that the authorities would veto the sale because of antitrust considerations. His sole problem was that he had only half of the $5.5 billion in cash that General Motors was demanding, and only until eleven in the morning of the following Saturday to find the rest. General Motors, according to press reports, indicated to News Corp. that if Ergen did not have the money by then, Hughes would be theirs.

On that Saturday, Steven Bandel, exhausted by several nights of little sleep, waited for news in Miami. Ricardo and Gustavo Cisneros, equally anxious, were in Madrid. They would speak at least ten times that day. Bandel recalls what happened: "On Saturday morning we received a call informing us that the decision was easy because the News Corp. offer was the only one GM had. They told us they foresaw no problems, and everything would be ready that afternoon. Then it was five o'clock, six o'clock...and they told us the meeting had been temporarily adjourned, which was strange."

Ergen, in a very bold move, had offered the equivalent of $2.75 billion of his shares in EchoStar as a guarantee for General Motors to lend him the money, so that he would have $5.5 billion in cash and the transaction would be concluded in his favor. He had made the offer very early on Saturday, and the board members had spent the day debating whether or not to accept it. It was somewhat irregular for the seller to finance the buyer, and an angry Murdoch said that at this stage of the game he was in no mood for an auction.

"Murdoch, who is a very skilled negotiator, did what he had to do and told the executives at GM: 'Either you decide today, or I withdraw my offer.' That was to force a decision," says Bandel. When General Motors adjourned the meeting without declaring a winner, Murdoch kept his word and fired off a press communiqué saying he had withdrawn his offer. General Motors had no alternative but to accept EchoStar's offer of almost 26 billion dollars, financed in part by General Motors itself.

The people at the Cisneros Group could not believe what had happened.

"We felt frustrated, surprised, depressed, in that order," says Bandel. "Depressed because the merger was the best outcome; it had been Gustavo Cisneros' vision for more than five years. We had succeeded in structuring a deal that was fair and viable for all parties, because if one wins and the other loses, it doesn't work. We created a structure in which everyone felt comfortable."

Murdoch lost because he could not solve the complex Latin American puzzle in time, and Ergen was able to score his last-minute goal. Bandel reflects on the incredible events that led to that October 27 meeting, and the questions that arise from it. If Cisneros and Murdoch had held their meeting on September 12, would Sky and DirecTV be joined today? What would have happened if Bandel had not received that last-minute offer to retransmit the World Cup in Mexico, which produced the objection from Televisa and the loss of five valuable days? "If the GM board had met two or three weeks earlier, the only proposal that would have been on the table would have been the one from News Corp., and this deal would have been closed."

Just as he was at the beginning of this process, Gustavo Cisneros is still confident that DirecTV and Sky will merge eventually. Some time will have to pass before the waters settle and matters can be seen clearly. The purchase of DirecTV by EchoStar meant a change in the balance of power in the entertainment world. The management of Vivendi Universal, Murdoch's important European rival, decided to invest in Charlie Ergen's project. Ergen did not have great Latin American ambitions, but by then the competition did. In addition, it was necessary to wait for the ruling of the authorities regarding the proposed merger of EchoStar-Hughes, which would continue operating with the name DirecTV, a ruling that eventually proved negative for EchoStar.

At the end of 2001, DirectTV Latin America had 1.5 million subscribers and was approaching its break-even point. Its growth, which began to accelerate between 1999 and 2001, showed that it was a formidable rival of cable in Latin America, which was very far from matching the rich offering of programs and the digital quality of DTH. Gustavo Cisneros' vision continued to be valid. He had lost an inning, but there was still a long way to go to complete the game.

In fact, recent developments in the saga have changed the panorama while simultaneously presenting new alternatives. In the United States, the EchoStar-Hughes transaction was blocked by the Department of Justice and the FCC. In the end, Ergen could not acquire DirecTV.

Meanwhile, the economic crisis in Latin America in 2002, the year in which it suffered its first recession in two decades, and less-than-expected subscriber growth, forced DirecTV to renegotiate the prices of contracts with its program suppliers. In January 2003, DirecTV tried to restructure its agreements with

Disney, HBO, KirchSport (the World Cup), and Clarín, among others, to allow a future profitable development for the company. Given the difficulty of reaching an agreement with the programmers and its key creditors, DirecTV Latin America filed for protection on March 18, 2003, under Chapter 11 of the U.S. bankruptcy code. The restructuring affected only DirecTV and not the local operators, such as Galaxy Entertainment of Venezuela, which continued normal operations.

The directors of DirecTV Latin America hoped that the end result would be a company with a solid financial position: all its debt capitalized or restructured and a structure of costs and expenditures adequate for confronting the dynamic Latin American market.

For its part, on April 9, 2003, Hughes announced an agreement in which News Corp. would acquire 34 percent of Hughes for $6.6 billion.

With News Corp. positioned to acquire control of Hughes, the option of merging the two satellite platforms in Latin America has been revived, and the possibility of a new period of negotiations based on the map of the initially proposed transaction remains open.

The story of this process continues. Cisneros is optimistic that a restructured and unleveraged DirecTV Latin America will be well positioned for the inevitable merger with Sky, a view that he has long held.

17. Transparency

> I would like my country to evolve toward the democratic center, and I am hopeful that this is going to happen.
>
> GUSTAVO CISNEROS

The Cisneros Group began as a group of companies with Venezuelan roots and international aspirations, and it gradually evolved into an international organization with a presence in Venezuela. But Cisneros had some surprises in store for those who thought his heart was closer to New York than to Caracas. As if to demonstrate that the Cisneros Group was still a force to be reckoned with in marketing, one of its companies in Venezuela developed an innovative strategy that would set a traditional monopoly reeling. The purchase of an old coffee plantation, a baseball team, and the creation of Vale TV, at a moment when the country was immersed in social and political upheavals, would further make explicit the deep-seated ties that link Cisneros to Venezuela.

By the early 1990s, the Cisneros Group had stopped operating as a centrally managed multipurpose entrepreneurial group, appropriate to the closed world of the 1970s. In a global economy, the axis of decision-making had to be moved from the center and greater autonomy given to the companies.

The new orientation was simple: each enterprise had to manage on its own. Those that could not succeed in this framework would be sold or liquidated.

Pizza Hut, Burger King, and Summa Sistemas (the exclusive distributor of NCR products in Venezuela) demonstrated sufficient autonomy to survive using their own resources. But Puro Pan, an inheritance from the days of Rockefeller, was liquidated because it could not operate independent of CADA, the supermarket chain. "We had to find the synergy without sacrificing the self-sufficiency of the group," explains Ariel Prat, the vice president for finances who worked on the transition, "because synergy means a channel of communication, but not an obligation or a relationship of dependency. Independence is achieved as you decentralize, because in this way you remove the excuse of the general manager who has to follow centralized orders. You no longer have the excuse that you did it because they told you to; you did it because this is your business."

Although the group was moving toward a decentralized model of management, there were certain functions within the group that remained centralized for strategic and cost reasons. For instance, the Cisneros Group maintains a legal department in Caracas that offers its services to the Venezuelan members of the group, so that each company does not need to create its own legal department or hire lawyers externally. These savings are shared and billed to the enterprises of the Cisneros Group, and they, in turn, are free to move to another "provider" if they wish.

There are other services that continue to be centralized, though in a manner different from the days of OCAAT and GURI. For example, the Group created an enterprise called Business Services Provider (BSP) in 1999. Using software from PeopleSoft, BSP can handle the administrative functions of a company, from the management of human resources to accounting, regardless of the industry involved. The manager of a firm makes a request via telephone, and BSP takes care of the rest. Everyone saves time, labor, and money. If general managers hire the services of BSP, it guarantees them a significant savings and the chance to concentrate on production and marketing, the heart of their business. BSP's investment in technology amounts to several million dollars, in addition to an annual payment to PeopleSoft. The advantage to the Cisneros Group is that it saves replicating administrative functions in all its companies, and the managers can focus on the company's business.

The Cisneros Group still functions in a centralized way when it is a question of important investments, as in the case of the transaction involving Drene shampoo, a well-known brand name in Venezuela, which was put up for sale by Procter & Gamble. It was an asset that suited FISA Kapina, the cosmetics branch of the Cisneros Group, but it was too expensive. To overcome this impasse, a price was agreed on with the multinational; FISA Kapina obtained the brand name under a licensing contract, and profits from the sale of the product covered the cost of the contract.

In a difficult economic climate, solutions like this allowed the Cisneros Group to keep its corporate health intact while continuing to participate in opportune deals.

Cervecería Regional is the best example of the success of the decentralization policy that Gustavo and Ricardo were implementing.

The Cisneros brothers acquired the brewery—founded in 1927—in 1992, with their cousin Oswaldo Cisneros. The brand was strong in Maracaibo, Venezuela's second-largest city, located in the west of the country in the state of Zulia, but it was not well distributed elsewhere in Venezuela. In fact, it had only 5 percent of the national market, but Cisneros wanted to use it as a point of departure for a Latin American beer project, and with an investment of $400 million, expansion soon began into other areas of the country.

As far as beer is concerned, Venezuelans are the Germans of Latin America; consumption is high, and there is general fondness for the product. At the end of the 1990s, Venezuelans consumed more than sixty-five liters per capita a year, more than Colombians, Panamanians and Mexicans. In fact, more beer is consumed in Venezuela than in Chile, Uruguay, and Argentina combined.

The beer market in the world has two peculiarities: it is dominated by local brands, and it gravitates toward a monopolistic situation. It is different from carbonated drinks, in which global brands like Coca-Cola or Pepsi-Cola predominate. Consumers embrace their national beers. Anheuser-Busch and Heineken are strong in their countries of origin but do not displace local products in Latin America.

Except for Mexico, in each country of Latin America there is one large brand that dominates the beer market, whether foreign or local. The combination of historic loyalty to a brand and the difficulties in creating a new distribution network seem to protect market leaders and known brands.

One of the few places where a smaller beer producer competed successfully with an established giant is, in fact, Venezuela: half a century ago, Polar, part of the business group of the Mendoza family, outstripped Cervecería Regional until it captured more than 90 percent of the market share. Gustavo and Ricardo Cisneros knew that gaining ground on Polar would not be easy.

Between 1992 and 1997, Cervecería Regional achieved internal growth because of improvements in distribution and in its Maracaibo plant, increasing its market share throughout the country from 5 percent to 9 percent. The great leap came after September 1997, when Gustavo Cisneros opened a new plant in Cagua, in the center of the country, which increased production capacity and allowed Cervecería Regional to add new distribution routes.

The key to the success of the beer business is marketing, a historic strength of the Cisneros Group. To compete with the Polar beer, it launched Catira. The word *catira* in Venezuela is used as a synonym for a blonde woman. As part of the market campaign for Catira, Cervecería Regional used a scantily clad statuesque woman who never shows her face on its billboards and advertisements. The image was accompanied by the provocative slogan: "I'm the other one," which in Spanish suggests "I'm the other woman."

In order not to lose momentum, another initiative as innovative as Catira had to be introduced in 2000. The directors decided to launch a new product but did not know if it should be a premium or a light beer. A visit to the United States, Colombia, and several Central American countries revealed that low-calorie beers were an interesting niche, although in Venezuela the segment amounted to barely 3 percent of the total market. An internal study said market share could double to 6 percent.

While alternatives were being discussed, the Cisneros brothers made a suggestion.

They wanted a beer in a clear bottle.

Beer in a clear-glass bottle complicated the manufacturing process. There is a reason why most beer is packaged in opaque bottles: exposure to sunlight alters its taste. Beer in transparent packaging relies on hops (the plant that gives beer its bitter taste) that have been specially treated to make it sun-resistant.

The complications in manufacturing were counterbalanced by the possibility of generating in Venezuela an effect similar to the one created in Mexico by Corona, a beer that is consumed all over the world.

The launching of Regional Light, Cervecería Regional's light beer in a clear bottle, is an example of the managerial style of Gustavo and Ricardo Cisneros. As opposed to the large multinationals that operate according to strict established procedures, in the Cisneros Group, managers have significant independence. Decisions regarding market sectors and the campaign for the new beer fell largely to José Rafael Odón, the president of Cervecería Regional, and Cristina Pieretti, the vice president for operations in Venezuela. "Cisneros makes you feel that you are part of this business; each of us feels that the Group is ours, there is nothing more powerful than giving a sense of ownership and responsibility to each executive," observes Pieretti.

There was a good deal of debate within the Cisneros Group regarding Regional Light. Some thought it was better to orient the brand name toward the traditional light-beer segment: women and people who wanted to limit their caloric intake. That was the profile of customers served by Polar Light. Others, however, argued that the light beer could achieve greater penetration if it were identified with a carefree, youthful life style (though it definitely would have less alcohol and fewer calories than its counterparts). Odón and Pieretti listened to the pros and cons and then chose the second option. "Beer is about self-gratification, refreshment, being with friends. Slimming down is at the bottom of the list of reasons for having a beer," said Odón.

The first Regional Light left the Cagua plant in November 2000. Gustavo Cisneros saw the clear bottles and the modern label—the typical medals and insignia were omitted—and he was delighted: "You're going to be short on production," he told Odón and Pieretti.

The Cisneros Group's marketing machine was set in motion. Cervecería Regional now dedicated 7 percent of its sales to advertising, in contrast to 3 percent when it was acquired in 1992. The goal was to turn the new brand into a desired object, because Regional Light cost 20 percent more than Polar Light, and 30 percent more than ordinary beers. To emphasize its transparent bottles, they began with the slogan "Flavor at first sight."

Regional Light turned out to be one of the most successful launches in Venezuelan history, perhaps since the time Antonio had and Diego Cisneros brought in Pepsi-Cola. By April 2001 it had achieved the sales goals that had been set for December. Cerveceria Regional finished 2001 with 40 percent of the light-beer market, a segment that grew, thanks to Regional Light, from 3 percent to 22 percent of the total, significantly better than the 6 percent marketing studies had projected. Just as Cisneros had anticipated, the plants could not satisfy demand. Odón and Pieretti estimate that few brands of beer in the world have had so meteoric a rise as Regional Light, which raised the total revenues of the brewery by 62 percent that year. Venezuelans even opted to drink more beer than before, up to seventy-six liters per capita, an increase of 17 percent.

Later, in July 2002, the Cisneros Group acquired 22 percent of Backus & Johnston, the largest brewery in Peru, and the sixth largest in Latin America. This investment reflected the Group's strategy of internationalization.

In mid-2003, the total investment of the Cisneros Group in Cervecería Regional was some 800 million dollars. Between 1992 and 2003, the number of liters of Regional beer in the market rose from 69 to 523 million; the brand's national market share rose from 5 to 28 percent; the production capacity of the various plants increased from 70 to 550 million liters a year; the number of products grew from two to five, with more products on the way; the investment in advertising rose from 3 to 7 percent (as a percentage of sales); and the number of distribution routes climbed from 136 to 1,000. The growth was astounding.

Following the success of Cervecería Regional, Gustavo Cisneros continued with new projects in Venezuela. A communications entrepreneur owning his own baseball team seems to be part of the game. Rupert Murdoch owns the Los Angeles Dodgers and Tom Hicks the Texas Rangers. The synergies are evident, because the sport continues to have a large fan base and can contribute a differentiating element to a television channel's programming.

Los Leones de Caracas—the Lions of Caracas— are to Venezuelan baseball what the Yankees are to New York, the Giants to San Francisco, or the Red Sox to Boston. A high percentage of Venezuelan baseball fans—and there are many of them—say they follow Los Leones, and with fifteen championships in its half-century-long history, it is the club in the local league that has received the most awards.

Discouraged by very unsatisfactory financial results—originating in the country's general economic decline, the Prieto and Morales families, the team's owners since the 1950s, were convinced the time had come to sell the team to a group that could give it more momentum. They hired a local investment banker, who in turn contacted Ariel Prat, the head of finance for the Cisneros Group in Venezuela.

Prat liked the idea of buying the team. Cisneros was also interested in the possibility. "Look into it...and let's see what happens," he told Prat.

At that moment the franchise was not very profitable, but in the eyes of Cisneros management, it had the potential to generate good cash flow in addition to providing the Group with a closer connection to the fans. Sixty percent of the team's income was derived from ticket sales, and the only outlet for selling tickets was the box office at the Universitario Stadium in Caracas. By increasing the number of ticket outlets, the franchise could increase the number of people attending the games. There were no special marketing promotions either, such as those directed toward children or senior citizens. As a consequence, the classic

final game with the team's archrival, the Navegantes de Magal-
lanes, filled the stadium with 25,000 people. But when the team
played against Pastora, there were only 2,000 spectators. Perhaps
the Cisneros Group could breathe new life into Los Leones.

The baseball season in Venezuela begins in October and ends
in January to make way for the Caribbean Series. With only eight
teams, this seems modest, but the advantage is that Venezuelan
players also play in the United States. The Caracas team alone
has eighty-five ballplayers scattered among American teams. This
keeps Venezuelans' interest high in one of the few sports—so far—
in which the country has generated world-class athletes, like Andrés Galarraga, Omar Visquel, and Bob Abreu, among many other
stars. In the last six years, more than sixty Venezuelans have reached
the major leagues, while in the previous sixteen years, forty-seven
achieved that goal.

The major points of contention in the negotiations involved
valuations—the sellers of Los Leones wanted $15 million, while
the analysts at the Cisneros Group thought that a little more
than half that sum was a fair price. In the first few months of
2001 their positions grew closer; in January, Cisneros paid $1.5
million to have exclusivity in the negotiations. By March they
reached a final agreement: almost $9 million, in the midst of a
good deal of confusion, because the news that Cisneros was
buying Los Leones encouraged others to make offers. Prat met
in his office with the forty shareholders from the Prieto and
Morales families—ranging from young people to grandmoth-
ers—for the entire day, until all of them were persuaded to give
their approval to the deal.

The acquisition gave Cisneros greater public exposure in his
own country, since Venezuelans are passionate about baseball.
The transaction, which involved a small amount of money compared to the Venezuelan magnate's other deals, acquired dispro-
portionate signficance in the Cisneros Group, and in the Cisneros
home. It was a recurrent theme in Gustavo's conversations with
his children. Managers were also following the deal very closely,
and when Cisneros asked for volunteers to serve as directors of
Los Leones, it seemed that the entire Cisneros Group wanted to

sign up. Ariel Prat was named president. Weeks before the contract was signed, Cisneros began to receive phone calls and e-mails congratulating him on the transaction.

On April 18, 2001, some five hundred people met at the Gran Meliá hotel for the official announcement of the sale. The local press had stirred up expectations, using terms like "a new time" and a "new stage" to describe the entrance of an entrepreneur of Cisneros' caliber onto the Venezuelan sports scene. The acquisition of rights to the World Cup by DirecTV hardly merited a few lines in the newspapers. Now Cisneros was going to be on the front pages of all the local and national newspapers.

For the occasion, the public relations team recreated a small stadium in the hotel's Salón Manzanares, with a green carpet to replicate the diamond and its bases. Cisneros was relaxed and wore the same clothing he had on during the rehearsals that morning: a white shirt with no tie, a checked beige jacket, and jeans. His casual appearance set him apart from the formality of the rest of the people on the podium, including the former directors of Los Leones.

He gave a simple, moving speech. He said this was "one more piece in the fascinating puzzle of baseball."

A reporter wanted to know how much he had paid for the club, and Cisneros' response was intentionally evasive. Another asked if he was going to build a new stadium. He would study it, he said. What would happen to the exclusivity contract to sell Polar at the stadium? It would be respected until it expired the following year, was his answer.

The next day, most of the newspapers published on their front pages a photograph of Gustavo Cisneros wearing a big smile and a Los Leones cap.

Cisneros would not be an absentee owner of the baseball team. On the contrary, he plunged into learning the details of its operation. Early in August, he and Ricardo had a long meeting with Prat. For Cisneros, baseball was a tool for public service, and he wanted to know the progress of the summer championship for children that the club was organizing. The Cisneros brothers shot questions at Prat. What impression did the fans have? How was the press treating the team? How was the hiring of new players going, and what about relations with major league teams? How much had been invested in improving the stadium? (Reply: $400,000.) Was the club keeping the promises made at the April 18 press conference?

The lion did not roar with the strength anticipated during the 2001–02 season. Attendance at the stadium rose by 4 percent to 240,000 during the entire season, which certainly was an achievement because the performance of Los Leones was poor: the ball club could not qualify for the league's second playoffs. Prat explained to a disappointed Cisneros that the team was suffering from tensions between the younger team members and the veterans who had played in the United States. "It was a team with an excess of egos," says Prat. The technical director was replaced and more prominence was given to the promising young players in the club. The changes had a rapid positive effect, and the public recognized this. For the 2002–03 season, which could not be completed due to political instability in the country, Los Leones began with the best record in five years. By the time play was suspended, the team was in first place in its division, with the second-best record in the league. The new players demonstrated their worth and became idols to those who followed the sport. Attendance increased by 25 percent, and Los Leones prepared for the next season, a team filled with potential stars and a proven spirit.

Like the Miss Venezuela pageant, Los Leones de Caracas signifies, over and above a business and image opportunity, the creation of an affective tie with the community, which is due—among other factors—to its seven minor league teams and the summer camps attended by some seven hundred children in the past two years. In 2002 the boys' team that represented the state of Miranda was crowned champion. As part of the plans for the Fiftieth Anniversary of Los Leones de Caracas, an album of baseball cards was published illustrating the five decades of the team's successes, with the proceeds donated to a local hospital.

Pieretti says that Cisneros bought Los Leones to promote a sport, imbue citizens with confidence, and stimulate young people to achieve. "Los Leones de Caracas are part of Venezuela, and the Cisneros Group is too."

But sports was not the only community tie for the Group.

In mid-1996, Cisneros went to see the Archbishop of Caracas, the late Cardinal Ignacio Velasco, to present him with an idea: he wanted the Catholic Church to join him in establishing a channel of "cultural entertainment," as an instrument of education and mass dissemination of culture. These were the first steps that would lead to ValeTV, an alliance between private television companies and the Catholic Church to generate a broadcast channel of cultural entertainment and education.

Gustavo Cisneros had already outlined this vision in his speech to the plenary meeting of the Pontifical Commission for Social Communications, which he delivered at Vatican City in 1987. He emphasized the relevance of telecommunications in general, and television in particular, for education and the dissemination of moral and cultural values. On that occasion, Cisneros cited the words of His Holiness Pope John Paul II, who had said that the media landscape is "an immense and fascinating terrain, which ought to constitute one of the principal fronts in the missionary commitment of the various ecclesiastic communities of each believer."

Cisneros had always encouraged the Church to use television to broadcast a message that was both instructive and entertaining. He explained his idea to Cardinal Velasco, who responded enthusiastically to the proposal.

The origins of ValeTV go back to the time when Diego Cisneros succeeded in having Venevisión defeat the powerful alliance of the Vollmer family with Goar Mestre in the late 1960s and early 1970s. The government inherited the signal left by Mestre, Channel 8. This meant that the original state signal, Channel 5, fell into disuse as the government focused its efforts on Channel 8.

Gustavo Cisneros felt the need for Venezuela to have a cultural channel, and he thought that Channel 5 could fill the vacuum. But for almost ten years Channel 5 either aired irregularly or duplicated Channel 8, which was a mixture of a commercial channel and a political tool for the government in office. Cisneros wanted private television to make a permanent contribution to the community, and a cultural channel seemed the ideal tool for the purpose.

For Gustavo Cisneros, purely educational channels, ones that teach multiplication tables, did not succeed with an open television signal because people quickly picked up their remote controls and changed the channel. But he was certain that a channel with high-quality documentaries would find acceptance. He knew that television was a medium of entertainment, and to carry out an educational function it would have to be engaging as well.

Monsignor Ignacio Velasco backed the idea. Subsequently, Cisneros presented the same proposal to President Rafael Caldera, who did not adopt it immediately but later accepted it with enthusiasm.

Then Cisneros gave Carlos Bardasano, the president of Venevisión, the job of proposing the project to all the private channels in the country and moving it forward. Marcel Granier at RCTV, and Omar Camero speaking for Televen, took the initiative and immediately joined the project.

President Caldera gave the concession to the Archdiocese of Caracas, while the operation was assigned to a nonprofit association made up of the three private channels. ValeTV went on the air on December 4, 1998, with the slogan "The world on a single channel," and four hours of programming.

ValeTV did not cost the government, the Church, or the taxpayers a cent. The channel marked the managerial debut of Guillermo, the oldest son of Gustavo and Patty Cisneros, who had recently turned twenty-seven. Working with María Eugenia Mosquera, the channel's general manager, he chose not to use well-known faces as moderators; the announcers on ValeTV are young—their average age is twenty-five. The personal touch is its minimalist image, accompanied by a female voice off-screen. Guillermo Cisneros selected the best documentaries from international producers, including BBC, ZDF, National Geographic, and TV France. He combined this with local content that raised the historical, social, and environmental consciousness of the Venezuelan viewing public.

The channel's innovative programming has been recognized at international competitions such as Emmy, Promax, Ondas (Spain), Caracol de Plata (Mexico), and Science and Technology (France).

The participation of Guillermo Cisneros gave the channel a special place in the hearts of his proud parents. Guillermo, who defines it as "Venezuela's audio-visual library," had situated ValeTV as the most watched of the group of thematic channels on broadcast television. Then too, ValeTV would be a unifying link with the other privately owned channels, which for the past twenty years had competed furiously among themselves, as well as with the Catholic Church.

For the private channels, ValeTV is proof that commercial television can make a contribution to society. Gustavo Cisneros believes that ValeTV fulfills a social and educational function, something that Venezuela needs, and is in line with his philanthropic interests, which attempt to use television to improve the education of Latin Americans. From Chile to Costa Rica, ValeTV is a topic of study by governments analyzing the possibilities of reproducing the experience of the channel in their own countries.

ValeTV, Cervecería Regional, and Los Leones demonstrated that Gustavo Cisneros had not become disconnected from his country, which he had loved passionately since childhood. He considered it part of his family inheritance. For this reason, Cisneros was deeply disturbed by what was happening in the nation in the early years of the new millennium, when a defiant and verbally abusive President Hugo Chávez divided Venezuelans in a way that had never occurred before in Latin America.

In 2002 the mood of management in the Cisneros Group was somber and apprehensive. In meetings with his executives, Cisneros considered the possibility of worsening economic difficulties in Venezuela in the face of an intensified political crisis. Cisneros viewed with particular concern the harassment of communications media and journalists by the Chávez government, and the increase in violence. He did not want that for his country, for it went counter to his democratic convictions and those of his father.

The first time Cisneros met Hugo Chávez in person was at a dinner the entrepreneur gave for him at Venevisión. Chávez had not yet been elected president, and Cisneros used the opportunity to explain his personal and business philosophy to a candidate who spent more time listening than talking, as someone who was present at the meeting recalls.

There were subsequent, sporadic contacts, which were always cordial. In mid-2001, on the occasion of the official visit to Venezuela by Jiang Zemin, then president of China, Cisneros brought the popular singer Julio Iglesias to a meeting with the two heads of state. Chávez and the Chinese leader, to the astonishment of Gustavo Cisneros and Iglesias, broke into song to demonstrate their musical gifts.

Cisneros believes that part of his work consists in maintaining contact with leaders. "If you want to participate in a nation's political, social and economic direction, it is important to have multiple links in various spheres of national life. I was correct in trying to influence that direction in order to create a more modern, liberal, and democratic Venezuela. We depend on democracy."

Cisneros did not ask for personal favors. Even during the family's most challenging times, for example when Ricardo Cisneros was being prosecuted because of the collapse of Banco Latino, Gustavo Cisneros asked the government for justice, not favors.

"I have seen Gustavo approach the governments in power with real concerns about education," says a high-ranking executive in the Group. Cisneros says to them, "I'll bring in this outside consultant," or "Why don't we improve the standard of living for police officers?"

"Gustavo Cisneros," says William Luers, a family friend and the former United States ambassador to Venezuela, "understood from a very early age that many Latin American politicians viewed the private sector with suspicion. It is Gustavo's unique intelligence that allows him to understand the mentality of certain people who think that capitalism is a corrupting force in society." Cisneros tried to influence the public sector in order to show the politicians that "the private sector can be a very positive influence on the development of society," says the diplomat. Cisneros' social vision is based on his belief in solidarity and in the existence of a legal framework that offers protection and opportunities to individuals, with laws that are the same for everyone and that codify the key principles of democratic life. This is the philosophy behind Cisneros' statement that, in his opinion, the best option is the democratic center, which represents the rejection of extremism on the left and the right, but at the same time is a manifestation of a sincere and staunch commitment to the defense of freedom. "I do not believe," Cisneros has said, "in a passive, insipid political center; I want a political center that is absolutely committed to individual freedom and democracy."

During those first encounters with Chávez, Cisneros told him that he believed in a Venezuela that took part in the first world, in a north-south economic union, in representative democracy, in free expression and free enterprise. They were the basic principles that the Cisneros family—father and sons—had defended for seven decades. Chávez's reply was that he agreed with those ideas and that he should be judged by his actions, not his words. He also expressed his desire for greater social equality, improved education, and the elimination of corruption. He said that public services had to improve.

Gustavo Cisneros agreed completely. Still, Chávez publicly attacked the Free Trade Zone of the Americas, a project backed by Washington that would liberalize trade and investments among the nations of the hemisphere. He considered the International Monetary Fund as something ominous that ought to disappear. Echoing Cuban revolutionary thought, he said he preferred "participatory" democracy rather than "representative" democracy. Cisneros initially had hopes that time would moderate Chávez's position. "I would like him to evolve toward the center, and I am hopeful this is going to happen," Cisneros said in August 2001.

But Chávez gave no peace to his opponents, describing them with some of his favorite epithets, such as "fascists," "filthy," "oligarchs," and "*jineteras*" (prostitutes), expressions that served only to deepen the division among Venezuelans. In spite of healthy oil prices, the economy was mired in growing insecurity in the courts and on the street. The wave of popularity and goodwill that carried Chávez to power in 1998 had disappeared, and in early 2002 the majority of Venezuelans opposed Chávez and his "Bolivarian" revolution. That year Venezuela was hit by the equivalent of the ten Biblical plagues. Panic overwhelmed investors, and the *bolívar* lost value in the midst of a flight of hard currency. High interest rates deepened a recession; the economy would contract almost 9 percent that year.

The confrontation reached its height on Thursday, April 11, 2002, when a huge opposition demonstration was fired on; nineteen people lost their lives and hundreds were injured. The president had asked the troops to use Plan Ávila—Venezuelan military code for using all necessary force to impose order—which in fact would have resulted in a massacre. The military commanders refused, and Chávez was finished.

Events were occurring at a dizzying rate, complicating the task of separating fact from rumor. Gustavo Cisneros was at Venevisión, along with his colleagues. The channel, as one of the principal communications media in the country, was a place where political, business, union, and intellectual leaders gathered in times of crisis, as many had done during Chávez's coup in 1992.

The union leader Carlos Ortega, a long-time representative of the organized labor sector, was there. Pedro Carmona, the president of Fedecámaras, was also present. He left the station shortly before two in the morning, saying he would spend the night at a hotel since his house was not considered safe. Consequently, everyone was astonished when Carmona appeared on the screens of national and international television channels some three hours later, broadcasting from Fuerte Tiuna, a military base, and stating that he was assuming power. Having a businessman take over the presidency at so complicated a moment was a dangerous sign, but the worst was yet to come.

The rumor was circulating among the diplomatic delegations that Carmona planned to dissolve the powers of the state, from the Supreme Court to the National Assembly. This meant that Carmona would lose all legitimacy and remain in power as a despot. Diplomats from the United States, Spain, and other nations warned that they were not prepared to support that kind of government. Despite fruitless efforts to locate Carmona and dissuade him from the idea, on Friday afternoon, on live television, in a ceremony to which neither Gustavo Cisneros nor any of his close associates were invited, Carmona announced the abolition of the National Assembly. Military leaders were horrified and decided to reinstall Chávez in the Miraflores Palace despite some counter-demonstrations in favor of Carmona.

Carmona's presidency had lasted barely forty-seven hours.

Chávez returned to power stating his commitment to dialogue and reducing animosity, but in the months that followed the dialogue did not go anywhere and the atmosphere again deteriorated.

There was great volatility in the streets when, in December, the opposition called for a work stoppage until Chávez was removed from power or had made a commitment to elections that would allow the people to express their will. But the stoppage failed and cost the ailing economy thousands of millions of dollars.

A triumphant Chávez—having already defeated an attempted coup and a strike—had recourse to an old Venezuelan tactic used to consolidate power, and in February he installed a system to control currency exchange.

The flow of dollars was cut off for thousands of businesses in the country, including the Cisneros Group. A sharpened dagger was placed at the throat of Venezuelan business, but this did not particularly concern Chávez, who was convinced that business-people formed the core of his political opponents.

Venevisión faced serious problems in paying for the basic elements of transmitting a television signal, from videotapes to canned programming. Only the lines of credit with foreign providers, who understood that the strangling of the private sector could not go on for very long, allowed the channel to operate with a semblance of normality.

"Chávez is harming Venezuelans with exchange controls," Cisneros told the magazine *Poder*. Then would Venevisión close? "Never." In spite of its losses? "That's right. Our commitment is to Venezuela."

Gustavo Cisneros is proud that his companies are sources of employment and well-being for his employees, a concrete way of contributing to the growth of his country in the midst of difficulties. Cervecería Regional employed almost 1,500 people, and another 10,000 worked for it indirectly. DirecTV Venezuela had 800 people on its payroll and another 3,200 working for it indirectly. Cisneros instructs his companies to make charitable donations as part of the social responsibility of the Group. DirecTV Venezuela donates equipment to shelters, schools, centers for social action, and even the Ministry of Defense so that those posted along the border can watch its programming and keep informed. For its part, Cervecería Regional disseminates popular culture, promoting and participating in fairs and other local celebrations in various places throughout Venezuela. Cisneros has made it clear that he does not intend to abandon his country.

atty Cisneros with the king of Spain and Hillary Clinton at the table of honor at the gala dinner held for
heir Majesties Juan Carlos and Sofía in Washington, D.C. (February 23, 2000).

he Cisneros family with the president of the World Bank, James Wolfesohn, fifth from left, and Nemir
irdar, president and CEO of Invest Corp., second from left, in Washington, D.C. on the occasion of the
eminar sponsored by the Fundación Cisneros, among other institutions, to deal with topics such as long-
istance education, overcoming poverty, and judicial reforms in the continent (May 16, 2000).

Cardinals Rosalio Castillo Lara and José Ignacio Velasco blessed the renewal of vows of Patty and Gustavo Cisneros at the celebration of their wedding anniversary (June 10, 2000).

Gustavo and Patty Cisneros with their three children, Adriana, Carolina, and Guillermo, at the celebration of the couple's thirtieth wedding anniversary, at the Hacienda Carabobo, their farm outside of Caracas, Venezuela.

A lover of tropical birds, President Jimmy Carter enjoying his hobby with his wife, Rosalynn, and the Cisneros couple, in the company of the Venezuelan ornithologist Gustavo Rodríguez, at the Hacienda Carabobo (July 27, 2000). Carabobo is a nature reserve for tropical birds and the organic cultivation of coffee, and is a center for the conservation of Venezuelan colonial art.

Patty Cisneros and family, at the Balbi Palace, in Venice, with the *Leone d'Oro di San Marco*, one of the most prestigious cultural awards in Europe, given to the Fundación Cisneros and its Orinoco ethnographic collection (November 2000).

Gustavo Cisneros, Peter Tinoco (executive chairman of the Fundación Cisneros), Patty Cisneros, and the secretary general of the OAS, César Gaviria, at the headquarters of the Organization in Washington, on the occasion of the signing of an agreement to work together to expand the Fundación Cisneros educational program AME (*Actualización de Maestros en Educación*, or Professional Development for Educators) (December 18, 2000).

A working session at the White House with President George W. Bush on the subject of free trade in the Americas (May 2001).

Cisneros has always maintained excellent relations with Mexican heads of state. Mexico is a key nation for the Cisneros Group's philanthropic and entrepreneurial relationships. The photograph was taken at a meeting between the Cisneros couple and President Vicente Fox (July 2001).

With Warren Buffet in Sun Valley, Idaho, at the annual meeting of international entrepreneurs in communications media (July 2001). Buffet is a key player in the world of international finance, and Cisneros considers him a gifted interlocutor.

With close friend Julio Iglesias. The occasion is the ceremony conferring on Iglesias the LARAS Person of the Year Award in Los Angeles (September 10, 2001). Cisneros presided over the event.

Cisneros receives the Emmy (International Emmy Directorate Award) in New York City (November 19, 2001). The most important award in the media industry was given in recognition of his entrepreneurial career in communications media.

Cisneros with President George Bush, on a private visit to Cisneros' Manaka encampment in the Venezuelan Amazon, where the two friends spent a few days of relaxation fishing for the famous peacock bass, which is found in tropical rivers (January 2002).

Meeting of the Columbia University Biannual International Advisory Council in Caracas.

Seated: George Rupp (USA), John Kluge (USA), David Rockefeller (USA), Lee C. Bollinger (president of Columbia University, USA).
First row standing: The Honorable Hilary Weston (Canada), Maria Kluge (USA), Lady Susy Sainsbury (England), Dr. Amira Badawi Nazer (Kingdom of Saudi Arabia), Gustavo Cisneros, Mingyi Wei (China), Dr. Walther L. Kiep (Germany), Patty Cisneros.
Second row standing: Kevin McManus (formerly of Columbia University, USA), Nancy Rupp (USA), Jean Magnano Bollinger (USA), Miranda Kaiser (USA), Hisham Nazer (Kingdom of Saudi Arabia).
Third row standing: Galen Weston (Canada), Dr. Ruth Fischbach (USA), Dr. Gerald Fischbach (USA) (January 25, 2002). Gustavo Cisneros is one of the co-founders of the Council.

Patty and Gustavo Cisneros converse with Jesús Soto, the internationally acclaimed Venezuelan artist, on the occasion of the publication by the Fundación Cisneros of the book *Conversaciones con Jesús Soto,* in Caracas (February 6, 2002).

With former Presidents George Bush and Carlos Salinas de Gortari, and former Prime Minister Brian Mulroney, at the Woodrow Wilson International Center for Scholars, in Washington, D.C., during a meeting celebrating the tenth anniversary of the creation of the North American Free Trade Agreement (NAFTA) (December 9, 2002).

A private audience with the president of Chile, Ricardo Lagos. The Cisneros Group has a strong presence in the communications media in Chile, through Chilevisión, DirecTV, and radio. and Cisneros praises the Chilean model of socioeconomic development as a positive example for the hemisphere (March 17, 2003).

Patty Cisneros on the occasion of receiving a doctorate of fine arts *honoris causa* from Wheaton College, her alma mater, in Norton, Massachusetts (May 2003). She is accompanied by Adriana, Gustavo, and Guillermo Cisneros.

A meeting of old friends: President Bill Clinton, David Rockefeller, and Bill Rhodes, senior vice chairman of Citigroup, in New York on the occasion of the award of the Gold Medal of the Americas Society to Gustavo Cisneros for his work on behalf of inter-American unity (June 3, 2003).

Cisneros with His Majesty Abdullah al-Hussein. The Cisneros couple attended the celebration of the tenth wedding anniversary of King Abdullah and Queen Ramia in al-Aqabah, Jordan (June 23, 2003). Cisneros considers the Jordanian monarch a reforming figure in the leadership of the Middle East.

Gustavo Cisneros with his pets Raz and Arrow in La Romana, Dominican Republic (August 2003).

With Emilio Azcárraga Jean and Jerrold Perenchio (center), two fundamental allies, at the Cisneros residence in New York, on the occasion of a reception given by Gustavo Cisneros in honor of Perenchio, president of Univision Communications (October 8, 2003). In 2003, Wall Street analysts estimated Univision's 2004 revenues at a total of $1.7 billion and an EBITDA of $590 million.

PODER

ISSUE 08 · MAY 2003   Intelligence for the Business Elite

The Economist: *Mexico's changing map*

The King of Entertainment

Everything you wanted to know about Gustavo Cisneros: his companies, his fight with Chávez and the future of his businesses. Exclusive interview.

Cover of *Poder* magazine (2003) proclaiming "The King of Entertainment." The article described Cisneros as "a risk-taker, a long-term player who has had his share of difficult moments, but in the end can be considered an unequivocal success."

Birthday celebration for Jesús de Polanco, owner of Spain's *El Pais* newspaper, at the Fourth Ibero-American Forum, at which intellectuals, politicians, and business leaders discuss the future of Iberoamerica and its relations with the world at large, in Campos do Jordao, Brazil (November 2003). Pictured are Isidro Fainé, Héctor Magnetto, Federico Reyes, Manuel Arango, Nélida Piñón, Alberto Ibargüen, Ray Rodríguez, Elena Esteves, Carlos Bardasano, Jesús Polanco, Carlos Fuentes, Leopoldo Rodés, Carmen Iglesias, Gustavo Cisneros, Ricardo Esteves, Juan Luis Cebrián, Roberto Teixeira, and Joao Roberto Marinho. Also attending the Forum were Carlos Slim, Francisco Pinto Balsemao, Julio María Sanguinetti, Enrique Iglesias, César Alierta, Roberto Civita, and Francisco Mezquita. Cisneros is one of the co-founders of the Forum.

Gustavo Cisneros with Spanish President José María Aznar, at the Palacio de la Moncloa, the president's office (February 2004).

Launch of the Spanish edition of *Gustavo Cisneros: Pioneer* at Casa de America, Madrid. Left to right: author Pablo Bachelet; Alfonso Cortina, president of Repsol, one of the largest oil companies in Europe; Ana Palacio, Spain's minister of foreign affairs; Gustavo Cisneros; and Fernando Henrique Cardoso, former president of Brazil (February 25, 2004).

Gustavo Cisneros receives the Woodrow Wilson Award for Public Service given by the Woodrow Wilson International Center for Scholars. The award is given to individuals who share President Wilson's vision of improving international relations through the open exchange of ideas. The award was presented by Lee H. Hamilton, president and director of the Woodrow Wilson Center. Cisneros was introduced by Alberto Ibargüen, the distinguished publisher of the *Miami Herald* (March 2004).

Launch of the Spanish-language edition of *Gustavo Cisneros: Pioneer* at the Club de Banqueros, in Mexico City. Left to right: Jesus Anaya, director of Planeta; author Pablo Bachelet; esteemed writer and intellectual Carlos Fuentes, who wrote the book's foreword; Gustavo Cisneros; telecommunications entrepreneur Carlos Slim; and prominent intellectual Sergio Sarmiento (March 11, 2004).

Paul K. Sugrue, dean of the School of Business Administration, University of Miami; Donna Shalala, president of the University of Miami; and Patty and Gustavo Cisneros, at the launch of the Spanish-language edition of *Gustavo Cisneros: Pioneer* in the United States. (March 31, 2004).

Gustavo Cisneros and Leonard Lauder, co-founder of the Joseph H. Lauder Institute of Management and International Studies, at the Wharton School of the University of Pennsylvania. Cisneros delivered the keynote speech on the occasion of the twentieth anniversary of the Alumni Association Global Business Forum at the Metropolitan Club, New York (April 3, 2004).

William F. Markey, Jr., president of The Wilmark Group and member of the Board of Trustees, Babson College, and Dr. Ralph Z. Sorenson, president emeritus, Babson College, who is receiving a diploma from Gustavo Cisneros in recognition of Sorenson's entrepreneurial achievements and personal commitment to Babson (Wellesley, Massachusetts, April 23, 2004).

Ricardo Cisneros, Carlos Slim, Mexican telecommunications entrepeneur; Martin Torrijos, president of Panama; Felipe González, former president of Spain; Leonel Fernández, president of the Dominican Republic and Gustavo Cisneros at "Casa Bonita," Cisneros' beach residence in the Dominican Republic (May 30, 2004).

18. The Vision

Gustavo Cisneros understood that he could not be a global player in all sectors. He counted on the verticalization of his business activity, and so far this book has principally been the story of how Cisneros endeavored to assemble the essential building blocks of his telecommunications and entertainment group—an ensemble in which each enterprise empowers the other. This is what the father had done when building an empire around Pepsi-Cola. This is what the son is doing with companies like Univision and DirecTV.

This chapter aims to place Cisneros' business motivations in a much broader context, one that includes the Venezuelan's vision of the Group's responsibility for the physical and sociopolitical environment. "We are not removed from the context of realities that surround us," he says. "We are within that framework, it influences us and we influence it. We want to function in a constructive way, aspiring to peace, stability, freedom, and progress for everyone."

The businesses of the Cisneros Group are not entities floating in a vacuum. For Cisneros, the entrepreneurial challenge consists of a constant adaptation to changes and the will to recognize and adjust to trends that point to the future. At an early stage, until the mid-1970s, the Cisneros Group owned industries, communications media, supermarket chains, and service enterprises in Venezuela—a little of everything in a country that seemed to be a source of opportunities as inexhaustible as its petroleum wealth. But even in the midst of this financial euphoria, Cisneros gradually began to open a path to the rest of the continent and the world. International expansion perhaps reached its height at the beginning of the 1990s, with the acquisition of Spalding and Evenflo, Galerías Preciados, and Paternoster Square.

But the world continued to change. What is termed globalization—which is, in essence, the multiplication of contacts among the nations that form the international system—came on the scene, and the countries of Latin America lowered their tariffs and privatized their national industries. They opened the floodgates to allow the entry of foreign investment and multinationals. Borders stopped being barriers to the flow of production, capital, and information, a phenomenon closely linked to the astonishing progress of communications networks. In the more advanced economies (with effects on other societies that are gradually moving in the same direction), we are witnessing an intensive transfer of production activity to the sector of information processing and services linked to the use of knowledge.

Gustavo Cisneros is aware that it is still necessary to confront the significant differences that separate the more advanced nations of the world from those that remain in conditions of underdevelopment, unable to realize their full potential. The gap in productivity between rich and poor nations, the accelerated growth in the world's population, the generational pyramid that shows the overwhelming predominance of the young in the so-called "developing world," are some of the challenges that constitute today's complex panorama of risks and opportunities. The challenge is pressing in Latin America, a region with the worst distribution of wealth in the world, where 43 percent of the population is poor, according to the World Bank.

In these times of transformation, economic productivity depends increasingly on the educational level of the people. Improving it will allow citizens access to information and to scientific and technological development. They will be able to create new jobs and efficient managerial methods, factors that are directly related to innovation in the field of knowledge. For Cisneros, new ways of organizing production, applying managerial talent to increase efficiency, understanding the changes in which we are immersed, and adapting adequately to them are the areas in which the challenges of the present and the future are found.

Cisneros wants to create opportunities that showcase people's creative energies and encourage investment in a secure environment in order to satisfy the needs and aspirations of humanity, which desires to improve its quality of life and reach higher levels of well-being. He is not tolerant of dictatorships or repressive governments. In a speech given in 1979, Cisneros denounced "the type of society in which the state has priority over the preferences and spontaneous actions of a free people." He found that nationalism "becomes a self-interested concept that makes an entire society look inward instead of projecting outward."

In 1982, in a speech delivered to a meeting of the World Advertising Congress in São Paulo, Brazil, he said, "No one will be surprised that my personal preference is to develop a society and an economy in which maximum importance is given to respect for the dignity and liberty of the individual." On that occasion he indicated his preference for "economic activity governed by the action of a free market and social solidarity."

"This is a question of a society in which the role of government is essentially focused on protecting the rights of citizens and promoting free choice and initiative within the legitimate state and under the rule of law."

"In this sense, free trade constitutes an important ally of nations in their struggle for liberty and progress, since global exchange becomes a powerful stimulus to motivate each individual," says Cisneros.

Gustavo Cisneros is aware that the confluence of changes is what explains their great impact: the struggle for freedom has joined the superiority of the free-market economy, which in turn has been empowered by the development of new communication technologies, the end result being a globalized planet.

He understands that oppressive political systems, closed societies, and centrally planned economies cannot halt the perennial human aspiration to freedom. He also knows that the new communication technologies have decisively eroded barriers to information.

These factors motivated Cisneros to make a qualitative leap. He concentrated his investments in telecommunications, information systems, and audiovisual communication content because he saw them as the vanguard of the trends that would define the sociocultural configuration of the twenty-first century.

Bringing this vision to fruition entailed Cisneros' moving from selling real estate in London, soft drinks in Caracas, and golf balls all over the world to distributing the Internet and television channels in Latin America and the United States.

The magnitude of this change of direction, and its impact as a function of the large trends in contemporary technology development, cannot be underestimated, even more so because Cisneros effected it in a perennially challenging Latin American setting, overcoming devaluations, political crises, and occasional controversies arising from natural business competition.

Each difficulty heightened the challenge, and Cisneros knows that the future will be as challenging as the past. "The new society of digital information, which is translated into multiple services through a single technological platform, demands a good deal of creativity and vision from business leaders in order to join new and traditional media in a single system of distribution capable of interaction," he once said in a speech.

Is there a brief, simple formula that can explain Cisneros' entrepreneurial success? Gustavo Cisneros insists that looking for this kind of formula would be a misleading and confusing exercise, since there are too many factors and variables that intervene in a process as complex and extensive as the corporate evolution of the Cisneros Group. There are, however, some central ideas, which in one way or another have already been described in this book. Gustavo Cisneros' achievements have been marked by the early identification of opportunities, the ability to make difficult decisions rapidly, the calculated acceptance of risk, the practical ability to execute projects, and the will to learn from both successes and errors and to correct mistakes.

Change has been a constant hallmark of the Cisneros Group and, obviously, any change brings inherent risks. Gustavo Cisneros accepts risk as something inevitable and necessary in the course of business, and he feels bound to assume it with equanimity, and with boldness tempered by caution.

The Cisneros Group gives priority to those areas in which it has the greatest experience, and to the premise that the consolidation of successes should, in general, take precedence over the initiation of new projects. Still, Cisneros always insists that when opportunities appear they must not be wasted. Furthermore, he repeats constantly that "you have to run your business; your business can't run you." What he means is that one has to act realistically in the face of both successes and difficulties: one should not "plug the holes" in companies that are losing money; one must assume the losses, change, look for options, innovate, attempt to move things forward, and if nothing works, one must close those companies. But one thing is certain: "You must not drain yourself dry," Cisneros reiterates.

In these matters, his brother plays a key role. "Ricardo evaluates without mercy each of the new projects. Getting through that filter is fairly difficult. The risks are there, and one has to take them. Even the mistakes we've made in the past became learning experiences, and I would dare to state that we emerged stronger from each of them. Our best projects have emerged from adverse circumstances. It is the combination of boldness and caution, of Ricardo's contribution and mine, when it is time to make decisions."

The two brothers complement each other to perfection, just as Diego Cisneros had imagined they would when he assigned each one his tasks in the Group. Bob Pittman, the former chief of operations at AOL Time Warner, sees the result from the outside. "Clearly, Gustavo is the visionary, the ambassador of the Cisneros Group to the world. Ricardo is the operator who dives below the surface to understand what is going on from day to day. But they have a marvelous relationship of mutual trust; they meet at the end of the day, compare their observations, and resolve problems. This gives them the ability to move quickly, and trust between brothers is the strongest tie that can exist. This range of knowledge and control permits them to be very flexible and agile. This does not mean that Gustavo doesn't know the details or that Ricardo is not focused on global topics, but each assumes the primary role that has been assigned to him. As a result, they operate very efficiently and quickly."

Another element that helps to reduce risk is having a focused organization with a sense of mission. Because of its growth and impact, by the mid-1970s the Cisneros Group had achieved a level of corporate expansion that made a clear articulation of its entrepreneurial mission imperative. A sense of strategic direction was defined in order to encourage the greatest identification and unity in the managerial team with regard to a shared vision. That mission has been summarized in this way: to develop and operate a diversified portfolio of enterprises with a multinational character, global reach, and strategic orientation; to respond to new opportunities in the world market by means of entry into new areas of business and the replacement or diversification, according to circumstances, of existing assets; and to look for business opportunities and complete commercial operations and transactions capable of generating greater earnings, such as the acquisition of undervalued assets in order to trade them or eventually integrate them into the Group.

Gustavo Cisneros maintains that the Cisneros Group, in addition to founding and promoting new enterprises, looks for businesses "that are doing well in order to improve them."

In the Cisneros Group, a business culture exists that is directed toward grouping the right people for carrying out specific tasks efficiently. Cisneros insists that flexibility and adaptability in managers and companies are key qualities for operating successfully in a variety of socioeconomic and cultural environments, which often are subject to dynamic, changing realities. He prefers managers who are at ease in Miami, Madrid, or Buenos Aires, and several of his closest associates have more than one nationality.

By integrating a diversity of managerial experiences, abilities, and aptitudes into a coherent entrepreneurial whole, the Cisneros Group has linked the tradition, personal relationships, and flexibility typical of a family business to the professionalism, discipline, and scope of a modern and diversified large corporation. This quality permits managers to launch, in a short period of time, a totally new product such as Regional Light, and defy an almost monopolistic brewery industry.

Even today, seven decades after Diego Cisneros began to operate a bus in Venezuela, the Cisneros Group continues to be in essence a family business. Guillermo Cisneros played a key role in the programming of ValeTV, the documentary channel run by ASOTV (Venevisión, RCTV, and Televen). Carolina, Gustavo's second child, worked in the Department of Special Projects at Venevisión and had special audience success with the program *Robinson, La Gran Aventura*, which in 2001 reached 40 percent of the audience. Adriana, the younger daughter, received her B.A. in art history at Columbia University and her M.A. in communications at New York University, in the United States. On the other hand, Eduardo and Andrés Cisneros, Ricardo's sons, have already begun to take part in the Group's operations.

But Cisneros insists on management with a good deal of autonomy and flexibility, and he considers this one of the assets that can guarantee the survival of the Group beyond its founders, which is one of the great challenges for every family enterprise. Cisneros cites three factors that an owner must consider in order to guarantee survival with each generation.

"First, you must have professional management. Second, you have to function like a public company, with transparency and accountability. And third, the family has to take very seriously its role as a good shareholder." A good shareholder, according to Cisneros, "is thinking about the next step after the Internet."

The job of turning the Cisneros Group into a vehicle akin to a public corporation is being developed at present by Gustavo and Ricardo Cisneros. In this regard, Gustavo observes: "We are trying to study how executive teams function in public and family companies."

Gustavo Cisneros is attracted by the idea of a broad, flexible structure in a Cisneros Group that imparts a sense of direction and a common entrepreneurial philosophy to multiple enterprises, some of them publicly traded on the market, all of them acting with autonomy.

What is of utmost importance, according to Cisneros, is developing a management structure that can respond to the unexpected, unpredictable, unusual situation that demands innovative responses without clear precedents. The theoretical study of management provides relevant indicators, but it does not guarantee that the person with purely academic training will be successful in the practical exercise of a complex and challenging art. Creativity, that supplementary and decisive ingredient, is also the result of a certain attitude and ethical view toward life that generates respect for people, loyalty, and a desire for service and self-improvement.

Stimulating innovation is fundamental, and in the Cisneros Group an internal atmosphere is encouraged that does not reward passivity but rather inspires experimentation with new ideas, plans, and concepts. One executive recalls how, in 1980, the Group arranged—with the enthusiastic participation of Antonio José Cisneros, Gustavo's brother—to plant onions in the area of the Guanipa Mesa in Venezuela. The idea was to bring down the price of the vegetable in December, when demand skyrockets because of its inclusion in the preparation of *hallacas*, the typical Venezuelan Christmas dish that consists of a cornmeal shell filled with stewed beef, pork, or chicken and wrapped in plantain leaves. Antonio José Cisneros had heard that the Israelis knew how to grow onions in semiarid places. Technicians from Israel were brought to Ciudad Bolívar, in southeastern Venezuela. The economic evaluations were attractive. Machines were installed that irrigated in drops, and imported special seeds. Then, a plague destroyed the plants, and the project was a huge failure; it had also been an innovative plan that exemplified the ingenuity of the Group.

Gustavo Cisneros is aware of and values the courage of individuals who dissent, in a reasoned way and with solid arguments, during the process of making corporate decisions. He recognizes as well that the willingness to take calculated risks also demands the ability to be tolerant of honest mistakes. The Cisneros Group rewards and compensates initiative and personal accomplishment, especially when these qualities are displayed in teamwork.

Cisneros' executives work hard, at times with almost impossible goals. One executive recalls that he had to review the numbers for the possible purchase of a brewery in Portugal while he was flying from Caracas to London.

In short, Cisneros maintains that the art of being a leader, of managing with success, creativity, and productivity, means stimulating and liberating the diversity of aptitudes present in the corporate environment where one operates, and establishing an adequate mix of the unique talents and abilities that each person can contribute. Managerial leadership, in other words, is translated as integrating a particular talent into a common effort.

For Cisneros, a true entrepreneur has to be a positive agent for social change, an agent who makes room for the creative labor of others, for self-improvement, and the improvement of those around him. That is the real definition of the entrepreneur: a creator of opportunities that enable society to move forward.

Throughout his life, Gustavo Cisneros has forged an identity as a bold international entrepreneur. That has been the work that captures headlines in the press. Less well known is his effort, often carried out in secret, to forge links between North and South America and between both continents and Spain.

In 2000, when Bill and Hillary Clinton received King Juan Carlos and Queen Sofía at the White House for a gala dinner, Antonio de Oyarzábal, who was then the ambassador of Spain to the United States, was pleasantly surprised to see Patty Cisneros seated beside the queen and the king. Gustavo Cisneros was also at the table, in animated conversation with the king. The ties of Gustavo and Patty Cisneros to Spain are long-standing. Gustavo Cisneros refers to the monarch as "a very impassioned person, a friend to athletes, businesspeople, world leaders, journalists. He is interested in everything."

Hillary Clinton later told the ambassador that she had wanted to seat the Venezuelans at the table of honor in recognition of what Gustavo Cisneros had done to bring the United States and Spain closer. "In the United States they understand that Cisneros is an outstanding representative of the Hispanic community, a paradigm of what the Spanish-American entrepreneur ought to be," says the former ambassador.

De Oyarzábal considered Cisneros "an excellent adviser." Spain was investing in Latin America and trading with Europe, but its ties to the United States were relatively weak. The ambassador appreciated how Cisneros helped to close the gap between North America and Spain. "Gustavo Cisneros accepts as gospel the idea that there is only a lake between Spain and the rest of America, and that lake is a nexus of unity, not separation," says de Oyarzábal.

He recalled that in 1998 Cisneros organized an annual conference at the Museum of Radio and Television in Madrid. He gathered together more than eighty notable figures, from Steve Case, who was then CEO of AOL, to former Secretary of State Henry Kissinger, and he invited them to the Spanish capital where they were received by the king and President Aznar.

One of Cisneros' key achievements as an outstanding figure in the media industry came principally from Univision. At the beginning of the third millennium, the channel had become the most visible face of the presence and influence of the Hispanic community in the United States.

Since 1992, when it was conceived essentially as a platform for transmitting soap operas, the channel had not stopped growing. In some cities, television news broadcasts in Spanish had more viewers than their English-language counterparts. The channel's management, encouraged by Cisneros as a board member, had approved the expenditure of $1.1 billion to buy USA Networks, with its thirteen TV stations. At the beginning of January 2002, these had been transformed into TeleFutura, Univision's second channel, which aims to capture younger viewers by offering, for example, more sports programming. As a consequence, most urban centers in the United States now have three broadcast channels in Spanish, and several more on cable. In the middle of that same year, Univision acquired a significant number of Hispanic radio stations.

With Univision, Cisneros took advantage of one of the most dramatic demographic phenomena to affect the United States since the great waves of immigration in the nineteenth century: the Hispanic phenomenon. According to the Census Bureau in the United States, in July 2003 the number of Hispanics, defined as people of Latin American descent regardless of race, had reached some 39 million. This meant that Latinos had surpassed African-Americans as the largest minority in the country.

There are more Hispanics in the United States than in any other country except Spain, Colombia, and Mexico. Projections indicate that the number will grow dramatically. By 2010, one in every five Americans—some 70 million people—will be of Hispanic origin.

The United States is still digesting the Latino phenomenon. Its commercial weight can be seen in the fact that many product labels already have text in Spanish. On one hand, politicians respect the Latino vote, although the community has not yet matured to the point where it can influence key decisions in its favor. A fraction of the Hispanics eligible to vote do so, which dilutes their impact at the polls. But politicians who aspire to national prominence have stopped waving the anti-immigrant flag as a way to gain votes.

The strength of Univision continues to grow through the already approved merger with Hispanic Broadcasting Corporation (HBC), the largest Spanish-language radio network in the United States, with sixty-three stations in fifteen of the principal Hispanic markets in the country. HBC also operates HBC Sales Integration, another extensive Hispanic radio network in the United States, as well as HBCi, a company that runs various community-oriented bilingual pages on the Internet. Univision is also developing its recording and music-publishing divisions. In June 2001, the firm acquired 50 percent of Disa Records S.A., based in Mexico, one of the most solid independent record companies in the Hispanic world. In April 2002, it bought Fonovisa, a leader in sales of Latino music in the United States and Puerto Rico. Recently, the sales of Univision Music Group averaged five of the first ten albums of Latino music on the weekly listing in *Billboard Magazine*, and included half the sales of Mexican regional music in the United States in 2002. By December of that year, the musical segment amounted to 6 percent of Univision's earnings. Added to this is the Internet business, through Univision Online, Inc., which operates the portal Univision.com, a site that provides content in Spanish aimed at Hispanics in the United States, as well as the general public in Mexico and Latin America. In its first year of activity (2001), Univision.com became the leading Web site for the Spanish-speaking public in the United States, according to surveys by Nielsen Media Research, and it maintained that position in 2002, attracting more than 200 commercial sponsors.

Univision fits perfectly into Gustavo Cisneros' vision, since the alliances that give him the greatest satisfaction are precisely those that allow him to strengthen the ties between Latin America and the rest of the world, starting with the dissemination of values, culture, and, of course, the Spanish language. Univision not only keeps the Hispanic community identified locally, but it also contributes to preserving the vitality of a language that is the most widely spoken in the United States after English.

Patty Cisneros, for her part, attempts to do the same thing, disseminating Latin American art and culture throughout the world. For Gustavo Cisneros, the enthusiasm generated in Germany and France by a show of the Fundación Cisneros' Colección Orinoco in 2001 "is a reward greater than any corporate success."

Cisneros' work in promoting understanding and cultural and socioeconomic unity among the nations of the Americas earned him the gold medal of the Americas Society in New York, an organization that is a leader in the work of promoting friendly relations among the various communities and countries that form the American hemisphere. The Americas Society grants this award to individuals who contribute to harmony, friendship, and cooperation among American nations.

In his speech accepting the prize in June 2003, in New York, Gustavo Cisneros said, "It has been a privilege to make use of the tools I have at my disposal to promote freedom of expression, access to information, and development in Latin America." Before more than six hundred people gathered at Lincoln Center—among them Bill Clinton, Henry Kissinger, César Gaviria (general secretary of the Organization of American States), and David Rockefeller—Cisneros pointed out that "our challenge is to empower the citizens of this hemisphere to maintain a dialogue with the global community."

William R. Rhodes, chairman of the Council of the Americas' board of directors, praised Cisneros as "an entrepreneur, an innovator, and a defender of democracy, free trade, and the rule of law." He called him a "true citizen of the Americas," who had "raised the profile of Latin America on the world business stage." Bill Clinton also addressed those present, referring to Gustavo Cisneros as his "good friend," and emphasizing that the Venezuelan entrepreneur was receiving the honor for his efforts in the task of integrating the Americas, maintaining democracy, and promoting freedom in the region. Further, in his remarks, the former president recalled the excellent relations that Cisneros had with Latin American presidents, always on the basis of development and prosperity for the area and its inhabitants.

For Gustavo Cisneros, the event was a culminating moment in a decades-long career devoted to serving the ideals of unity among nations.

Cisneros is certain that his group's confidence in and commitment to the hemisphere will be rewarded over the years.

19. The Balance

Gustavo Cisneros likes to think in broad terms. The Internet is not merely a communications tool; it is something that can close the educational gap in Latin America as compared to the developed world. His companies are not simply machines that produce cash flows and maximize shareholder value. They generate jobs, satisfy consumers, and entertain viewers. Globalization is not simply the fall of the barriers that separate countries; it is an opportunity to bring Venezuela and Latin America closer to the rest of the world.

Gustavo and Patty Cisneros also perceive their work—their mission—in broader terms, which they define as "the social balance." Beyond the positive contributions made by the Cisneros Group's companies through creating jobs or making donations, the Cisneros family wants to contribute directly in areas that range from education to the preservation and promotion of culture.

"Gustavo in the business world, and I in the cultural world, are both trying to strengthen understanding between Latin America and the globalized world," says Patty. This is part of what she calls "the social responsibilities of the Cisneros Group."

The Fundación Cisneros, created through the initiative of Patty, Gustavo, and Ricardo Cisneros, is a private philanthropic institution, headquartered in Venezuela, which defines itself as committed to the development of programs that are based on the conviction that education and freedom of thought are the elementary foundations of every democratic society. Its programs center on education, culture, and the environment.

Fundación activities include diverse programs based on two major collections—one of objects from the Venezuelan Amazon, the other of mostly modern Latin American art; a music program that includes a school for young Venezuelan musicians; and administering AME and cl@se, among other educational initiatives. The organization was created by a combination of fortuitous circumstances, the drive of Patty Cisneros, and the entrepreneurial sense of Gustavo Cisneros.

The seeds of the Fundación Cisneros were the works of art that Patty began collecting thirty years ago "for the pleasure of looking at them and being surrounded by beautiful things." She acquired pieces by Spanish, French, and Swiss artists such as Joan Miró, Pablo Picasso, André Derain, Josef Albers, and Max Bill, among others.

She also began collecting works by Latin American artists, most of them modern and contemporary, and realized that she had assembled a coherent collection, known today as the Colección Cisneros. The Colección also includes works from the Colonial period, and a selection of Latin American landscapes from the seventeenth to twenty-first century, which were created by local artists as well as by others from North America and Europe who traveled to the region.

Today the Fundación's art initiatives, based on the Colección Cisneros, include much more than bringing exhibitions to Venezuela. The Fundación organizes its own exhibitions at major museums throughout the world, lends works to museums for their exhibitions, runs an effective visual-awareness program for schoolchildren—originally developed by The Museum of Modern Art in New York (MoMa) and adapted for Venezuelan students—maintains an educational Web site, and funds trips by curators from MoMA to various countries in the region, among other activities.

Patty Cisneros has ensured that education is at the center of the activities of the Colección Cisneros. The school program, for example, uses slides of works from The collection, along with other work, as a means of improving critical-thinking and expressive-language capabilities in schoolchildren.

The teachers ask the students questions. "What do you see? What do you think?"

The pupils respond: "I see big green leaves; I see flowers; I see an egg."

Since the activity is not graded, what is accomplished, as Peter Tinoco has remarked, is "stimulation of the critical sense, development of intelligence, and confidence in oneself."

If the origin of the Colección Cisneros was the product of a gradual accumulation of works, the same could also be said of the Colección Orinoco, the collection of objects from the Venezuelan Amazon.

Gustavo and Patty Cisneros have loved the jungle since they were very young. Sport fishing is one of Gustavo Cisneros' favorite pastimes, a fondness that he sometimes shares with international figures and personal friends, such as former president George Bush and the actor Michael Douglas. He takes them to his camp, called Manaka, in the Venezuelan Amazon. His guests leave deeply affected. They take away the impression of having been in one of the most beautiful places on earth.

When they were still practically newlyweds, Gustavo and Patty Cisneros began to explore the Orinoco River. The area of Venezuela is triple the size of Germany, and the Orinoco divides the country in two, just as the Mississippi separates east from west in the United States. The river is born in the Sierra Parima, on the border with Brazil, in the extreme south, and it flows for 1,678 miles in the form of a "C" until it empties into the Atlantic in the northeast of the country. To the north of the great river lie the urban centers, located in a small strip along the coast. To the south lie the regions of Amazonas and Guayana. Both occupy half the territory of the country and are full of mysterious, overwhelming places.

People who have accompanied the Cisneros family on their trips to the jungle cannot find the words to express what they have experienced. "It's a miracle; the beauty of Venezuela is unique in the world. There are sacred mountains that rise in the middle of plains that extend for hundreds of miles, it's something... incredible," says Guillermo de la Dehesa, a banker who is a friend of Cisneros.

Although it is called the Gran Sabana, or the Great Savanna, the Venezuelan jungle is, in reality, on a kind of forest carpet from which rise the *tepuyes*—hills that have been eroded by natural forces for hundreds of millions of years. Their flat tops reveal wide plateaus that are home to exuberant fauna and flora. Their craggy flanks are composed of dramatic granite formations, multicolored vegetation, and countless waterfalls. The plateau of the Marahuaca *tepuy*, in the extreme south of the country, covers an area of 92 square miles, and inspired Sir Arthur Conan Doyle to write *The Lost World*. On one of the faces of another *tepuy*, the Auyantepuy, is the Salto Angel, or Angel Falls, whose waters fall almost 3,211 feet, three times the height of the Eiffel Tower.

The jungle defies any effort to know it. Four centuries ago, the famous English pirate and explorer Sir Walter Raleigh searched it for the legendary city of El Dorado. He was the first of a series of subsequent expeditionaries that includes Humboldt, Bonpland, and William H. Phelps. The logistics of an expedition south of the Orinoco is the equivalent of "planning the conquest of Everest," says Patty, great-granddaughter of William H. Phelps.

One way to make more intimate contact with the Venezuelan Amazon is to navigate its rivers in *curiaras*, the dugout canoes made by native peoples. There one forgets about comforts and ordinary life: each trip is an adventure. One of the most memorable, Cisneros recalls, occurred in 1988. An excursion in a helicopter revealed a zone with settlements of Yanomami, one of the thirteen ethnic groups that inhabit the area.

On this occasion, the Yanomami received Gustavo Cisneros, Patty, and their children with warm embraces. The community was typically small: barely 125 people. Patty recounts nights in the *shabonos*, the Yanomami dwellings. "We went to sleep at ten at night, which is the time they go to bed, and everything was silent. No one spoke. Not even the dogs barked. From our hammocks we could see the stars. They live in harmony with nature."

According to indigenous customs, Gustavo Cisneros gave Doshamoshatheri, the chief of the community, the gift of a machete. Doshamoshatheri understood that Gustavo Cisneros was the visitors' leader, and in turn he gave him a necklace of boars' teeth, a rare adornment highly valued by shamans. Despite his small stature, Doshamoshatheri had an air of severity, underscored by his lower lip, which held the tobacco leaves he chewed continually. There was a welcoming ceremony, during which the visitors and their hosts ate plantains, river crabs, and caiman meat. The Cisneros family spent three nights in the Yanomami settlement and was overwhelmed by the experience.

For them the Orinoco is a retreat, a place to share with close friends. On another trip they took David Rockefeller and his wife, Peggy, in a helicopter to see Sarisariñama, the gigantic natural cavern approximately two-thirds of a mile in diameter and 1,148 feet deep. Holding on to nets, the Cisneros family and the Rockefellers went slowly down to the bottom, where the air is so thick that small clouds of vapor are formed when one breathes. Unique species are found in the interior, caught in time. An executive at the Cisneros Group describes it as "a journey to the center of the earth, with a window to the sky." David and Peggy Rockefeller were amazed at everything and celebrated everything, as if they were children. "They were ideal travel companions," says Patty Cisneros. David Rockefeller would describe the experience as the most intense of his life.

On another occasion, Cisneros flew in a helicopter down to the bottom of Angel Falls with the American architect Richard Meier, the designer of the Museum of Contemporary Art in Barcelona and the Getty Center in Los Angeles.

As modernization makes its way to all parts of the world, the Cisneros family has been saddened to see how contact with civilization has modified many of the original customs of the Amazonian ethnic groups. The hunting weapons used by the men began to incorporate pieces of plastic. The women rejected their clay pots for the convenience of metal utensils. Members of communities farther to the north ride motorcycles and wear t-shirts with the names of rock bands.

Patty and Gustavo Cisneros took on as their own the mission of protecting what they consider a historical legacy of their country. They began to collect necklaces of teeth, feather crowns worn by the wise men of the Ye'kuana communities, and long arrows. In 1988, they purchased the collection of Venezuelan explorer Edgardo González Niño; by the end of 2002, Patty Cisneros had carefully catalogued more than two thousand ethnographic objects from twelve different societies. The Colección Orinoco also has an archive of 300,000 photographs of explorations of the Venezuelan south.

In 2000, some 200,000 viewers in Bonn, Germany, were able to see more than four hundred of these objects in an exhibition entitled *Orinoco Parima: Indian Societies in Venezuela*. The show led Patty to a prestigious cultural prize, the *Leone d'Oro di San Marco*. In 2001, the *New York Times* described her as "a serious student of the ethnographic art of the Amazonian basin." Early in 2002, she would receive the medal of the Legion of Honor from the French government for her work in preserving the treasures of the Orinoco River basin.

For Patty, being a collector goes beyond the accumulation of works. She believes it is a position that carries social and cultural responsibilities. She once was asked what the responsibility of the collector was. "There are two kinds of responsibilities," she said, "what we owe to the collection itself and what we owe to the cultural community. We have to think that the collection is itself 'another work.' It is one of 'our' works, in continuous gestation, which gives us as many satisfactions as the work it demands of us. It supposes a complex series of actions: circulation of the works, their reproduction, loans, visits, all the things we must learn."

In the final analysis, the Colección Cisneros and Colección Orinoco attempt, in the words of Patty Cisneros, "to project into the world the richness of the cultural legacy in our midst, which has local significance and universal importance."

"The origin of Mozarteum was Zubin Mehta," says Patty Cisneros, referring to the famed conductor and to the music center located in Salzburg, Austria. "He came to Venezuela in the middle of the Malvinas war. Sentiment against the United States was very strong here, and he arrived with the New York Philharmonic and filled the Poliedro in Caracas for four nights, with 25,000 people attending each night."

Mehta subsequently went to Buenos Aires and gave a free concert on the Avenida 9 de Julio, the city's principal thoroughfare. "I understood the importance culture has for creating bridges," says Patty, recalling that tour. "The development of a country has to go hand-in-hand with its cultural development."

Gustavo and Patty Cisneros promoted the creation of the Centro Mozarteum, administered by the Fundación Cisneros and dedicated to the professional growth of young musicians. Recently the center created a school for the study of the violin and the viola, aimed at talented young Venezuelan musicians, particularly those of limited means. In addition, the Centro Mozarteum offers the public the opportunity to hear works of classical music, and grants scholarships so that two hundred young musicians can attend classes in music institutes in Europe, the United States, and Latin America.

The Cisneros family has maintained "a good friendship over time" with Mehta, says Patty. They have gone on vacation together, but with Gustavo "they always talk about international affairs. That is Zubin's passion."

In July 1998, Gustavo and Patty Cisneros bought the Hacienda Carabobo, an old coffee plantation in the mountains to the south of Caracas. The hacienda combines two of their enthusiasms: nature and colonial art.

A little more than an hour by car from the Venezuelan capital, and located at the top of a mountain in the interior range, the farm is surrounded by cedars, mangoes, and acacias. It is a place where nature and Venezuelan history meet. Formerly, its secluded spots offered a perfect hiding place for the armed men who ambushed royalist armies in the period of Independence. Residents affirm—echoing legends passed down over time—that no less a personage than the Liberator, Simón Bolívar, spent the night at the hacienda on route to the famous Battle of Carabobo (1821) that won Venezuela's independence. In the twentieth century, the hacienda suffered a slow deterioration, until the owner prior to the Cisneros family attempted to restore it to its past splendor, carrying out an agro-industrial project with nurseries and laboratories for performing genetic research. The hacienda was restored, but even so the project suffered losses. When he acquired the hacienda, Cisneros had a very clear sense of what to do with it.

He liked the idea of the Hacienda Carabobo once again producing the crop to which it owed its existence. Like Colombia, Venezuela had been a coffee-producing country for years, ever since the colonial period. In fact, in 1919 coffee brought in 212 *bolívares* for each *bolívar* provided by oil. But the strengthening of Venezuelan currency by the boom in crude made the Venezuelan coffee industry uncompetitive, and the farm fell into disuse.

Cisneros ordered the corresponding feasibility studies, and the numbers were promising. The organic method of cultivating coffee is laborious and costly, since it uses natural fertilizers and pesticides, which are produced in the surrounding area. The plant grows more slowly—a serious challenge for Cisneros' natural impatience—but its shoots are hardier and more robust. The experts estimated that the final cost would be 50 percent higher than for ordinary coffees, but the price paid for a premium organic coffee—highly prized in specialty stores in the United States and Europe—could be as much as five times higher than that of other coffee.

In July 1999, the seventy-eight employees of the Hacienda Carabobo began to plant the first bushes of the *Typica, Bourbón,* and *Catuai* varieties on 104 acres of the hacienda. In the harvest of 2001 some experimental beans were produced. The flavor was deep and aromatic. The first commercial production was planned for mid-2002, a year in which production reached 1,100 pounds. The following year the harvest increased tenfold to 11,000 pounds, and for 2004, the farm managers projected a production of over 17,000 pounds.

When something makes Gustavo Cisneros enthusiastic, he plunges into it as if he were a diver searching the ocean's floor for treasure. In his office on the hacienda there are various volumes about coffee, from *Las aventuras del café,* by Felipe Farré, to *Uncommon Grounds: The History of Coffee and How it Transformed Our World,* by Mark Pendergrast.

Cisneros likes to go around the hacienda and inspect the growth of the coffee plantings. One of his favorite outings is to climb a nearby hill—which he nicknamed the "great peak"—from the top of which one can see certain parts of Caracas. It is a forty-minute walk through a wooded highland with unforgettable views.

Coffee production is only one part of the Hacienda Carabobo, which received the international certificate that classifies it as an "organic" farm. Gustavo and Patty Cisneros were equally intent on exalting its historical richness, turning it into a small sanctuary for four hundred years of Venezuelan history. A simple table is an authentic piece of the cabinet-maker's art, with elaborate turnings and joints. In another room one can appreciate *San José,* a painting by the Venezuelan artist José Lorenzo Zurita (1695–1753).

Patty Cisneros defines it as a place for "preserving the essence of the Latin American."

The furnishings on the hacienda are original, and those that had been destroyed, like the altar and the benches in the chapel, were restored according to the instructions of experts. The salons, the rooms, all the many spaces of the house are conceived, designed, and reconstructed with a fine aesthetic sense and respect for Venezuela's historical past and artistic legacy.

The Hacienda Carabobo is an intimate and special place for Gustavo and Patty Cisneros. When the couple celebrated their Pearl Anniversary on June 10, 2000, approximately one hundred friends, including Cardinals Rosalio Castillo Lara and Ignacio Velasco, were invited to the hacienda. It was a simple, moving celebration organized by their children.

Patty would describe it as one of her "most beautiful moments."

According to Antonieta López, a childhood friend of Patty Cisneros, and the current vice president for corporate affairs in the Cisneros Group, "Patty is a person filled with curiosity who clearly defines her interests and delves into them deeply. Patty does not fit the mold of the woman accompanying the man. The two of them enrich each other."

Beyond realizing projects such as the Fundación Cisneros, including its activities involving the Colección Orinoco and Colección Cisneros, Patty Cisneros plays a more subtle role as a support for her husband. Many years ago she recognized in Gustavo Cisneros the quality he had of surrounding himself with positive, dynamic people. She works to generate a positive atmosphere at home. "He is positive; he refuses to surround himself with negative people," says Patty. "There is no negativity. Even today, if you go to him with a problem, you have to have the solution at hand."

Gustavo believes that this partnership with his wife is the best he has created in his life. "Patty is an integral part of everything I do," says Cisneros. "She is a person of firm ethical principles and deeply rooted values; she is totally dedicated to her family and philanthropic activities. We are a team, and what has been achieved we have done together."

Afterword

In November 2003, Gustavo Cisneros was working to advance his vision of an American continent united with Spain and Portugal, all of them closely associated in the process of economic development.

On the weekend of November 7–9 he was with friends at Campos do Jordao, 5,576 feet high in the Paulista mountains in the south of Brazil. In a town that resembled the Swiss Alps, more than sixty entrepreneurs, intellectuals, politicians, and diplomats met for the Fourth Ibero-American Forum. They discussed administrative details, such as the cities where the next Ibero-American Forums would be held, and the system for accepting new members, and of course, weighty matters like the economic and political paths Latin America should follow.

Once a year the Forum brings together outstanding personalities from the political, business, and cultural arenas in Latin America, Spain, Portugal, and the Hispanic community in the United States to discuss the challenges of the future. They do this behind closed doors and without the press. Their resolutions are not published. Each person takes home the reflections presented there and implements them as circumstances and options emerge.

The welcoming address was delivered by Carlos Fuentes. "The world has changed a good deal since we met for the first time, in Mexico City, at the end of the year 2000," said the Mexican writer, one of the founders and organizers of the Forum.

At that time, he recalled, those attending were celebrating the promise of a new international order. "Today, we deplore the proximity of a New International Disorder."

Democracy allows political freedom, but it does not necessarily generate employment, health, and security. "We are threatened by disillusionment," he stated.

Still, the content of the discussions revealed a panorama of ideas and perceptions which, as is usually the case with regard to Latin America, made manifest a horizon of light and darkness, expectations and difficulties that are part of the reality of so diverse a continent with so complex a history.

Cisneros, in his contributions, framed an optimistic perspective on Latin America. He said that "in spite of difficulties, people continue to show democratic convictions, a rejection of dictatorial and collectivist formulas, and a firm commitment to human rights and freedom." He was aware that those attending the Forum had to "respond to the challenge of social justice." He was concerned about the possibility that nations might be seduced by "demagogic and radical messages, which instead of improving matters only help to make them worse."

"These are the dangers that are there," he observes, "threats that have not disappeared and that demand of democratic leaders, entrepreneurs, and all of us who love freedom a responsible, concerted course of action to accelerate growth and increase employment, equality of opportunities, and access to healthier and more satisfying lives for the great majorities on the continent." In his keynote presentation, Cisneros made clear his uneasiness regarding the situation in Venezuela, but at the same time he reaffirmed his confidence in the democratic calling of his compatriots and their will to find a constitutional, peaceful, and electoral solution to the country's crisis.

On the economic front, on the other hand, the prospects seemed better.

Argentina was recovering from its traumatic devaluation of the previous year. Interest rates in Brazil, the second driving force in Latin America after the United States, were decreasing, which augured a return of economic growth.

The panorama was very different from that of August 2001, more than two years earlier, when negotiations to unite DirecTV and Sky experienced their first difficulties. At that moment the world economy was stumbling over serious obstacles, which would be exacerbated by the reverberations of the attacks on September 11. Latin America was about to have its first year of diminished growth in almost two decades.

Now the horizon was clearing. The alliance between Cisneros and Rupert Murdoch in Latin America was moving ahead, needing only the approval of U. S. regulatory agencies for the merger of the two platforms and the official announcement of the transaction to take place.

Cisneros' wager on the American hemisphere, with an emphasis on the United States, Canada, Mexico, and Brazil, was still valid.

A few days after his meeting in Brazil, Cisneros went to Miami to participate in a crucial ministerial meeting aimed at furthering negotiations for the Free Trade Area of the Americas (FTAA). President George W. Bush encouraged the creation of an entrepreneurial colloquium, the Hemispheric Leadership Council, with the idea of examining the problems of development that impact on the trade agenda, such as poverty, unemployment, and the modernization of agriculture. At President Bush's suggestion, Gustavo Cisneros would be one of three entrepreneurs responsible for presiding over the constitution of the Council, along with Armando Codina, president of the board of directors of the Codina Group, and Richard Wagoner, president of the board of directors and delegated adviser of the General Motors Corporation.

At this meeting, held on November 20, 2003, Cisneros delivered the introductory address and spoke again at the closing session. His message was direct: governments and the private sector must redouble their efforts in the hemisphere and correct the structural imbalances that have stood in the way of the rapid advance of well-being on the continent.

For Gustavo Cisneros, the Americas would inexorably become united through free trade, which he considered the driving force behind economic growth. He understood, however, that the United States had to take into account the asymmetries of power and wealth that separate it from Latin America. He liked the idea that Washington would support projects in infrastructure that would increase the competitiveness of the region's economies.

Cisneros maintained that Latin America and the Caribbean are the natural partners of the United States and Canada in their efforts to expand mutual prosperity: "Other markets in Asia may be larger, but they will become natural competitors of the United States."

The hemispheric meeting did not end in failure, as many had feared. Even though the United States and Brazil had differences over the degree of the FTAA's scope, both agreed on a format for negotiations—scheduled to conclude before January 1, 2005—which left the door open for countries to choose the degree of commitments they wished to assume. But the thirty-four countries that participated in the process—the entire hemisphere except Cuba—reiterated their commitment to the FTAA, a very important fact since just a few months earlier, in Cancún, Mexico, negotiations to lower trade barriers in the world had experienced a clearly disheartening course, to some extent counteracted by the positive results of the subsequent meeting in Miami.

Within the FTAA, many details were still in the air but the countries were still talking. Cisneros understood this. He knew about difficult negotiations.

His alliance with Murdoch well underway, the entrepreneur was ready to find a strategic association for AOL Latin America in order to strengthen its position in the market. Univision was continuing to rise. In mid-November the company became a media giant, with a stock market valuation that exceeded $10 billion, when it completed its acquisition of Hispanic Broadcasting Corporation, renamed Univision Radio. In conjunction with the Univision Web site, the most frequently visited by the Hispanic community, this constitutes a fundamental instrument for any advertisers who want to bring their message to the more than 40 million Hispanics who live in the United States. The potential is large because three out of five advertisers still do not specifically direct their campaigns to the Hispanic consumer in the United States.

In the course of this year, Cisneros and Carlos Slim, the Mexican mogul and an important partner of Televisa, with whom Cisneros maintains a cordial relationship, have formed a group of fathers and sons from the most important private business organizations in the region. The idea is for them to meet and discuss their particular problems, such as philanthropic foundations, macroeconomic growth, and the fight against poverty. A first meeting was held in Mexico.

With regard to his country, Cisneros—as we have already seen—is optimistic. He says: "The successful democratic exercises of 2003 and 2004 point to a surmounting of the political crisis." This, he maintains, "will stimulate a better climate for investments, increased levels of employment, and the opening of a period of reconstruction and reconciliation that will make possible a decisive struggle against poverty in the country."

Cisneros insists: "All of this must be achieved within a framework of tolerance, with a basis in dialogue and a sincere democratic vocation for living together in a civilized way. The high oil prices in 2004 will also ensure heavy consumer demand in the economy."

In other fields, where a good part of the best efforts of Patty and Gustavo Cisneros are concentrated, the year also closed with encouraging results and prospects. Patty Cisneros points out the recognition by the first World Meeting of the Information Society (sponsored by the United Nations and Secretary General Kofi Annan, which met in Geneva in December) of the AME program for training teachers in Latin America, an initiative widely praised by participants in eight countries in the region—Argentina, Colombia, Costa Rica, Ecuador, Mexico, Panama, Peru, and Venezuela. The program, which now reaches some 250 schools is sponsored by the Fundación Cisneros with the participation of DirecTV Latin America.

Patty and Gustavo Cisneros feel legitimate pride in having set in motion a project of this importance, which proposes to help confront the scourge of poverty, gradually and efficiently, through education and by encouraging responsibility and achievement in each individual in solidarity with his or her community.

In short, Gustavo Cisneros feels confident about the progress of the Cisneros Group and the success of the philanthropic projects to which he and his wife and family are committed: "We are where the future will be," Cisneros declares.

Bibliography and Sources

Head, Heart, and Courage

Luongo, José Silva, *De Cipriano Castro a Carlos Andrés Pérez (1899-1979)*, Monte Avila Editores Latinoamericana, 2000.

Diego Cisneros, Una Vida por Venezuela, Fundación Diego Cisneros, 1990.

Morón, Guillermo, *Breve Historia Contemporánea de Venezuela*, Fondo de Cultura Económica, México, 1994.

Yanes, Oscar, *Pura Pantalla*, Editorial Planeta, 2000.

Ulanovsky, Carlos, Silvia Itkin, and Pablo Sirvén, *Estamos en el Aire, Una Historia de la Televisión en la Argentina*, Editorial Planeta, 1999.

Krampner, Jon, "On the Edge at 50, The Big 3 TV Networks Can't Savor Their Anniversary," *Los Angeles Times*, May 17, 1998.

Glueck, Grace, "A Universe of Art, Centered in Boston," *New York Times*, August 17, 2001.

The Apprentice

Diego Cisneros, Una Vida por Venezuela, Fundación Diego Cisneros, 1990.

Krampner, Jon, "On the Edge at 50, The Big 3 TV Networks Can't Savor Their Anniversary," *Los Angeles Times*, May 17, 2001.

"El Amor en la Competencia de TV," *El Universal,* June 11,1970.

Mannion, Jim, "Gustavo Cisneros, Forceful Young Man Is Driving Element in Fast-Moving Entrepreneurial Group," *Daily Journal* (Caracas), October 29, 1976.

The Boys

Yanes, Oscar, *Pura Pantalla,* Editorial Planeta, 2000.

Fernández, Claudia, and Andrew Pasman, *El Tigre Emilio Azcárraga y su Imperio Televisa,* Editorial Grijalbo, 2000.

Mazziotti, Nora, compiler, *El Espectáculo de la Pasión, la Telenovela Latinoamericana,* Ediciones Colihue, 1995.

Ulanovsky, Carlos, Silvia Itkin, and Pablo Sirvén, *Estamos en el Aire, Una Historia de la Televisión en la Argentina,* Editorial Planeta, 1999.

"Pentacom No Impone Criterios al Estado," *La Verdad* (Caracas), March 8, 1975.

Silva, Simón, "Directivos de Pentacom en el Consejo Nacional de la Industria Petroquímica," *El Mundo* (Caracas), March 14, 1975.

"Venezuela: Can it Cash in on its Petrochemical Potential?" *Chemical Week* March 16, 1975.

"Los Secretos de Pentacom," *Revista Bohemia,* March 31–April 6, 1975.

"Pedro Tinoco Hijo: El Proyecto Pentacom es de Utilidad para el País," *El Universal,* April 3, 1975.

"La Petroquímica Puede Ser Factor Esencial de Relevo Para Nuestra Producción Petrolera," *La Verdad* (Caracas), April 16, 1975.

"Retirado el Proyecto Pentacom," *El Nacional,* May 3, 1975.

"El Rey de Entretenimiento," *Poder,* May 2003.

A Quarry of Talents

Morón, Guillermo, *Breve Historia Contemporánea de Venezuela,* Fondo de Cultura Económica, México, 1994.

Torres, Gerver, *Un Sueño para Venezuela. ¿Cómo Hacerlo Realidad?* Liderazgo y Visión AC in association with Banco Venezolano de Crédito, November 2000.

Diego Cisneros, Una Vida Por Venezuela, Fundación Diego Cisneros, 1990.

Lowenstein, Roger, "Latin Power: In Venezuela, Name of Cisneros Connotes Wealth and Influence—Closely Tied to Government, Family Controls Many of Nation's Businesses—Like a Horatio Alger Story," *Wall Street Journal,* February 2, 1985.

Keaveny, Jake, "Scalpel Perfects Venezuela's Production Line Beauty Queens," *Sunday Times* (London), December 8, 1996.

Omestad, Thomas, "In the Land of Mirror, Mirror on the Wall Venezuelan Women Vie To Be Fairest of Them All," *U.S. News & World Report,* July 23, 2001.

Olson, Alexandra, "Venezuela's Men Seek the Beauty Pageant Limelight, Too," *Associated Press Newswires,* November 22, 2000.

Rohter, Larry, "Who Is Vainest of All? Venezuela," *New York Times,* August 13, 2000.

Wilson, Peter, "Gowns of Renown," *Chicago Sun-Times,* May 13, 2001.

Efficiency and Effectiveness

Picker, Ida, "Can Venezuela's Gustavo Cisneros Make His Media Strategy Pay?" *Bloomberg Latin America,* May 26, 2000.

Harman, Danna, "All the King's Men," *Jerusalem Post,* June 4, 1999.

Dror, Yehezkel, "True-Believer's Terrorism," *Jerusalem Post,* April 7, 1996.

Ashkenazy, Daniella, "Crystal Ball, Crystal Clear," *Jerusalem Post,* March 8, 1991.

Izenberg, Dan, "Machiavellian with a Moral Mantle," *Jerusalem Post,* December 21, 1989.

Multiplying Businesses

Colbert, David, *Eyewitness to Wall Street, Four Hundred Years of Dreamers, Schemers, Busts and Booms,* Broadway Books, New York, 2001.

Geisst, Charles R., *Wall Street: A History,* Oxford University Press, New York, 1997.

Chernow, Ron, *The Death of the Banke: The Decline and Fall of the Great Financial Dynasties and the Triumph of the Small Investor,* Vintage Books, New York, 1997.

Delaney, Paul, "Ex-U.S. Banker, 82, Still Active Abroad," *New York Times,* August 24, 1987.

Dullea, Georgia, "The Evening Hours," *New York Times,* June 13, 1986.

Lenzner, Robert, "Creative Giving: A Wealth of Names: David Rockefeller Sr. Is the Ultimate Rainmaker. The Former Chase Chairman Sets No Boundaries Between Business and Philanthropy," *Forbes,* January 1, 2000.

"The Rockefellers: End of a Dynasty?" *Fortune,* August 4, 1986.

Birger, Larry, "Venezuelan Conglomerate Sets up Shop in Coral Gables," *Miami Herald,* December 22, 1980.

Williams, John D., "Forstmann Little Is Making a Name in the Leveraged-Buyout Business," *Wall Street Journal,* March 7, 1984.

Vise, David A., "Forstmann Turns 'Pepper' to Gold," *Washington Post,* February 2, 1986.

Hilder, David B., and Randall Smith, "Mr. Forstmann Goes to Washington: LBO Rivalry Menaces Deals," *Wall Street Journal,* August 9, 1989.

Bartlett, Sarah, "LBO Giants Building Their War Chests Again. Forstmann Little and Kohlberg Kravis Seeking Funds from Institutional Investors," *New York Times,* December 3, 1990.

Hylton, Richard D., "How KKR Got Beaten at its Own Game," *Fortune,* May 2, 1994.

Machan, Dyan, "A Hero Among Barbarians," *Forbes,* July 6, 1998.

Devaluation

Guerra, José, and Julio Pineda, *Trayectoria en la Política Cambiaría en Venezuela,* Banco Central de Venezuela, Vicepresidencia de Estudios, February 2000.

Sabino, Carlos A., *Fracaso del Intervencionismo, Apertura y Libre Mercado en América Latina,* Editorial Panapo de Venezuela, C.A., Caracas, 1998.

Pensamiento Empresarial de Carlos Enrique Cisneros Rendiles, Asociación Venezolana de Ejecutivos y la Fundación Diego Cisneros, Caracas, 1984.

Lowenstein, Roger, "Latin Power: In Venezuela, Name of Cisneros Connotes Wealth and Influence—Closely Tied to Government, Family Controls Many of Nation's Businesses—Like a Horatio Alger Story," *Wall Street Journal,* February 2, 1985.

A Diamond on the Floor

Martín, José Luis, Carlos Martínez Shaw, and Javier Tusell, *Historia de España, La Edad Contemporánea,* Grupo Santillana de Ediciones, 1998.

Barmash, Isadore, "Spalding, Two Other Units are Sold by Q Holdings," *New York Times,* September 20, 1984.

"El Grupo Cisneros Mezclará Supermercados, Tiendas y Venta de Computadoras para Reactivar Galerías Preciados," *El Universal,* December 17, 1984.

Bowers, Brent, and Ana Westley, "Spain Sorts Out Fake from Real Rumasa Assets," *Wall Street Journal,* April 20, 1984.

Vitzthum, Carlta, "Galerias Preciados Files for Protection from Its Creditors," *Wall Street Journal,* December 19, 1994.

Washington Post, "Spain to Sell Chain to Venezuelan Firm," December 6, 1984.

Vitzthum, Carlta, "Mountleigh Sale of Galerias Raises Questions about the Spanish Buyers and Their Backers," *Wall Street Journal Europe,* November 2, 1992.

Vitzthum Carlta, "Galerias Preciados Files for Protection from Its Creditors," *Wall Street Journal,* December 19, 1994.

Gooch, Adela, "Spain's Largest Department Store Group Sold to Rival," *Guardian* (London), June 10, 1995.

Vitzthum, Carlta, "El Corte Inglés Bid for Galerias Chain Appears Favored," *Wall Street Journal,* May 26, 1995.

"Spaniards Protest Buy-up of Property by Foreigners," *The Economist,* November 26, 1987.

Barsky, Neil, "Park Tower Realty Enters Partnership for Site in London's Financial District," *Wall Street Journal,* November 3, 1989.

"London's Great Property Grab," *The Economist,* September 30, 1989.

Idudu, Ogale, "Developer Has a Vision for a London Eyesore—Paternoster Square Project to Complement St. Paul's," *Wall Street Journal Europe,* November 12, 1999.

Syal, Rajeev, and John Waples, "Prince Backs New Vision for Paternoster Square," *Sunday Times* (London), November 16, 1997.

Lebow, Joan, "Big Japanese Developer Joins London Project," *Wall Street Journal,* February 9, 1990.

Heathcote, Graham, "Prince Scorns Plan for Cathedral Area," *Associated Press,* September 18, 1990.

Marcom, Jr., John, "Architecture: The Prince Had a Point," *Wall Street Journal,* July 26, 1988.

Koring, Paul, "Modern Architectural Style Provokes Wrath of Prince," *Globe and Mail* (London), December 3, 1987.

The Storm

Wise, Carol, and Riordan Roett, *Post-Stabilization Politics in Latin America, Competition, Transition, Collapse,* Brookings Institution Press, Washington, D.C., 2003.

Sabino, Carlos A., *Fracaso del Intervencionismo, Apertura y Libre Mercado en América Latina,* Editorial Panapo de Venezuela, C.A., Caracas, 1998.

Oppenheimer, Andrés, "Simmering Woes Hit a Boil in Venezuela," *Houston Chronicle,* March 5, 1989.

Tejera, María, "Rioting Leads Venezuela to Curb Rights," *Associated Press,* January 3, 1989.

Riding, Alan, "Venezuela Riots Reflect Region's Instability Due to Debt Crises," *New York Times,* March 2, 1989.

Collett, Merrill, "Venezuela's Dispossessed Saw Chance to 'Get Mine'; Backdrop of Riots Is Economic Overhaul," *Washington Post,* March 3, 1989.

Charters, Ann, "Letter From Caracas. From Avenida Bolívar to Avenida Beirut," *Business Week,* March 20, 1989.

"Venezuela: Coup Attempt Aggravates Economic Problems," *Chronicle of Latin American Economic Affairs Latin American Database/Latin American Institute,* December 10, 1992.

"Coup Fever in Venezuela," *New York Times,* December 5, 1992.

"Venezuela Still Edgy: Will There Be Coup No. 3?" *New York Times,* December 3, 1992.

Robberson, Todd, "U.S. Help Important in Blocking Coup, Venezuelans Say," *Washington Post,* December 2, 1992.

Ball, Carlos, "Seeds of Venezuelan Revolt Found in Social Provisions," *Wall Street Journal Europe,* February 13, 1992.

Farah, Douglas, "Venezuelan Mutineers Drew Wide Backing; 133 Officers Held; Civilians Show Sympathy," *Washington Post,* February 6, 1992.

Greene, Merilyn, "Pérez Remains in Control," *USA Today,* February 5, 1992.

Yarbro, Stan, "Loyal Troops Seize Venezuela Coup Leaders," *Los Angeles Times,* February 5, 1992.

"Memorias de un golpe delatado," *El Universal,* May 9, 1999.

Escobar, Gabriel, "Venezuelan Ex-Plotter Turns Cult Politician; Cashiered Colonel Now Invoking Bolívar," *Washington Post,* July 24, 1994.

"Bad to Worse: Venezuela," *The Economist,* July 9, 1994.

Robberson, Tod, "Suspended Venezuelan Chief to Face Trials," *Washington Post,* May 22, 1993.

Barber Ben, "The Gang That Couldn't Find the Right Video-tape," *Baltimore Sun,* January 19, 1993.

"Web Ventures, Despite Setbacks, Find Success in Latin America," *Wall Street Journal,* June 5, 2002.

That Marvelous Hispanic Spirit

Hift, Fred, "Steamy Spanish-Language Soaps Gain Fans," *Christian Science Monitor,* January 14, 1992.

Fernández, Claudia, and Andrew Pasman, *El Tigre: Emilio Azcárraga y su Imperio Televisa,* Editorial Grijalbo, 2000.

Diehl, Jackson, "Brazilian TV Challenges US Hold on Soap Operas," *Washington Post,* May 3, 1984.

Pollack, Andrew, "The Fight for Hispanic Viewers, Univision's Success Story Attracts New Competition," *New York Times,* January 19, 1998.

Lippman, John, "Hallmark Cards to Sell Univision TV Network," *Los Angeles Times,* April 4, 1992.

Hendricks, Mike, "Hispanics Object to Sale of Univision. The Buyers of Spanish-language TV Are Reason for Challenges to Proposed Deal with Hallmark," *Kansas City Star,* April 25, 1992.

Puig, Claudia, "Univision Sale Raises Concerns Television: The Presence of a Mexican Magnate in Investment Group May Affect the Spanish-language Network's Programming Balance, Observers Say," *Los Angeles Times,* April 27, 1992.

Frankel, Mark, "Univision Fears Losing Independence," *Newsweek,* May 10, 1992.

Moffett, Matt, and Johnnie L. Roberts, "TV Titan: Mexican Media Empire, Grupo Televisa, Casts an Eye on U.S. Market—CEO Emilio Azcárraga's Bid For Univision Holdings Would Be a Beachhead—Opponents Lobby at the FCC," *Wall Street Journal,* September 30, 1992.

Patton, Susannah, "Spanish-Language TV Battle Heats Up–Telemundo Steps Up Pressure on Univision in U.S. Market," *Wall Street Journal,* October 31, 1994.

Dolan, Kerry A., "Muchas Gracias, Congress: Congress Passes Laws. Folks Like Jerry Perenchio Get Rich by Figuring Ways Around Them," *Forbes,* October 7, 1996.

Levaux, Janet Purdy, "The New America: Univision Communications Inc.," *Investor's Business Daily,* November 26, 1996.

Sheridan, Mary Beth, "Company Town Mexico's Media Baron Steps Down From TV Empire Communications: The Legendary Mogul Turns Over Grupo Televisa to His Son Because of Health Problems," *Los Angeles Times,* March 5, 1997.

"Rodven Gives PolyGram Greater Latin American Market Share," *Financial Times,* October 25, 1995.

Cisneros, Gustavo, "Retos de la integración hemisférica," Ediciones de la Fundación Cisneros, Caracas, 1995, pp. 4-5.

With Our Heads Held High

Vera, Leonard, and Raúl González, *Quiebras Bancarias y Crisis Financieras en Venezuela: Una Perspectiva Macroeconómica,* Banco Central de Venezuela, Caracas, 1999.

Ojeda Reyes, Yolanda, "Crisis Política Precipitó Debacle Bancaria," *El Universal,* January 13, 1998.

García, María Yolanda, "Están Confirmados 139 Autos de Detención," *El Universal,* February 28, 1998.

Freed, Kenneth, "Venezuelan Bank Collapse Threatens Nation's Future Finance: Banco Latino's Failure Is Worst Ever in South America. Analysts Fear a Social Explosion," *Los Angeles Times,* February 14, 1994.

Birger, Larry, "Venezuelan Conglomerate Sets Up Shop in Coral Gables," *Miami Herald,* December 22, 1980.

Sanders, Richard, "A Really Big Bank Bust; Venezuela's Crash of the Century Is Still Crashing," *Washington Post,* March 19, 1995.

Moffett, Matt, "Venezuelan President's Drastic Moves Are Short-Term Fix for Ailing Economy," *Wall Street Journal,* June 29, 1994.

Escobar, Gabriel, "Venezuelan Economy In Crisis; Currency's Decline Threatens Stability," *Washington Post,* June 27, 1994.

Gómez López, Gustavo, "Letters to the Editor: Bank Driven to Failure For Political Reasons," *Wall Street Journal,* April 12, 1994.

"Organización Cisneros aclara vínculos con el Banco Latino," *El Nacional* (Caracas), February 6, 1994.

Ball, Carlos, "The Americas: Bank's Failure Signals End of Cronyism in Venezuela," *Wall Street Journal,* February 4, 1994.

"Miami or Bust. Former Executives of Venezuela's Banco Latino Sued by New Executives for Financial Mismanagement in Florida," *The Economist,* July 1, 1995.

"Like Thieves in the Night," *Euromoney Magazine,* September 15, 1996.

Globalized Television

Crespo Ortiz, Gonzalo, "Latin America: Cable TV's Days Are Numbered," *Inter Press Service,* April 4, 1995.

Cole, Jeff, "GM's Hughes, Latin American Concerns Form Partnership to Offer Satellite TV," *Wall Street Journal,* March 10, 1995.

Walley, Wayne, "Cisneros: Future Lies in Telecommunications," *Electronic Media,* March 13, 1995.

Dolan, Kerry A., "Gustavo versus Rupert: Rupert Murdoch Has Big Plans for the Latin American Market. So Does Venezuela's Gustavo Cisneros," *Forbes,* October 5, 1998.

Robichaux, Mark, "Dishing It Out: Once a Laughingstock, Direct-Broadcast TV Gives Cable a Scare–Pizza-Pan-Size Receivers are Hot Sellers; Prices Plunge as Four Million Sign Up—One Man's Satellite Dream," *Wall Street Journal,* July 7, 1996.

"DBS Services Accepted—Finally—By the Broadcasting Community," Phillips Business Information, Inc., *Satellite News,* April 26, 1993.

Malkin, Elizabeth, and Ian Katz, "Satellite TV Comes Down to Earth: Sky and Galaxy Had High Hopes, But Profits Are Now Far Away," *Business Week,* April 12, 1999.

"Galaxy, Tevecap to Restructure DirecTV's Brazil Operations," *Dow Jones Business News,* May 19, 1999.

Whitefield, Mimi, "Galaxy Latin America Watches Satellite TV Venture Take Off," *Miami Herald*, September 15, 1997.

The Swan's Triumph

Sellers, Patty, "How Coke Is Kicking Pepsi's Can," *Fortune*, October 28, 1996.

"La Reina de las Colas," *Semana* (Bogotá), August 27, 1996.

Sellers, Patty, "Who's In Charge Here? Coke's Sales Are Weak. Its Stock Is Down. Its Execution Is Lousy. And One More Thing...," *Fortune*, December 24, 2001.

Greising, David, "I'd Like the World To Buy a Coke. How Roberto Goizueta Shook Up the Status Quo and Created a Global Powerhouse," *Business Week*, April 13, 1998.

Charan, Ram, "Managing To Be Best. The Century's Smartest Bosses Have Influence Beyond Their Companies," *Time*, December 7, 1998.

Collins, Glenn, "How Venezuela Is Becoming Coca-Cola Country," *New York Times*, August 21, 1996.

Deogun, Nikhil, Joel Millman, and Thomas T. Vogel, Jr., "Acquisition Makes Panamco a Major Coke Bottler in Caracas," *Asian Wall Street Journal*, May 14, 1997.

Deogun, Nikhil, "Venezuelan Bottler Must Pay PepsiCo for Coke Defection," *Wall Street Journal*, September 4, 1997.

Hillman, Leslie, "PepsiCo's Main Venezuelan Bottler Switches to Coke," *Bloomberg*, August 16, 1996.

Saporito, Bill, "Parched For Growth, Pepsi Had a Grand Plan for Global Expansion. Alas, Coke was Thirstier," *Time*, September 2, 1996.

Oram, Roderick, "Cola War Hots Up in Venezuela as Pepsi Loses Plant," *Financial Times*, August 17–18, 1996.

"Venezuela—Major Market Lost by Defection, Pepsi Plots Next Step," *Associated Press*, August 18, 1996.

Frank, Robert, "PepsiCo Asks Venezuela to Block Pact Between Its Ex-Bottler and Coca-Cola," *Wall Street Journal*, August 20, 1996.

Oliver, Thomas, "Palace Intrigue at Coca-Cola Co.: Is Keough Power Behind Throne?" *Atlanta Journal*, July 31, 2001.

Hays, Constance L., "Coca-Cola Is Battling To Consolidate Its Recent Gains Over Pepsico in a Turf War in Venezuela," *New York Times*, December 18, 1998.

Fisher, Daniel, "Gone Flat; How Can Coca-Cola Get Its Fizz Back?" *Forbes*, October 15, 2001.

Lipin, Steven, "KKR Agrees To Buy Majority of a Unit of Cisneros Group," *Wall Street Journal*, August 16, 1996.

Bishop, Jerry E., "Spalding's New Golf Ball Aims for Improved Slice of Market," *Wall Street Journal*, January 31, 1986.

Dubashi Jagannath, "On the Ball: Spalding Sports Worldwide Links Its Sales Force with a State-of-the-Art Computer System," *Financial World*, June 11, 1991.

Sullivan, Pat, "Golf Balls: Flights of Fancy," *San Francisco Chronicle*, July 6, 1991.

Richards, Rhonda, "Spalding's Commercial Drive. Top-Flite Puts New Spin on Golf-Ball War," *USA Today*, November 20, 1992.

Scannel, Kara, "Deals & Dealmakers: KKR's Touch Appears Faded after 25 Years—Takeover King Has Trouble Raising Money—Stock Market Made It Harder to Find and Acquire Hidden, Undervalued Gems," *Wall Street Journal*, June 19, 2001.

Atlas, Riva D., "What's an Aging 'Barbarian' To Do?" *New York Times*, August 26, 2001.

The Internet

Gunther, Marc, "What Does AOL Want? Growth, Growth, and More Growth," *Fortune*, July 23, 2001.

Yang, Catherine, Ronald Grover, and Ann Therese, "Show Time for AOL Time Warner: Bob Pittman's Job Is To Implement the Biggest Merger in U.S. History. That's a Tall Order," *Business Week*, January 15, 2001.

Bachelet, Pablo, "Ciudadano Cisneros: El Empresario Venezolano Cree Que el Futuro de los Negocios de Comunicación

Se Centrará en la Televisión. La Apuesta Es Alto Riesgo,"
AméricaEconomía, June 18, 1998.

Darrigrandi, Isabel, and Pablo Bachelet, "La Alianza que Cambiará Internet," *AméricaEconomía*, January 28, 1999.

Colitt, Raymond, "UOL Makes Capital Out of Steve Jobs' Business Model," *Financial Times*, August 31, 2001.

Gunther, Marc, "You've Got Merger: Understanding AOL's Grand Unified Theory of the Media Cosmos. The Sky's the Limit for AOL Time Warner. But Getting the Company Off the Ground Might Take Rocket Science," *Fortune*, August 1, 2001.

Karp, Jonathan, "AOL Hangs Touch in the Dicey Latin Market—Internet Service Provider Calls Its Numbers Solid, in More Ways Than One," *Wall Street Journal*, September 5, 2001.

Boudette, Neal E., and Stephanie Gruner, "In Europe, AOL Isn't a Dominating Factor," *Wall Street Journal*, December 21, 2000.

Lee, Jennifer, "In the US, Interactive TV Still Awaits an Audience," *New York Times*, December 31, 2001.

Emling, Shelley, "Media Goliath Confident of Vision Skeptics Wonder if AOL Time Warner's Multiple Services Will Be Quickly Embraced," *Atlanta Journal-Constitution*, January 6, 2002.

"AOL Colaborará con Fox en la Educación por Internet," *Novedades*, July 12, 2000.

Benechi, Mario, "AOL Busca Ganar el Terreno Perdido," *El Cronista*, August 9, 2000.

Faber, J.P., "The Last One Standing Wins," *LatinCEO*, September, 2000.

Kapadia, Reshma, "AOL Time Warner Sharpens Foreign Focus," *Reuters English News Service*, December 5, 2001.

Faber, J.P., and Reese Ewing, "Cisneros Goes Online," December 2000.

King of Content

Paxman, Andrew, and Claudia Fernández, *El Tigre, Emilio Azcárraga y su imperio Televisa*, Editorial Grijalbo, Ciudad de México, 2000.

Vivo Chaneton, Roberto, and Roberto Cibrián Campoy, *Negocios en Red, El Management de la Nueva Economía*, Grupo Editorial Norma, Buenos Aires, 2001.

Alm, Richard, "Will New Hicks Strategy Pay Off? Company Hopes To Restore Investors' Faith after Recent Losses," *Dallas Morning News*, December 9, 2001.

Serafini, Dom, "Where Is the Cisneros Group Going?" *Video Age International*, January 1, 2000.

Vitzthum, Carlta, "Technology & Health Spain's Two Digital-Television Platforms to End Battle, Set Up Join Company," *Wall Street Journal Europe*, July 23, 1998.

Green, Jennifer, "Which Spanish DTH Service Can Survive?" *Electronic Media*, January 25, 1999.

AFX News, "Vivendi's Messier 'Optimistic' Over Via Digital, Canal Satelite Merger," June 2, 1999.

Huang, Keith, "Telefonica Media Aims To Be Content King of Latin America," *Dow Jones International News*, February 4, 2000.

Rolfe, Pamela, "Telefonica Gets It—Spanish Operator Adopts a Content/Platform Strategy," *Tele.com*, April 17, 2000.

Beresford, Mark, "European Media Giants Eye Up Spanish TV Prize," *Dow Jones International News*, May 28, 2001.

Paxman, Andrew, "CTG Embraces Group Philosophy," *Variety*, March 31–April 6, 1997.

Paxman, Andrew, "Globally Mobile, Cisneros Amasses Cash for Satellites, Star of the Future," *Variety*, March 31–April 6, 1997.

García, Beatrice, "Multimedia Merger Completed," *Miami Herald*, September 25, 2001.

Conniff, Tamara, and Nicole Sperling, "Univision Snares Key Output: Deals Bring It Televisa, Venevisión Programs Through 2017," *Hollywood Reporter*, January 21, 2001.

Sutter, Mary, "Crossing The Border: Televisa, Univision Pact On Content, Pay TV," *Daily Variety*, December 21, 2001.

An Obstacle Course

Goldman Rohm, Wendy, *The Murdoch Mission, The Digital Transformation of a Media Empire*, John Wiley & Sons, Inc., New York, 2002.

Caulk, Steve, "Entrepreneur Par Excellence; Echostar's Charlie Ergen Takes on a Billion-Dollar Deal With Barely A Flinch," *Rocky Mountain News*, December 8, 2001.

Bilotti, Richard A., Sarah Simon, Celeste Mellet, and John McMahon, "Lunch with Rupert Murdoch in London," *Equity Research, Morgan Stanley Dean Witter*, North America, June 18, 2001.

Ortiz, Fiona, "Televisa, Azteca Threaten To Drop World Cup," *Reuters English News Service*, December 11, 2001.

Harding, James, "Echostar Win GM Tricked News Corp., Say Its Executives: Played Them Along To Give Ergen Time To Put Together a Deal," *Financial Times*, October 30, 2001.

Harmon, Amy, and Jennifer Lee, "Deal Bolsters Satellites as Cable TV Competitors," *New York Times*, December 17, 2001.

Hudson, Kris, "Deal Ends 4-Day Roller-Coaster Ride," *Denver Post*, November 4, 2001.

Transparency

García Castro, Alvaro, and Pedro Benítez, *Hacienda Carabobo, Una pequeña historia de Turgua y el café en la segunda mitad del siglo XIX*, Fundación Cisneros, Caracas, 1999.

Morón, Guillermo, *Breve Historia Contemporánea de Venezuela*, Fondo de Cultura Económica, México, 1994.

Rivas, Jorge, *Arte del Período Hispánico Venezolano en la Hacienda Carabobo*, Cuaderno 00.5, Colección Patty Phelps de Cisneros, Caracas, May 2000.

"Vale TV: Una Ventana al Mundo," *El Universal,* Estampas, Caracas, October 14, 2001.

The Vision

Richert, Giuseppe, *La dimensión económica de las comunicaciones en un mundo globalizado,* CEPAL/CLADES, Santiago, 1996.

"Gustavo Cisneros y el desafío de competir," *Producto,* August 2001.

Leonhardt, David, "The Imperial Chief Executive Is Suddenly in the Cross Hairs," *New York Times,* June 24, 2002.

Frank, Robert and Robin Sidel, "Overbought: Firms That Lived by the Deal in 90s Now Sink by the Dozens—Serial Acquirers Are Struggling To Pay Debts, Sell Assets; At Tyco, 700 Buys in 3 Years—Pressure To Seek Bigger Game," *Wall Street Journal,* June 6, 2002.

Esterl, Mike, "Web Ventures, Despite Setbacks, Find Success in Latin America," *Wall Street Journal,* June 5, 2002.

The Balance

Cantz, Hatje, *Orinoco—Parima, Comunidades Indígenas del Sur de Venezuela,* Colección Cisneros, Fundación Cisneros, 2000.

Al Encuentro de los Indígenas de la Amazonia Venezolana, Orinoco, Colección Cisneros. Exposición Ciudad de Biarritz, Fundación Cisneros, 2001.

Moonan, Wendy, "Jungle Fever Strikes a Collector," *New York Times,* March 30, 2001.

García Castro, Alvaro, and Benítez Pedro, *Hacienda Carabobo. Una pequeña historia de Turgua y el café en la segunda mitad del siglo xix,* Ediciones de la Fundación Cisneros, Caracas, 1999.

Rivas, Jorge, *Arte del período hispáñico venezolano en la Hacienda Carabobo,* Ediciones de la Fundación Cisneros, Caracas, 2000.

List of Individuals Interviewed

Susan Ainsworth
Luis María Ansón
Plácido Arango
María Ignacia Arcaya
Carlos Ball
Steven Bandel
Carlos Bardasano
José Casas
Gustavo Cisneros
Guillermo de la Dehesa
Lelia Delgado
Antonio Díaz
Ligia Echeverría
Johnny Fanjul
Alba Fernández
Víctor Ferreres
Manuel Fraíz Grijalba
Peter Gabriel
Luis Emilio Gómez
Ralph Haiek
Eduardo Hauser
Antonio Herrera Vaillant
José Antonio Ituarte
Bill Keon
Kelsy Kolch

Luis Vicente León Vivas
Antonieta López
José López Silverio
Raúl López
William Luers
Elizabeth Marichal
Fausto Massó
Violy McCausland
Dennys Montoto
Guillermo Morón
María Eugenia Mosquera
José María Nogueroles
Rafael Odón
Estanislao Pérez
Gerardo Pérez Puelles
Patricia Phelps de Cisneros
Cristina Pieretti
Bob Pittman
Ariel Prat
Beatrice Rangel
Luis Regalado
Aura Rengifo
José Antonio Ríos
Alejandro Rivera
Arquímedes Rivero

David Rockefeller
Leopoldo Rodés
Rodolfo Rodríguez Miranda.
Rafael Romero
Consuelo Sánchez
Harvey Schwartz
Ramón Solórzano

Osmel Sousa
Peter Tinoco
Jesús Urdaneta
Ricardo Valladares
Roberto Vivo
Sandra Zanoletti

Index

Abreu, Bob, 246
Albers, Josef, 271
Annan, Kofi, 285
Anselmo, René, 129, 132
Arango, Plácido, 97, 194
Arias, Óscar, 111
Armstrong, Michael, 71, 151,
    153, 154, 155, 157, 158
Azcárraga Jean, Emilio, 207, 208
Azcárraga Milmo, Emilio, 43,
    129, 130, 131, 132, 133, 134,
    135, 137, 155, 157, 158, 159,
    167, 195, 207, 211, 223
Azcárraga Vidaurreta, Emilio, 23,
    129
Aznar López, José María, 266

B

Babson, Roger, 29
Bacardis, the, 40
Balzac, Honoré de, 9
Bandel, Steven, 70, 73, 139, 147,
    189, 194, 204, 205, 220, 227,
    228, 229, 230, 231, 232, 233,
    234, 235, 236
Banderas, Antonio, 201
Barba, Carlos, 126, 131, 133

Bardasano, Carlos, 67, 70, 72,
    126, 138, 147, 189, 214, 219,
    220, 231, 250
Becker, Boris, 201
Beltrán, Héctor, 43, 100
Ben Gurion, David, 65
Berlusconi, Silvio, 127
Bermúdez Martínez de Castro,
    María Luisa, 19, 20
Betancourt, Rómulo, 23, 24, 27
Bill, Max, 18, 271
Blaya, Joaquín, 130, 134
Boada, Claudio, 97
Bolívar, Simón, 276
Bonnet, Brother, 26
Bonpland, Aimé, 273
Bosch, José (*Pepín*), 27
Botín-Sanz de Sautuola y García
    de los Ríos, Emilio, 97, 197
Botín-Sanz de Sautuola y García
    de los Ríos, Jaime, 97
Boyer Salvador, Miguel, 97
Brando, Marlon, 132
Brillembourgs, the, 32
Büchi, Hernán, 214
Bush, George H., 121, 272
Bush, George W., 283

C

Cabello de Requena, Edith, 149
Caignet, Félix B., 126
Caldera, Rafael, 143, 144, 250
Callaway, Howard H., 184
Calloway, Wayne, 175
Camacho, Mayela, 61
Camero, Omar, 250
Cardoso, Fernando Enrique, 162
Carey, Chase, 228, 229, 230, 231, 232
Charles of England, Prince of Wales, 16, 92, 104, 106
Carmona, Pedro, 254, 255
Carratú M., Iván, 120, 122
Case, Steve, 191, 193, 197
Castillo Lara, Rosalio, 278
Castro, Fidel, 23
Chávez Frías, Hugo, 12, 13, 122, 123, 124, 251, 252, 253, 254, 255, 256
Cisneros, Andrés, 263
Cisneros, Carlos Enrique, 208, 214, 215, 218, 219
Cisneros, Eduardo, 263
Cisneros, brothers, 20, 26, 30, 57, 72, 77, 82, 83, 84, 88, 90, 91, 102, 103, 114, 117, 118, 142, 143, 144, 146, 149, 164, 170, 192, 205, 241, 242, 247, 261
Cisneros, family, 32, 33, 38, 84, 117, 140, 146, 174, 177, 178, 179, 180, 181, 184, 200, 253, 270, 274, 276, 277
Cisneros Bermúdez, Antonio, 19, 20, 21, 22, 32, 33, 38, 171, 244
Cisneros Bermúdez, Diego, 15, 19, 20, 21, 22, 23, 24, 25, 26, 27, 28, 29, 30, 31, 32, 33, 34, 35, 37, 38, 39, 40, 42, 63, 64, 71, 75, 77, 79, 81, 85, 90, 108, 115, 121, 158, 171, 172, 173, 174, 178, 193, 223, 244, 249, 261, 263
Cisneros Fajardo, Oswaldo, 38, 39, 82, 118, 174, 175, 176, 177, 178, 179, 180, 182, 183, 187, 241
Cisneros, Patricia (Patty) Phelps de, 11, 17, 18, 36, 51, 52, 60, 78, 111, 142, 167, 232, 250, 265, 268, 270, 271, 272, 273, 274, 275, 276, 278, 279, 285, 286
Cisneros Phelps, Adriana, 51, 162, 232, 263, 278, 286
Cisneros Phelps, Carolina, 51, 263, 278, 286
Cisneros Phelps, Guillermo, 36, 51, 162, 250, 251, 263, 278, 286
Cisneros Rendiles, Anita, 97, 98
Cisneros Rendiles, Antonio José, 41, 55, 66, 146, 264
Cisneros Rendiles, Carlos Enrique, 41, 55, 146
Cisneros Rendiles, Diego Alberto, 41
Cisneros Rendiles, Gerardo, 41
Cisneros Rendiles, Marion, 98, 99, 100
Cisneros Rendiles, Ricardo, 15, 30, 34, 38, 39, 40, 41, 42, 56, 61, 62, 68, 77, 80, 82, 86, 89, 90, 97, 98, 99, 102, 103, 107, 115, 117, 118, 119, 141, 142, 143, 144, 145, 147, 148, 149,

170, 174, 176, 178, 184, 187,
192, 193, 197, 204, 205, 235,
241, 242, 243, 247, 252, 261,
262, 263, 270
Civita, Roberto, 159, 160, 161,
162, 165, 166
Clark, Lygia, 18
Clegg, Anthony, 99, 100, 101,
102, 105, 107
Clinton, Bill, 11, 216, 265, 269
Clinton, Hillary, 265, 266
Codina, Armando, 283
Correa, Gilberto, 135
Crawford, Joan, 24
Cruz Diez, Carlos, 18
Cuzcó, Enrique, 43

D

Davies, Jack, 199
Dávila, Guillermo, 59
Dehesa, Guillermo de la, 11, 272
Delgado, Maite, 61, 135
Delgado Parker, 160
Derain, André, 271
Díaz Bruzual, Leopoldo, 86
Diana of Wales, Princess, 105
Diller, Barry, 34
Dilworth, J. Richardson, 71
Dolan, Charles F., 153
Doshamoshatheri, chief of the
Yanomami, 273, 274
Douglas, Michael, 199, 272
Doyle, Arthur Conan, 13, 273
Dreiser, Theodore, 9
Dror, Yehezkel, 65, 66, 67

E

Eisenberg, Shoul, 70
Eisner, Michael, 34
Enrico, Roger, 176, 179, 181, 182

Ergen, Charlie, 19, 226, 227,
230, 231, 235, 236, 237
Ertegun, Nesuhi, 59
Escámez, Alfonso, 97

F

Fajardo, Carmen, 180
Fanjul, Johnny, 30, 31, 44, 66
Farré, Felipe, 278
Feria, Al, 90
Fernández, Eduardo, 110
Fernández, Lorenzo, 45
Ferreres, Victor, 72, 164, 165, 205
Fiallo, Delia, 45, 126
Forstmann, Nicholas, 81
Forstmann, Teddy, 81, 82
Forsythe, William, 22
Fox, Vicente, 200, 201
Fraíz-Grijalba, Manuel, 127, 128
Frei Ruiz-Tagle, Eduardo, 162
Friedman, Milton, 27
Fuentes, Carlos, 9-13, 281

G

Gabriel, Peter, 66, 67
Galarraga, Andrés, 246
Galbraith, John Kenneth, 55
Gallegos, Rómulo, 13
García Márquez, Gabriel, 126
Gates, Bill, 230
Gatica, Lucho, 25
Gavin, John, 212
Gaviria, César, 121, 269
Godó y Muntañola, Javier de,
209
Goizueta, Roberto, 71, 171, 172,
175, 176, 177, 178, 180, 181,
182, 183, 184, 187
Goldenson, Leonard, 24, 34
Gómez, Juan Vicente, 21

Gómez, Luis Emilio, 70, 147
González, Alberto, 216
González, Humberto, 98, 100
González Márquez, Felipe, 55, 94, 95, 96, 97, 99, 101, 111, 121
González Niño, Edgardo, 275
Granier, Marcel, 250
Guevara, Ernesto (*El Che*), 30
Guillot, Olga, 25
Gutfreund, John, 106

H

Haiek, Ralph, 218
Handley, Ricardo, 216
Hanks, Tom, 198
Hauser, Eduardo, 70, 189, 190, 191, 193
Havel, Vaclav, 119
Hayek, Friedrich, 27
Hayek, Salma, 201, 202
Herington, Charles, 199
Herrera Campins, Luis, 86
Hicks, Thomas (*Tom*), 70, 205, 209, 212, 213, 214, 216, 217, 218, 220, 221, 245
Hitler, Adolf, 12
Hughes, Howard, 153
Humboldt, Alexander von, 273

I

Iglesias, Julio, 71, 231, 252
Infarinato, Ruth, 202
Irimia, José, 40
Ivester, Douglas, 171, 177, 181

J

Jiang Zemin, 252
Jiménez de Cisneros, Diego, 19
Johnson, Magic, 201, 202

Jordan, Michael, 71
Juan Carlos I, King of Spain, 18, 96, 265
John Paul II, Pope, 249

K

Kendall, Donald, 173, 174, 175, 176
Keon, William, 103, 104, 106
Keough, Donald, 176
Kissinger, Henry, 266, 269
Kravis, Henry, 186, 187, 226
Kreutzberger, Mario (*Don Francisco*), 134
Kuczynski, Pedro Pablo, 94

L

Lescure, Pierre, 210
Little, William Brian, 81
López, Antonieta, 278
Luers, William, 252
Lufkin, Dan, 92, 93
Luksic, Guillermo, 162
Lula da Silva, Luiz Inácio, 222
Lusinchi, Jaime, 87

M

Macaya, Javier, 170, 172
Magnetto, Héctor, 160, 162
Malone, John, 230
Mandela, Nelson, 119
Marinho, Joao, 155
Marinho, José, 155
Marinhos, the, 44, 156, 157
Marinho, Jr., Roberto, 155, 156
Marinho, Sr., Roberto, 23, 127, 155, 156, 157, 158, 159, 167, 208, 223
Martínez, Mario, 52

Martos Sánchez, Rafael (*Rafael*), 59
Massa, Jorge, 97, 98
Matta, Roberto, 18
McCausland, Violy, 71, 170, 172, 179
McGrath, Kevin, 161
Mehta, Zubin, 275, 276
Meier, Richard, 274
Meir, Golda, 65
Melliet, Guy, 61
Meneghel, Xuxa (*Xuxa*), 134
Menem, Carlos, 162, 216, 217
Mestre, Goar, 23, 24, 25, 43, 44, 86, 160, 195, 249
Meyers, Jesse, 181
Miró Ferrà, Joan, 18, 271
Moneta, Raúl, 216, 217
Monsanto, Julieta, 37
Monsantos, the, 32, 33, 38, 39, 172
Monsanto, Roberto, 32, 37, 39
Moore, George, 75, 76, 77, 79, 81, 95, 96, 108
Morales, family, 202, 245, 246
Moreta, Fernando María, 28
Morón, Guillermo, 110
Mosquera, María Eugenia, 250
Murdoch, Rupert, 16, 18, 19, 153, 154, 155, 156, 157, 158, 159, 167, 205, 223, 224, 225, 226, 227, 228, 229, 230, 231, 232, 233, 235, 236, 237, 245, 283, 284
Mussolini, Benito, 12

N

Newman, Rick, 220
Noble, Ernestina, 160

O

Ochoa Antich, Fernando, 122
Odón, José Rafael, 115, 243, 244
Ortega, Carlos, 254
Oyarzábal, Antonio de, 265, 266

P

Palacios, Bárbara, 61
Pao, W. K., 78
Parises, the, 32
Parsons, Richard, 197, 204, 205
Pellicer, Luis Antonio, 39
Pendergrast, Mark, 278
Perales, José Luis, 59
Perenchio, Jerry, 131, 132, 133, 208
Pérez, Carlos Andrés, 45, 46, 47, 110, 111, 112, 114, 120, 121, 122, 123
Pérez, Estanislao, 32, 34, 39, 40, 73, 97, 98, 100
Pérez Benítezes, the, 32
Pérez Jiménez, Marcos, 27
Perón, Juan Domingo, 12
Phelps, family, 36, 43
Phelps, William, 36, 51
Phelps, William H., 36, 273
Picasso, Pablo R., 18, 271
Pieretti, Cristina, 64, 199, 243, 244, 248
Pirko, Tom, 182
Pittman, Robert, 193, 194, 195, 196, 197, 199, 200, 204, 205, 261
Prat, Ariel, 240, 245, 246, 247, 248
Prieto, family, 245, 246

Q

Quayle, Dan, 111

R

Ramírez, Paco, 100
Raleigh, Walter, 273
Rangel, Beatrice, 72
Reed, John, 216
Regalado, Luis, 100
Rendiles Martínez, Albertina, 19, 21, 23, 26, 27, 35, 85
Reyes, Alfonso, 12
Reyes, Gerardo, 120
Rhodes, William R., 119, 269
Ríos, José Antonio, 67, 68, 73, 91, 147, 195
Rivera, Alejandro, 42, 82, 137, 184, 189
Riviera, Joaquín, 61
Rockefeller, Abby Aldrich, 78
Rockefeller, David, 66, 75, 77, 78, 79, 81, 111, 239, 269, 274
Rockefeller, John D., 78
Rockefellers, the, 49, 50, 71, 78, 90, 111
Rockefeller, Nelson, 49, 78, 197
Rockefeller, Peggy, 274
Rockefeller, Rodman, 49, 50
Rodríguez, José Luis, 59
Rodríguez García, Rodolfo, 58
Rodríguez Miranda, Rodolfo, 58, 72, 126
Roosevelt, Franklin D., 49
Ross, Steve, 194
Rossi, Juan, 202
Rothschild, Mayer Amschel, 81
Ruiz-Mateos, José María, 94

Ruttenberg, Derald, 81
Ryan, Meg, 198

S

Sáez, Irene, 61
Salcedo, José Joaquín, 51
Sánchez, Ángel, 61
Sánchez, Consuelo, 155, 156, 161
Sanguinetti, Julio, 162
Santiago Atencio, Adriana Catalina de, 36
Santo Domingo, Julio Mario, 138
Scardino, Marjorie, 223
Schlesinger, Arthur, 55
Schwartz, Harvey, 49, 50
Silverman, Henry, 134
Simpson, John, 106
Sinclair, Christopher, 182
Slim, Carlos, 11, 285
Smith, Michael, 226
Sofía of Greece, Queen of Spain, 265
Sosa, Arturo, 86
Soto, Jesús Rafael, 18
Sousa, Osmel, 60, 61
Spalding, A. G., 93
Statons, the, 184

T

Tata, J. R. D., 78
Taylor, Elizabeth, 132
Tinoco, Pedro, 38, 39, 47, 49, 50, 57, 80, 109, 141, 142, 146, 169
Tinoco, Peter, 69, 70, 168, 272
Tonito, Guido, 72
Torres-García, Joaquín, 18

U

Uribe, Alberto, 183

V

Valladares, Ricardo, 30
Vargas, Ernesto, 161, 165, 166
Velasco, Ignacio, 249, 250, 278
Velasco, Rafael María, 21
Villalonga, Juan, 209, 210, 211
Villanueva, Luis, 126
Visquel, Omar, 246
Vivo, Roberto, 217, 218, 219, 220, 221
Vollmer, family, 24, 25, 43, 249
Volpi, Alfredo, 17

W

Wagoner, Richard, 283
Walters, Barbara, 71
Wasserman, Lew, 131, 132
Watson, Tom, 66
Wertheimer, Robert, 30
Whitehead, Edward, 27
Wolfensohn, James D., 170
Wren, Christopher, 103

Z

Zanoletti, Sandra, 64, 119, 146, 147
Zedillo, Ernesto, 157, 201
Zingg, Margarita, 61
Zurita, José Lorenzo, 278